LATIN AMERICANISM

Cultural Studies of the Americas

Edited by George Yúdice, Jean Franco, and Juan Flores

Cultural Studies of the Americas

Volume 3

AMERICA

LATIN

NISM

Román de la Campa

University of Minnesota Press
Minneapolis — London

Some parts of individual chapters have been published previously,
in different versions, in the following articles and chapters.

"On Latin Americanism and the Postcolonial Turn,"
Canadian Review of Comparative Literature, Steven Tötösy de Zepeteknek
and Sneja Gunew, eds. Special Issue on Postcolonial Literatures:
Theory and Practice, vol. 22, nos. 3–4, 1995. Reprinted by permission.

"Postmodernism and Revolution: A Central American Case Study,"
in *Late Imperial Culture,* Román de la Campa, E. Ann Kaplan, and
Michael Sprinker, eds. London: Verso, 1995. Reprinted by permission.

"Resistance and Globalization in Caribbean Discourse:
Antonio Benítez-Rojo and Edouard Glissant," in
A History of Literature in the Caribbean, A. James Arnold, ed. Vol. 3.
Amsterdam: John Benjamins Publishing Company, 1997.
Reprinted by permission.

"Cultural Studies, Globalization, and Neoliberalism," in
The Politics of Research. E. Ann Kaplan and George Levine, eds.
Copyright 1997 by Rutgers, The State University.
Reprinted by permission of Rutgers University Press.
New Brunswick, N.J.: Rutgers University Press, 1997.

Published by the University of Minnesota Press
111 Third Avenue South, Suite 290
Minneapolis, MN 55401-2520
http://www.upress.umn.edu

Printed in the United States of America on acid-free paper

Library of Congress Cataloging-in-Publication Data

De la Campa, Román.
Latin Americanism / Román de la Campa.
p.   cm. — (Cultural studies of the Americas ; v. 3)
Includes bibliographical references and index.
ISBN 0-8166-3116-6 (hc). — ISBN 0-8166-3117-4 (pb)
1. Latin American prose literature—20th century—History and
criticism.   2. Criticism—Historiography.   I. Title.   II. Series.
PQ7081.D262   1999
868—dc21   98-56167

The University of Minnesota is an equal-opportunity educator and employer.

10 09 08 07 06 05 04 03 02 01 00 99   10 9 8 7 6 5 4 3 2 1

Contents

Preface

The transit of cultural signs between peripheral practice (Latin America) and metropolitan theory (Latin Americanism), as well as the system of academic exchanges that administers these signs, are responsible not only for the circulation of analytic tools, but also for the criteria that regulate their value and reception according to the predominant tendencies established by certain discursive hegemonies.
Nelly Richard, "Bordes, diseminación, postmodernismo: una metáfora latinoamericana de fin de siglo"[1]

This book attempts to examine the main criteria at play in the reception and codification of literary Latin Americanism today. It understands that field as a community of discourses that has gained particular force during the past few decades, mainly in the United States, but also beyond. It argues that the most significant method of critique behind postmodern, postcolonial, subaltern, and cultural studies approaches—despite their possible or avowed differences—is to be found in the poststructural legacy of deconstruction and its related metanarrative critiques. It understands this legacy to have generalized, in the sphere of literary analysis, into a powerful but unquestioned practice that I call *episthetics:* that uncertain interplay between epistemology and aesthetics, from which criticism turns into a writing, and language metaphors translate into an immanent sense of rhetorical praxis and agency.

In this project, I have sought to rehearse a critique of the preferred *episthetic* moves within literary Latin Americanist practices today, how they inform and authorize many other methods and theories that go under different names, including, of course, postmodern and postcolonial epochal constructs. It could be said that what I attempt to do in this book is to unearth the political implications often ignored by this theoretical legacy as it manifests itself through Latin Americanism. If so, I would suggest that I see that legacy as both necessary and insufficient, as having reached a point of exhaustion even as it continues to inform new work, in short, as a critique that both conditions and threatens the possibilities of more critical approaches at our neoliberal moment of global order.

Mine is not the first register of this exhaustion, nor will it be the last call for going beyond it. In one of the few transnational attempts to offer a comparative outline of global cultural relations, Lisa Lowe and David Lloyd declare the need for a new "politics of culture."[2] They emphasize the need for such an intervention "insofar as neither the postmodern conception of the transnational nor the liberal assumption of the congruence of capitalism, democracy, and freedom is currently adequate to address the ubiquity and variety of alternatives."[3] My more specific concern is how deconstructive modes of literary analysis collude or collide with this apparent dead end in the context of literary Latin Americanism.

The reader will thus find many moments in this book dedicated to readings of Latin American literature informed by deconstruction, with their corresponding post-turns. At times this effort will appear to betray a certain fascination for the very object of scrutiny. That apparent contradiction is a necessary one. My purpose is not to turn literary deconstruction into a bête noire, or to deny its momentous impact, but rather to behold its own set of taboos and traverse its unsuspected blind spots within Latin Americanism. That look at the other side of the language metaphors and their growing academic narrative motivates my recurrent reference to an episthetic legacy. I know that deconstruction is much more than a form of literary exegesis, but I also know that it has been particularly congenial to the latter kind of appropriation. My critique aims to stay within that limited field of dissemination.

Readers may also observe that my critique of methods of self-enclosure carries on, hypercritically, throughout every chapter of this book, particularly in the beginning pages. They will also notice that my calls for more culturalist, social, economic, and feminist groundings of Latin America in all forms of Latin Americanism are also primarily intended to show what is missing, forgotten, evaded, avoided, or repressed in deconstructivism, rather than providing a tried and true alternative path. Indeed, this book may well be just a map of our critical labyrinth inspired by the power and intensity of the most well traveled cul-de-sacs.

All chapters begin with a theoretical prelude in which different aspects of our theoretical legacy are examined. These are followed by a more detailed discussion of key texts, critical as well as literary, which inform the production and articulation of Latin America as a constellation of discursive constructs. Of primary concern is how these discourses negotiate the conflictive links between literary and cultural analysis; the local in global times; the here, the there, and the in-between loci of enunciation; gender; modernity, postmodernity, and alternative modernities; the colonial residue; and loci of legitimation. I do not embrace culturalist paradigms without some reservations that call for the need to historicize how they are applied, yet my project is also not quite driven by cultural materialism. On the other hand I am profoundly intrigued by Derrida's newfound need to revisit Marx, and I eagerly continue to explore modes of transcultural discourse in Latin America in spite of their historic pitfalls. What this book does, insistently, is to hover around the most familiar critical tropes of our times—totalization, identity, selfsame, essentialism, transparency, fixity—not merely because they are powerful tools, but rather to unhinge their complicity with a still universalist, and increasingly triumphant, pretense of free-floating positionality.

Chapter 1 begins with a discussion of the ambivalent postcolonial turn in Latin Americanism and then moves backwards and sideways to more established postmodern, boom, and postboom forms of criticism. In many ways, this chapter also serves as an introduction for the entire book. The discussion is structured around a key intervention by Gayatri Chakravorty Spivak that is taken in two separate directions: first to register the tensions inherent to her deconstructive-feminist-diasporic postcoloniality, but then to deploy that same critique against the grain of Latin Americanist discourses also inspired by various forms of deconstruction: de Manian, postmodern, and subaltern studies. The main literary presuppositions at work across postmodern, subaltern, and postcolonial studies are examined, as well as their fusion into a recurring common theme of Latin American modernity as a failed, expendable tradition. Also explored are the possibly different routes provided by transculturation and new feminist work being produced in Latin America, particularly in their capacity to yield a differing reading of postmodern culture.

Chapter 2 attempts to give way for the return of the repressed. Latin American revolution is read through Jorge Luis Borges, not to unearth a political specter but to rehearse the narrative entanglements of an incredibly rich and self-referential Latin American discursive history. A different type of postmodern critique is thereby suggested, one that brings revolution to deconstruction, not the other way around. Che and Sandino are thus brought to Borges, as narrative strands unprotected by literary and political canons, into a broader, hopefully freer, sense of textual historicity. That rereading, thoroughly steeped in alternative histories of modernity that neither privilege nor dismiss revolutionary stories, moves on to a discussion of critical and creative texts and interventions, including Julio Cortázar, Eduardo Galeano, Joan Didion, Che, Borges, Sandino, and Chiapas.

Chapter 3 explores performative approaches to hybridity. It begins with an exploration of Judith Butler's and Homi K. Bhabha's respective theories of gender and postcolonial performativity, exploring their deconstructive premises and probing their corresponding sense of cultural politics. The chapter then traces the history of Latin American transculturation, throughout the twentieth century, in terms of its own modes of articulating discursive theory. The chapter grapples with the possibilities for a Latin American cultural studies able to deconstruct identitarian longings without erasing the theoretical legacies of its modern period; hence, the closer look at transculturation, whose own performative work remains largely ignored. The work of Néstor García Canclini, Ángel Rama, and Fernando Ortiz is discussed in detail as a changing, ongoing, culturalist Latin American intervention that attempts to theorize modernity in alternative and conflictive ways. Finally, the chapter suggests the importance of a transmodern understanding of Latin American cultural history, and how that might alter current notions of postmodernity and performative principles.

Chapter 4 has various related aims. Its overarching organization shows a contrast between postmodern and postcolonial readings of the Caribbean as articulated by two major theoretical sources: Antonio Benítez-Rojo and Édouard Glissant. From there the chapter's other aims evolve. The Caribbean, often forgotten by Latin Americanism, or reduced to a handful of authors easily read as Latin American, is here taken as a key site of postmodern and postcolonial rhetorical figures. Lyotardian notions of the sublime, de Manian approaches to literary history, religious syncretism, and Derridean critiques of orality—these and other frequent critical tropes are introduced into a close reading of these two Caribbean writers. The chapter concludes with a comparative critique of the central postcolonial figure of mimicry, as derived by Homi K. Bhabha from Frantz Fanon's work. The chapter brings that notion into play alongside analogous but different figures, such as *choteo* and *diversion,* thereby forwarding postcolonial deconstruction to a broader critique involving the work of Benítez-Rojo and Glissant, as well as Achille Mbembe and Bhabha.

Chapter 5 returns specifically to the work of Ángel Rama. The purpose this time is not transculturation theory but *The Lettered City,* a profoundly defiant text in which Foucauldian concepts are first engaged to redraw the cartography of Latin Americanism. Rama's posthumous work is here understood as a singular text still largely unread, even though it corresponds in many ways to the episthetic legacy, albeit in unorthodox, if not heretical, ways. Jacques Derrida's notion of orality and Michel Foucault's critique of epistemic constructs are brought to bear on the discussion of Rama's book. Particular attention is paid to Rama's attempt to articulate the links between writing, the social, and Latin America's deeply entrenched colonial order. Ernesto Laclau's deconstructive critique of society as separate from the social is introduced to probe literary modes of conflating the two. Finally, Rama's text is brought into a direct dialogue with the contemporary work of Harold Bloom and Richard Rorty in the context of globalization and the crisis of literary studies. Bloom's idea of a transnational Western canon, and Rorty's notion of North Atlantic Postmodern Bourgeois Societies are contrasted to Rama's deconstructive cartography of the Real City.

Chapter 6 arrives at a set of questions implicit throughout this book: Is the language of theory, particularly its troping of the theorist as a free-floating scanning subject, somehow complicit with the utopian tropes of globalization? Are the principles of undifferentiated difference in hyper-criticism somehow analogous to the hyperbolic relativism of technocultural discourses? Are the linguistic turns of the language metaphors strictly bound to a syntactic plane that evades semantics or is unable to read what Roth Ruthrof calls the "intersemiotic and heterosemiotic" planes? Is that linguistic cul-de-sac in any way a symptom of a naive realism in which "mere differentiation and its current technical expression, the binary digital, act both as a vast and highly efficient retrieval system and as an attractive screening syntax against critical analysis"?[4]

I thus move past Latin Americanism in this last chapter, without leaving it altogether, toward the question of how postmodern writing and metanarrative critiques, in spite of their obvious value, can be seen to resonate with the cultural needs of global capital on a larger plane. Martin Hopenhayn's critique of postmodernism in its interface with Latin American neoliberalism is brought into play, as well as Nelly Richard's instantiation of a Latin American feminist critique of metropolitan postmodernity. Harold Bloom and Richard Rorty are discussed again, this time in terms of their profound and contradictory expression of alarm regarding the turn toward cultural studies in the American academy. Chapter 6 also returns to Derrida's *Spectres of Marx,* this time with a special emphasis, given his own sense of alarm with the dangers facing deconstruction. Arif Dirlik's work on postcolonialism and Chinese Confucian capitalism is engaged as a possible companion to Derrida's current work, in spite of the differences between the two. The contradictory edges of postmodern cultural and literary studies are discussed in light of these two theorists, as well as the possibilities of theoretical work able to move beyond language metaphors.

Acknowledgments

In writing this book, I must acknowledge many debts. They begin with Dania Saa, whose presence in my life and work is a constant source of inspiration, as well as with Alejandro and Cecilia de la Campa, who continuously teach me the most unexpected lessons in life.

I have many colleagues to thank, particularly those for whom friendship never gets in the way of a demanding reader. They are the indispensable kind. I begin with Michael Sprinker, whose uncompromising intellectual rigor is an inspiration. I am particularly indebted to him for the time he took to read various parts of this manuscript with great patience. Malcolm Read, Neil Larsen, Ann Kaplan, and Antonio Vera León have also been incisive interlocutors to whom I am grateful. Many other friends and colleagues have provided me with insights, encouragement, and questions. They include Mabel Moraña, James Arnold, George Yúdice, Sonia Mattalía, Elizabeth Monasterios, Juan Flores, Jean Franco, Gastón Lillo, and Katherine Popeney-Hart. None of these scholars, of course, is in any way responsible for my views, choices, or obsessions.

Institutional support is never to be underestimated. The Humanities Institute, the Comparative Literature Department, and the Hispanic Languages and Literature Department at Stony Brook have been more than instrumental in the creation of a truly collegial climate. A special word about our students: A good number of graduate students in Hispanic studies, comparative literature, English, and other disciplines have helped me sharpen my thinking and pursue different directions; and our undergraduates, many of them Latin Americans, Latinos, or occupying positions in between, have been a source of constant inspiration. It is always striking to find in them an unquenchable thirst for knowledge regarding Latin American cultural history that is much more than academic.

I should not list them separately, but one of the central claims of this book is that specialists working in Latin America can spell a difference in how we think, write, speak, and even feel Latin Americanism from afar. My specific debt is to Alberto Rodríguez Carucci, Arturo Gutiérrez, Susana Marchán, Ricardo Kalimán, Guillermo Mariaca, Néstor García Canclini, Fernando Balseca, and Juan Dushesne. I should add that my ongoing dialogue with various organizational sites in Venezuela, Mexico, Cuba, Argentina, Ecuador, Colombia, and Bolivia is indispensable to me, most particularly those institutions that provide alternatives to such established sites as LASA (Latin American Studies Association) and the Modern Language Association. The future of the field may well rest in the possibility of turning these and other Latin American institutions into corresponding Latin American loci of legitimation for all Latin Americanist discourses. I owe that experience to JALLA (Jornadas Andinas de Literatura Latino-americana), Bienales Mariano Picón Salas, CELARG (Centro de Estudios Latinoamericanos Rómulo Gallegos), Instituto de Literatura Mariano Picón Febres, and the Revista Iberoamericana Institutes.

A special thanks to Lisa Freeman, former director of the University of Minnesota Press, for her interest in this project.

Finally, I would like to declare my debt to the work of many critics, writers, and scholars with whom my writing intersects, particularly those whose work is critiqued in this book. I am a true believer in the possibility of learning through scholarly dialogue and debate. Without their contributions, this book could not have been written.

1
Latin Americanism and the Turns beyond Modernity

In the emerging production of new discourses and modes of perception, negation aims to keep both its sides: the critique of totality (the general order) and the affirmation of that which denies totality (the interstitial or peripheral). One could object, however, that there is no dialectical relation between the two parts of negation: the dominant order is not liberated or left behind by interstitial flares. Instead, one could posit that the "interstitial-emancipatory" coexists with the "general-coercive," without abolishing it or disputing its hegemony.

Martin Hopenhayn, Ni apocalípticos ni integrados:
Aventuras de la modernidad en América Latina

It is not often observed that the current status of Latin American literary studies closely corresponds to the arrival of new theoretical paradigms in humanistic research. Today, the widening scope of Latin Americanism claims the attention of a growing body of English-writing critics and scholars, including a considerable number of diasporic, postcolonial, and new immigrants from Latin America and other parts of the world. More than a field of studies, or the literary articulation of a hybrid culture, Latin American literature and criticism are perhaps best understood as a transnational discursive community with a significant market for research and sales in the industrial capitals of the world. Current critical debates about gender representations, theoretical shifts, modes of periodization, and new comparative frameworks—indeed, all the paradigms brought to bear on canonical literatures within the Euro-American academy—now incorporate Latin American literature without exception. U.S. research universities continue to invest in Latin American studies often in concert with a developing interest in related areas such as Hispanic and Latino studies, and with a considerable emphasis on contemporary literature and performative culture. New anthologies of multicultural and global literature generally feature Latin American samples. Indeed, if there is a postmodern canon, Borges and Gabriel

García Márquez are thought to constitute its very center, and Rigoberta Menchú's testimonial narrative its multicultural margin.

Recent theoretical insights have brought into question national and regional boundaries as well as ethnic and linguistic points of origination, but the "coming of age" of Latin Americanism through the medium of English—the lingua franca of globalization, deconstruction, and postcolonial discourse—also has significant ramifications.[1] Clear examples can be found in the processes of scholarly legitimation. Many of the most forceful texts of Latin American criticism have been written in English; conversely, major Latin American contemporary works of fiction and criticism in Spanish, as well as Portuguese, often achieve worldwide reception largely through English translations;[2] debates over subaltern subjectivity and curricular reform based on Latin American testimonial literature and magic realism carry on, mostly in English, in the American academy;[3] and new theoretical constructs informed or inspired by Latin American literature—such as John Barth's discovery of a postmodern literary style, Hans Robert Jauss's revision of German reception theory, and Fredric Jameson's notion of a Third World national allegory—have evolved from a somewhat limited exposure to contemporary masters such as Borges or García Márquez, often without accounting for differences between them or their relation to Latin American culture as a whole.[4]

For Latin Americanists, it is becoming increasingly pertinent to ask what sort of academic object we construct and, in the process, how our self-inscriptions might situate us. We have become experts at detecting the identity drive of Latin American discourses claiming autochthony, nativism, exotic locality, and any other form of fixed bearing, leaving our own complicity as situated subjects bound to social and disciplinary interests beyond scrutiny. Considerable attention has been given to Benedict Anderson's critique of the modern nation by literary critics, but "Latin Americanism," as well as other objective correlatives for less-than-modern societies, can also draw significantly from Edward Said's reflections on nations and regions as the production of disciplinary objects.[5] If the nation is an imagined community we conjure into existence, how do we describe those "other" nations or regions we construct in the process of teaching and writing about them from discursive communities anchored in Europe or North American societies? "This seemingly natural and spontaneous availability of Latin America as a subject for discourse is no doubt partly a holdover from the colonial past," writes Neil Larsen in *Reading North by South*.[6] Nelly Richard, in *La estratificación de los márgenes* (Border stratification), one of the most incisive texts of Latin American deconstruction, warns that the growing academicist archive of decentering theories may turn Latin American and feminist "difference" into "predictable supplements."[7]

Of course, even a cursory attempt to conceptualize Latin America in a comprehensive way is bound to challenge any critical approach. Latin American textuality is a repository that should require a serious engagement with work done in at least four major sites—Latin America, the Caribbean, the United States, and Europe. To find such a range of critical and theoretical sources in any given critic is difficult, and perhaps even more so if Latin America remains all too easily extrapolated from regional, or even national, points of reference and expertise. In recent times, one thinks of Ángel Rama's work as an exceptional effort, particularly when it comes to combining Euro-American theory with a close reading of the major Latin American cultural traditions: Andean, Caribbean, Southern Cone, and Brazilian. Nonetheless, with so many potential authors, countries, and cultural traditions, the richness of Latin America's textual production belies the notion of an all-encompassing entity often portrayed by critical works and anthologies, including those committed to a discourse of difference. The market totalizes in its own way. Moreover, unlike the Caribbean discourse of Frantz Fanon, C. L. R. James, and Édouard Glissant that is often cited in postcolonial criticism, Latin American literature in translation was brought into the canon at an earlier turn in theoretical debates. It reached center stage during the sixties and seventies, particularly with the translations of the so-called narrative boom exemplified by Carlos Fuentes, Gabriel García Márquez, Mario Vargas Llosa, and Julio Cortázar, among others, and the incorporation of Borges's earlier work as the master code. Thus by virtue of its proximity, if not correspondence, to the advent of new critical paradigms in humanistic scholarship since the sixties, the study of Latin American literature became quite invested in structuralist, semiotic, and deconstructive modes of reading, or in a literary understanding of postmodernism that is by and large removed from extraliterary postmodern social constructs, and more so from postcolonial entanglements. In addition, the field has been further mainstreamed along new aesthetic lines by the marketing of Latin American *testimonio* and magic realism that now includes women writers such as Rigoberta Menchú, Isabel Allende, and Laura Esquivel, among others.

It is not surprising, therefore, that postcolonialism has been met with some early skepticism, if not confusion, by the more or less established schools of Latin American criticism in the United States. In addition, one must bear in mind that this initial response comes at just about the time when the full implications of postmodernism as a sociopolitical reality are being felt in Latin America through the neoliberal political regimes that came about in the eighties. Beatriz Sarlo's *Escenas de la vida posmoderna* dramatizes just how different this sense of lived postmodernism can be from the celebration of its literary embodiment.[8] Martin Hopenhayn, whose *Ni apocalípticos ni integrados* provides the most systematic Latin American critique of postmodernism, reminds us that "there is something attractive in the idea of learning to unlearn, in the invitation to contemporaneity, in the vitality of forgetfulness. But, is this levity what we want to claim as an aesthetic for our everyday lives?"[9] By and large, literary critics have ignored or eschewed the work of social scientists and philosophers living in Latin America, for whom postmodernism constitutes an ongoing debate of multidisciplinary nature and considerable political ramifications, as is evident in the work of Sarlo, Richard, Hopenhayn, and anthologies such as *Cultura política y democratización.*[10]

There are, to be sure, some notable exceptions. The marketing of boom writing and criticism, for example, has come under review in the work of critics in the United States, among them Doris Sommer and George Yúdice; and the need to approach Latin American postmodernity as a cultural political project that must step beyond the traditional practice of poststructural literary studies has been observed by John Beverley, Neil Larsen, and Jean Franco, among a few others. But the postmodern gaze on Latin American literary topics remains much closer to a utopian poststructuralist critical practice whose link with the life-world and other forms of culture remains quite distant, if not wholly unreconciled. Postmodern topics of interest have developed, such as postboom forms of narrative, as well as *testimonio* writing, but they can also encompass much of what has been written since the mid-1970s, including newer work from boom writers such as Vargas Llosa himself, new women's writing, and rereadings of writers such as Borges and Severo Sarduy in a more contemporary light.[11] Despite debates that tend to isolate one or another of its major elements, the field remains relatively fluid in its postboom/postmodern/subaltern/postcolonial slippages, even though, as a critical practice, barring the exceptions noted earlier, Latin Americanism in the American academy remains caught in preferences surrounded by well-known binaries such as realist/fantastic, symbolic/postsymbolic, and referential/literary, identity/difference, political/aesthetic—a somewhat traditional literary debate that generally avoids asking how lived postmodernity compounds such polarities. On the other hand, as a marketing practice, postboom criticism may be seen as a jockeying for position in sales and promotions of discourse on Latin America in the U.S. academy. In that marketing sense, the postboom enterprise does indeed correspond to a postmodern heightened awareness of the need for academic disciplines to package its objects of study. One would expect Latin Americanist critiques of postcolonialism, therefore, to be as varied and contradictory as the field itself, if not more so. For scholars invested in the study of Latin American colonial discourses, for example, resistance to postcolonial theory has generated an important historiographical debate on whether the first two centuries after the Spanish conquest classify as colonialism, though it remains somewhat removed from considering its theoretical implications.[12] For critics closer to structuralist and Marxist methods, postcolonial writing constitutes no more than an extension of the already established postmodern paradigm.[13] Conversely, scholars operating from the firmness of poststructural or postmodern literary perspectives have seen postcolonialism as having little to add to deconstructive Latin American criticism.[14] For critics invested in *testimonio* and its deconstruction, links between subalternity theory and postcolonialism are being explored.[15] Others yet have seized the opportunity to suggest a closer dialogue between Latin American studies in its broadest sense (social sciences as well as literary studies) and the newer field of Anglo-American culturalism that is often implicit in postcolonialism.[16]

These are welcome, and in most cases valuable, entanglements. After all, they speak to the central questions regarding postcolonialism: Does it constitute an extension, if not an intensification, of deconstructive work on the plane formerly occupied by Third World tropes, as seen in the work of Gayatri Chakravorty Spivak, Homi Bhabha, and Gyan Prakash? Can it entail a more radical challenge to postmodern and deconstructive critical thought, as argued by critics such as Henry Giroux, Neil Lazarus, and R. Radhakrishnan? Is it merely a derivative by-product of a new and still Western master code, a position advanced in the work of Arif Dirlik and Aijaz Ahmad?[17] Latin American cultural and literary studies may well compose a fertile testing ground for these questions, given its extraordinary plurality of nations, traditions, languages, and diasporas, on one level, its century-and-a-half history of neocolonial struggles and modernizing revolutions on another, and its proximity to Western literary indexing of postmodern textuality on yet another. In any event, the field is ripe for studies of a broader historical and theoretical range, perhaps even for a disciplinary shift toward a Latin American comparativism that will not be bound to a narrow canon of authors and a strict metropolitan definition of literary intertextuality.[18] It seems ironic, and perhaps emblematic, that, excepting studies such as Neil Larsen's *Reading North by South,* the often-noted debate between Fredric Jameson and Aijaz Ahmad—distinguished nonspecialists—appears to have brought greater attention to the position that Latin American literature holds on the contemporary global scale than the work of so many specialized scholars.[19] The only other current debate, that of *testimonio* subalternity, has more to do with important but mostly internal debates of multiculturalism in the American academy than with Latin American entanglements. The possibility of a transnational dimension to the study of the Americas remains a distant future, but Latin Americanism is already caught in its uncharted territory.

Many questions remain unasked, insufficiently explored, or caught in either/or critical motifs. Does the Latin American literary boom of the sixties and seventies constitute a form of early postmodern textuality, or is it a lingering form of high modernism? Has the Western canon replenished itself through the translation and the intertextual influences of a few, mostly male, Latin American novelists? Is there a contradictory process of double coding that allows Latin America to read itself differently than Europe or North America read themselves through the same texts? Do postboom forms of writing such as *testimonio* literature constitute postmodern engagements? Can they also spell the return to identity politics or to a realist fiction of earlier epochs? Does the growing corpus of women's writing, fiction as well as theory, require different paradigms from the postmodern and postcolonial constructs? Do critical diasporas of Latin American origin trained in the United States read differently? Do they alter the way Latin American literary values are administered and codified? Are there differences between postmodern, postcolonial, and peripheral modern types of readers? Are Latino texts produced in the United States directly transferable to the study of Latin American literature? Can the literature and criticism of the postcolonial world as well as feminism instantiate, or challenge, entrenched historical or political voids in postmodern theories of reading? If so, how is this a reshaping of Latin Americanism? Is the field of Latin American critical discourses a world of multiple loci of enunciations where all methods and approaches coexist more or less equally in a new market of multiculturalist or postcolonial bliss, without much debate or attempts to probe each other's assumptions?[20]

This essay explores many of these questions by examining the conditions of possibility for postcolonial criticism within the existing constellation of Latin American postmodernism and deconstruction. The latter are taken to be, by and large, the most important discursive elements at work in either construct. My focus should be seen as part of a broad and increasingly fertile terrain within Latin American literary studies in which many scholars are involved, as exemplified by a wealth of publications. English-language sources include various anthologies of cultural criticism (*The Real Thing: Testimonial Discourse and Latin America, On Edge: The Crisis of Con-*

temporary Latin American Culture, The Postmodernism Debate in Latin America, Latin American Identity and Constructions of Difference), as well as a debate sponsored by the *Latin American Research Review, Callaloo,* various issues of *Poetics Today,* a special issue of *Modern Language Quarterly,* and a couple of issues of *Revista Iberoamericana* on Latin American cultural studies and on the work of Ángel Rama, among others.[21] Spanish sources include, since 1992, various special issues of *Nueva Revista de Crítica Literaria, Nuevo Texto Crítico,* and *Papeles de Montevideo,* as well as many critical anthologies, such as *Teoría y política de la construcción de identidades y diferencias en América Latina y el Caribe, Posmodernidad en la periferia, Las culturas de fin de siglo en América Latina, Cultura y Tercer Mundo,* and *Culturas en Globalización.*[22]

This list does not include the work of individual scholars that will be discussed more directly throughout the essay. It also does not aim to be exhaustive or to ignore the Portuguese and Caribbean aspects of this postmodern/ postcolonial gaze on Latin American criticism. Indeed, the work of the Brazilian critic Roberto Schwarz is of growing importance. The Caribbean's postmodern/postcolonial splippage is the topic of another chapter that concentrates specifically on the work of Antonio Benítez-Rojo and Édouard Glissant. Another important site of critical production is found in various new bilingual journals from Puerto Rico (*Postdata, Nómada, Bordes*) as well as the border zones of El Paso (*Puente Libre*) and Miami (*Apuntes Postmodernos/Postmodern Notes*). Such a flurry of new scholarship clearly goes beyond the study of postmodernism as a literary style that continues to inform a somewhat established scholarly tradition in contemporary Latin American literature. One could also include important new European journals such as *Latin American Cultural Studies.*[23] Together, these efforts come closer to providing a sense of the living aspects of postmodern logic, a contradictory exchange with the life-world that includes concerns over the globalization of cultural forms as well as their tendency to absorb all spaces of contestation and resistance. These pages are meant as explorations in the context of such ongoing research.

The Postcolonial Radical

In "Representing the Colonized: Anthropology's Interlocutors," Edward Said reminds us that First World appropriation of as yet unconquered spaces belies First World claims to ideological neutrality, in the very technical expertise and epistemological refinement with which its contemporary academic discourses textualize, and in their disregard for political and historical specificity.[24] Said thus appears to challenge postcolonial thinking into a recognition of elements that postmodernity finds problematic or simply outdated: imperialism, peripheral modernity, neocolonialism, and other structures of inequality give way to a focus on complicitous participation of all subjects in the construction of power, on identity as an obstacle to a freer and more fluid postmodern ontology, and on writing as a place where otherness can be explored and even experienced from within regardless of position, gender, or even class. Said's own attempt to theorize the subaltern calls for acknowledging a realm of otherness that is "constitutively different," and for recognizing the still unmet anti-imperialist challenges implicit in the work of Third World writers such as Fanon and Aimé Césaire, whose "models or representations of human effort in the contemporary world" still carry relevance.[25] One could question whether Said wants to contain Fanon and Césaire to the times invoked in their colonial discourses, or whether his orientalist model requires an either/or epistemological structure that no longer obtains in the predominant strands of contemporary theory. But his critique still raises important questions, such as whether postcolonial readings of Fanon and Césaire are all too willing to forget the specific nature of not-so-distant colonial struggles, or whether a strictly rhetorical account of otherness is tantamount to a new form of benign neglect. This has become a key question for other critics as well, most notably Henry Louis Gates Jr., whose essay "Critical Fanonism" vividly depicts the ahistorical tendencies of postcolonial theorizing.[26]

A different look at contemporary critical approaches toward the Third World is found in Gayatri Chakravorty Spivak's emphasis on combining a concern for decolonization with deconstructive work as such. In her most explicit and perhaps controversial attempt to distinguish postcolonial writing from the new wave of interest in Latin American literary canonization, she writes:

> The radicals of the industrial nations want to be the Third World. Why is "magical realism" paradigmatic of Third World literary production? In a bit, and in the hands of the less gifted teacher, only that literary style will begin to count as ethnically authentic. There is, after all, a reason why Latin America qualifies as the norm of "the Third World" for the United States, even as India used to be the authentic margin for the British. It is interesting that "magical realism," a style of Latin American provenance, has been used to great effect by some expatriate or diasporic subcontinentals writing in English. Yet, as the Ariel–Caliban debates dramatize, Latin America has not participated in decolonization. Certainly this formal conduct of magical realism

can be said to allegorize, in the strictest possible sense, a socius and a political configuration where "decolonization" cannot be narrativized. . . . In the greater part of the Third World, the problem is that the declared rupture of "decolonization" boringly repeats the rhythms of colonization with the consolidation of recognizable styles.[27]

Spivak clearly points to the reductionist practice of a critical process whereby Latin American literature becomes a monumentalized style that claims to account for the voice of the native, a generalized Third Worldness marketed for literary and critical reproduction by the "radicals" of industrialized nations. Leftist and liberal critics become particularly complicitous in constructing Third World identities: (1) through First World academic appropriation of the Other's fixed place as producer of "national allegories" that are presumably no longer available in Western postmodernism; (2) by looking on foundationalist traditions that inform Third World texts as models of authenticity for subaltern stories whose representation can be guarded from the distance. The decolonizing or postcolonial intellectual that Spivak calls for would be more conscious and critical of how this transaction with the "voice of the native" takes place, though not necessarily free of contradictory entanglements. He or she would be a different "radical," though clearly one who still speaks for the other, or at least someone who is able to transfer that other to the space of writing itself, without claiming to speak for anyone in particular.

But what to make of Spivak's extraordinary claim that "Latin America has not participated in decolonization"? It would seem to make sense only if we read that region strictly along the lines of the "magical realist" ideology she aims to deconstruct. In her attempt to critique this rather facile form of referentiality, Spivak somehow fails to acknowledge the existence of a Latin America that speaks through differing voices, most particularly from within, but also through First World diasporic and immigrant articulations like her own. She makes no effort to document, or imagine, a vast region with a rich, though far from successful, history of attempts to decolonize that inform more than a century and a half of culture and literature. One doubts that she means that decolonization can only begin now, from postcolonial interventions made in First World institutions. Her Latin America gets locked into the mirror of its own reception through critical tropes that also flow uncritically, particularly in the U.S. academy. After all, terms like "magical realism" ("carnivalesque," "neobaroque," and "hybridity" may also deserve similar scrutiny) have lost much of their initial explanatory value.[28]

They have become buzzwords loosely associated with an exotic and undifferentiated multiculturalist flavor.

To be fair, Spivak's aim does not seem to be Latin American literary history as such, but rather a critique of Fredric Jameson's Third World construct, as well as his failure to deconstruct how some Marxist critics working in the First World position themselves in the process of producing literary criticism. Under scrutiny are Jameson's attempt to theorize "national allegory" as the Third World's literary correlative to the First World's postmodern cultural logic, as well as his subsequent work on Third World film and narrative representation based on Latin American magical realism.[29] Theorizing the entire Third World with one totalizing stroke, as Aijaz Ahmad's often-quoted response to Jameson's national allegory construct makes clear, fails to account for a historically and culturally more complex Third World, or even to question the accuracy of the term. Most important, by overemphasizing the need for realism in the literature of "developing countries," Jameson's attempt to show how national allegory constitutes a use-value for Third World texts that is difficult to appreciate for First World readers truncates the Third World's diverse relationships with modernity, a history that has also produced a literature informed by hybrid modern and even postmodern inscriptions.

In contrast to Jameson, Spivak proposes a postcolonial mode of critique and textuality in which "you take positions in terms not of the discovery of historical or philosophical grounds, but in terms of reversing, displacing, and seizing the apparatus of value-coding."[30] This she defines as a form of "founding catachresis," a "claim for which no adequate referent exists." Rather than an assertion of "spurious identity," it involves an epistemological vigilance, "an incessant re-coding of diversified fields of value" that becomes the "deconstructive predicament of the postcolonial": the need for such an intellectual to "say 'no'" to the luck "of having access to the culture of imperialism," while still recognizing that "she must inhabit it, indeed invest it, to criticize it."[31]

Spivak's image of a postcolonial critic places the danger of assuming a fixed identity, as woman or subaltern, under the regimen of incessant critique and constant self-questioning, yet it also seems to suggest a somewhat more political edge to postmodern notions of ambiguity and dispersal. Spivak's postcoloniality, a designifying construct accented by feminism and traces of Third World culture, attempts to make a claim for the elusive, if not wholly absent, referent of postmodernism. The embodiment of this claim is found in the diasporic intellectual armed with deconstructive competence, a would-be commuter between First and Third World subject positions, a self-conscious native speaker of English as a second language, indeed, a scandalous intruder upon Western metaphysics. One assumes that Spivak does not intend this claim to be identified with an origin, even though the specific "in-betweenness" of having come from the Third World (but being no longer bound to it), or that of being a woman under a contested Western patriarchal order, manifestly (though not prescriptively) informs it. A sense of referentiality for this critical position is thus suggested, albeit a deconstructive one that is at odds with its own trace of origins.

This sense of discursive referentiality solicits questions about critics whose work remains anchored in their Eurocentric native space and intellectual male tradition. Could they perform postcolonial criticism? Indeed, Spivak has herself raised these questions about Jacques Derrida and Michel Foucault in her often-cited essay "Can the Subaltern Speak?" How would they manage to construct such liminality except through deconstruction, if neither birth nor accident has produced access to a hybrid state thus defined? Then again, if deconstruction proper is the only medium through which "doubleness" is obtained in general, regardless of cultural or national bearings, is it always already postcolonial, or does postcolonialism make claims on deconstruction that are distinctive? This unresolved ambiguity in her work is also evident in Homi Bhabha's own attempt to articulate a postcolonial sense of "politics" and cultural "Third Worldness" that could claim a bit more specificity than First World Derridean deconstruction, though it often seems readily in concert with a mainstreamed postmodern rhetoric of writing and troping.[32]

It could therefore be argued that Spivak's concern to provide a clear antithesis to Jameson's construct produces a blindness of sorts, for she fails to register another conceptualization of Third World literature that today is arguably more prevalent in the United States than Jameson's: Latin America as the quintessence of postmodern textuality—a discursive community bound by an allegory of pure difference, which translates all forms of referential specificity into writing, errancy, and rhetorical liminality. Works utilizing this model are often imbued by references to Borges's masterful writerly stories and deconstructive moves, or by an ongoing appraisal of writerly experimentation in more contemporary Latin American writers, which is then seen as the essence of postmodernity.[33] The generally unsuspected relationship between this reading and Jameson's construct has been succinctly outlined by Jean Franco:

> The juxtaposition of disparate discourses, the use of pastiche, perhaps helps explain why U.S. critics so eagerly embrace Latin American

novels as postmodern. But incorporation into postmodernism is no more satisfactory than Jameson's Third World national allegory. Indeed, the two recuperative gestures seem to be motivated by the same operation of extrapolation. Extrapolation reduces the complexity of intertextual allusions and deprives texts of their own historical relations to prior texts. It implies a view of Latin American literature either in opposition to the metropolis or as part of the metropolis's postmodern repertoire. Yet novels such as Augusto Roa Bastos's *Yo el Supremo* and Edgardo Rodríguez Juliá's *La noche oscura del Niño Avilés,* which defy facile recuperation as national allegory or as the postmodern, demand readings informed by cultural and political history.[34]

Would Spivak's notion of a postcolonial critic, owing largely to deconstructive insights, differ from such postmodern readings as clearly as it does from the referentially bound notion of magical realism? How would she or he keep from extrapolating cultural and political history, or sustain the complexity of historical relations to prior texts? It may well be, as Spivak contends, that multiculturalism, ethnic discourses, and magic realism deserve greater scrutiny because they foster "the production of a neo-colonial discourse" by allowing "disciplinary support for the convictions of authentic marginality by the (aspiring) elite."[35] It is not clear, however, that postmodern deconstructive criticism has been any less productive in constructing marginality—for itself, if not for others—from the act of reading and writing, in its search for an internal sense of "otherness" that somehow supplants what Said would call the "constitutive other."

These questions carry considerable promise precisely because they rehearse many of the contradictions inherent in the notion of postcoloniality. Arif Dirlik, in perhaps the most biting critique of the "postcolonial aura" to date, pinpoints many of its ambiguities and imprecisions, even while underscoring the relevance of the global framework that informs it:

> One might go so far as to suggest that, if a crisis in historical consciousness, with all its implications for national and individual identity, is a basic theme of postcoloniality, then the First World itself is postcolonial. To the extent that the Euro-American self-image was shaped by the experience of colonizing the world (since the constitution of the Other is at once also the constitution of the Self), the end of colonialism presents the colonizer as much as the colonized with a problem of identity.[36]

Dirlik begins with the consideration that postcolonialism, as informed by the poststructuralist/postmodernist paradigm, may well correspond to the growing genre of academic First World theoreticism—another empowering discourse for well-paid intellectuals working in the West, in this case claimed by those with Third World credentials. On the other hand, Dirlik does acknowledge the material and conceptual need for the rise of such a field. Postcolonialism arose not just in the immediate context of British postcolonial history, but as a "response to a genuine need, the need to over-come a crisis of understanding produced by the inability of old categories to account for the world," which makes it "possible to conceive of the future in ways other than those of Euro-American political and social models."[37] But postcolonialism, he argues, has not taken up this opportunity. Its self-refer-ential program of subject theory, discursive historicity, and close readings has rendered critics incapable of grasping contemporary Third World prob-lems in broader conceptual terms. At best, Dirlik concludes, postcolonial-ism "resonates"—from a distance and at the level of the individual subject—with the cultural transformations brought about by the advent of global capitalism. In general, postcolonialism systematically shuns any notion of the structure that continues to link the Third and First Worlds and requires that we theorize them together. At worst, it responds more to First World intellectual careerism than to the needs, social or conceptual, of those parts of the world implied by the term *postcolonial.*

Dirlik's powerful review of postcolonial theory insists on the latter's deepest aporia: a continuous critique of the Eurocentric epistemological tradition that fails to account for capitalism as structure, particularly in its present global form, or for the roles that "modernization" and "the nation" may still play in developmental strategies that are very much wanted, and perhaps needed, in the so-called postcolonial world.[38] What discourses can critiques of Western master narratives provide that address those needs? What is truly striking about Dirlik's critique, however, is how indistinguish-able it becomes from a critique of postmodernism proper. Indeed, toward the end of his essay, Dirlik affirms that postcolonialists have merely re-phrased postmodern precepts. At this point, however, one wonders why he did not focus on the latter more directly or draw them into his set of con-clusions more sharply. In its immediate attempt to expose how derivative and opportunistic a handful of postcolonialists appear to him, Dirlik's cri-tique disavows its own promise of transferability toward the source of the problem he seeks to define.

The value of postcolonial theory, as well as that of its critics, may ulti-mately rest on how it intensifies and mediates the contradictions it shares with the more generalized and prestigious body of critical methods and theories: poststructuralist deconstruction and postmodernist critique of master narratives. On a different plane, however, it is unclear how notions of postcoloniality informing the current Anglophone critique of the British colonial legacy in India, parts of Africa, and the Caribbean can be transferred to regions like Latin America or African America, whose experiences with colonialism and neocolonialism are markedly different and which have a history of decolonization that long antedates current theoretical globalizations. At times, one can sense the potential for a clash between the British and Hispanic literary traditions, jockeying to see which will constitute the true precursor for a new global literary order. At other times, the postcolonial is just confused with postindependence periods. Postcoloniality has, however, a wider frame of reference beyond the "strict chronologies of history tout court," as Ella Shohat has argued.[39] Its other referential emphasis corresponds to "the disciplinary advances characteristic of intellectual history" at a time in which Third World thinking is being challenged and redefined by global economies. "The unarticulated tension between the philosophical and the historical teleologies in the 'post-colonial,'" she adds, "underlies some of the conceptual ambiguities of the term."[40]

The Latin American Postmodern Canon

The ambiguities of postcolonial criticism are profound, and will likely continue to nurture important debates, but it seems already clear that they accentuate the uncertain interplay between history and theory inherent to all postmodern discourses. That ambiguity, often rendered as the very site of ludic or transgressive potential for rhetorical performance, unearths new challenges when applied to residues of colonialism in fields of study such as Latin American literature and cultural studies. As stated earlier, this field has been primarily influenced by poststructural readings in the United States. In the influential work of Djelal Kadir and Roberto González Echevarría, for example, the force of Paul de Man's method of close readings has been brought to bear on major authors such as Alejo Carpentier, Carlos Fuentes, Octavio Paz, and Jorge Luis Borges. Such a critical program has also inspired new and often innovative readings of nineteenth-century and colonial times, indeed, the entire field of Latin American and Caribbean literature. By now it stands as an important, if not dominant, alternative to earlier structuralist, nationalist, and dependency-theory approaches to Latin American literature, particularly in the United States. Yet, this strand of deconstructive Latin Americanism remains closely bound to a literary form of epistemology that is far removed even from the cultural politics implicit in its own epistemological challenges to modernity. An engagement with Latin America's debate on postmodern culture, as well as more recent postcolonial discourses, cultural studies, and feminism, is likely to bring greater depth to this field, and perhaps bridge the boundaries between a Latin America constructed from U.S. universities and critical discourse that draws closer to the Latin American cultural life-world. The recent history of the disciplinary divide in various Latin Americanisms has been outlined by John Beverley and José Oviedo:

> In the context of the crisis of the traditional Left and the waning of the right-wing military dictatorships imposed to contain its force in the 1970's, the theme of democratization has played the same role in the Latin American discussion of postmodernism as the shift in aesthetic-epistemological paradigms did in Anglo-European postmodernism. The impulse for the latter came mainly from the humanities and art criticism; in Latin America, it has come from the social sciences, with, however, this proviso: that in assuming the problematic of postmodernism, the Latin American social sciences have also begun to assume the obligation to take on problems that were posed initially in the humanities, particularly in advanced literary and cultural theory.[41]

But the problematic of postmodernism in Latin American literary studies, as Beverley himself has shown in *Literature and Politics in the Central American Revolutions,* is not prone to take on postmodernism as a cultural debate either.[42] Indeed, a strictly humanistic (i.e., literary) understanding of postmodernism has become a Western (or perhaps American) luxury of sorts, because few developing societies seem able to fund literary criticism as such, or have the deep structure of research universities invested in literary studies. The stability of full-time teaching positions and well-financed research opportunities dedicated to the study of Latin America in Euro-American institutions since the mid-1980s could not find a greater contrast in Latin America itself, where even countries such as Venezuela, known for its support of humanistic studies, have witnessed severe contractions and neoliberal regimes such as Chile's, in spite of their lauded economic strides, have yet to invest significantly in the production of critical or cultural spaces. Such research has been severely limited in all of Latin America, where part-time adjunct positions are the norm. One could safely estimate that there are more professors of Latin American literature remunerated at middle-class levels in New York and California than there are in all of Latin America. Needless to say, the ranks of exiles, expatriates, and other forms of diasporic "in-betweenness" have increased, but unlike those of a generation ago, today's Latin American academic migrants are younger, often trained in the United States, and fully aware of the need to engage Latin Americanism in English as much as in Spanish or Portuguese. Their academic future demands it. There are few, if any, loci of legitimation for such influential strands of Latin Americanism in Latin America itself.

As one would expect, scholarly construction of disciplinary objects relies primarily on social and academic institutions of support, although Latin Americanism cannot be simply divided into neat categories of here and there, particularly with so many diasporic Latin Americans commuting between the borders. Crossover influences are increasingly felt in the work of women writers and critics, as well as in culturalist approaches to Latin America itself that are not bound to narrowing identitarian readings. As mentioned earlier, previews of this task can be found in the work of critics such as Julio Ramos, Jean Franco, Beatriz Sarlo, George Yúdice, Roberto Schwarz, John Beverley, Mary Louise Pratt, Walter Mignolo, Hugo Achugar, José Rabasa, Sylvia Molloy, Antonio Cornejo-Polar, Juan Duchesne, Doris Sommer, and Néstor García Canclini. In the work of Jean Franco, for example, Latin American history, culture, and literature, as well as feminism, are enlightened by postmodern theories without succumbing to its conflationary pressures. She writes that the history of Latin American narrative, most particularly through García Márquez, "rather than an allegory, has become the terrain of conflicting discourses" that have "made visible that absence of any signified that could correspond to the nation."[43] Spivak's notion of catachresis again becomes curiously useful here, with perhaps a more specific sense of a historical bind: Latin American narrative is read within its own (postcolonial?) claim for which no fixed referent exists; it is a literature that both calls for and problematizes the construction of nation-states as the solution to Latin America's identitarian quest.

Modernizing discourses continue to inform the culture of postcolonial societies even when modernization theory no longer enjoys the explanatory power it once did. Both modernist and postmodernist cultural understandings are challenged by this nonsynchronous sense of history, a source of doubling that calls for more than choosing between realist or textualist readings. A crucial example is found in García Márquez's classic *One Hundred Years of Solitude*. It could be argued, on the side of realism and identity formation, that the more or less linear account of imperialism and foreign hegemony that involves Macondo's passage into Latin American modernity instantiates otherness as "constitutive Others," to use Said's term. Conversely, the novel allows an opposite reading, as a self-seeking "otherness" transferred to the acts of reading and writing implicit in the character of

Melquíades, whereby the reader discovers the novel's own Borgesian writing of itself. But these are not mutually exclusive: both codes are explicitly evident in forms of emplotment that continue to invoke conquest and colonialism, neo-colonial struggles, failed revolutionary struggles, cycles of default modernity, as well as the literary transgression of those apparent historical forces.[44] Realist enclosures have failed to produce comprehensive readings of Latin American literature by ignoring the self-referential aspects of Latin America's astounding literary originality, as well as its capacity to deny simple longings for transcendental signifieds. But the celebration of literary subversion since the boom period may also require greater scrutiny in its attempt to deny the flip side of this double coding—a critique of Latin America's discourses of modernity specific enough to complicate Euro-America's self-critique of master narratives.

How, in short, have the poststructuralist allegories of reading been deployed in the study of Latin American literature? As noted earlier, this has become an influential paradigm whose epistemological underpinnings seem to challenge, in the name of difference, all forms of discourse except itself. Its cul-de-sac logic has not gone unnoticed. In *The Voice of the Masters,* Roberto González Echevarría reluctantly acknowledges its potential limitations:

> Deconstructive criticism's indiscretion, like charity, begins at home, since in practice it self-deconstructs as it deconstructs. If in this it resembles fiction—which not only narrates, but tells us how—such a resemblance is not accidental. I am not unaware that such a position implicitly reintroduces an authoritative claim; it invents a supercritical consciousness that winds up the mechanism and leaves it ticking, apparently on its own. This may well be the blind spot of deconstructive criticism, but, as we shall see, it is one that it shares with postmodern literature.[45]

Yet, a mere detection of this apparent aporia may be unhelpful, because it seems content to invest itself through it by conflating deconstructive criticism with postmodern literature, leaving both in somewhat ambiguous territory. Such a festive blind spot makes urgent the need for a critique of the poststructural/postmodern slippage, particularly as this paradigm has been domesticated by literary criticism. That distinction may well define the "postcolonial difference," for it is in that space that the inscription of "others" and the world of politics are generally kept from resurfacing beyond deconstructive decodification. How, for example, do the postmodern/poststructural categorical critiques of language, culture, and history—indeed, all forms of cognition known heretofore—end up sealing themselves in a hermetic domain of privileged literary/grammatological discourse? What kind of intertextuality does this paradigm demand for the broad array of cultural and social texts that articulate historical unfolding?

A closer look at the Latin Americanist version of this forceful construct is perhaps best done through the outlines of Djelal Kadir's *Questing Fictions* and *The Other Writing*. At the root of Kadir's work is the notion of Latin American literature as the quintessence of nonrepresentational discourse. Kadir posits that a continuous rhetorical force is situated in the semantic abyss created by the discovery of America, from which Latin America's texts have derived. "Latin America rediscovers [in the nineteenth century] simultaneously its 'true' [colonial] fictions and the rebellious impulse to forge, to fabricate a new historical-political 'truth' of liberation and democracy, which time proves, and continues to prove, as yet another fiction of linguistic extravagance and rhetorical errancy."[46] "Latin America has been variously a pretext and a text that for five hundred years now has been generating a panoply of fictions about and from within itself. In this protracted cohabitation, fictionality (of fictions and of theories) and Latin America could be considered as functionally synonymous."[47]

According to this outline, broadly deployed with mild variations by Latin Americanist deconstructivism in general, the errors committed in the process of colonizing (taming, nominalizing, inscribing) the New World in the name of preestablished notions (nomenclature, signifieds, representational schemes) become a sort of "original transgression" from which Latin America's texts flow through the nineteenth century down to the present. The lack of correspondence between the linguistic and conceptual frameworks of the conquering and conquered worlds turns into a ruling principle of error, aided by neocolonial attempts to modernize that are also prone to repeated error. This combination is exemplified by the constant search for identity that has historically characterized Latin American textuality (history, literature, politics). Errancy, absence, lack of a center, confusion, search for identity, desire to name the abyss—all become signifiers that govern and inform Latin American literature and writing. Hence, Latin America becomes the best example of a contradictory search for and confirmation of an epistemological absence, because it cannot help but—to quote Djelal Kadir's celebration of this condition—"founder on the slippery ground of heterogeneity, desultoriness, raving polysemia, and unmitigated dissemination."[48]

Spivak's notion of catachresis, that "claim for which no referent exists," could be deployed here once again, as a way of complicating Latin America's brushes with modernity. But instead of defining a struggle against an imperial tradition that encumbers the critic's own contradictory attempts to simultaneously invest and resist it, to "leave the wound open," as Spivak is wont to say, Kadir's deconstruction extols the semiological virtuosity implicit in Latin America's errant history as a new master code for understanding Latin America; hence, the canonical value of errancy for a postmodern poetics that thrives on the unmitigated premise that writing—particularly that which attempts to articulate social and economic claims—can be denied any pretense of pertinence, except as literary conceit. In this dominant strand, deconstruction thus slips into a celebration of a discursive performance that mimics epistemic negation as literary prowess. The oppositional promise of Spivak's catachresis is thereby lost, perhaps owing to its strictly virtual promise as "incessant re-coding of diversified fields of value."[49] A new Latin American postmodern aesthetics comes to life nonetheless, and a history of more than five hundred years is periodized into one epoch bound by a single wayward epistemological force. Dirlik's critique becomes directly applicable here as well, because Kadir's discursive historicity, while attempting to avoid the pitfalls of structural periodizations, slips into its own set of diachronic idealizations.

To ground Latin America's literature, or any literature, in a foundational moment, or event, would seem wholly contradictory to the poststructuralist philosophy of language that informs deconstructive criticism. Even when defined as sheer negation, however, as texts that can only mirror their rhetorical nature following a key moment of epistemic dispersal, this notion still betrays a sense of origination, if not a sort of essentialism. Such a philosophy of language fails to grasp how societies, particularly societies that defy the normative notion of entry into modernity, continuously resemanticize history according to material and spiritual needs. It is a blindness that arises precisely at a time when Third World texts are increasingly consumed by First World readers, partially because of their artistic merit, but also because these texts seem to evoke a social, cultural, and ethnic hybridity that speaks to internal changes within the Western life-world. Moreover, if the so-called errant quest that informs Latin American writing constitutes an intransitive grand signifier, a repository of stories never capable of affirming any particular signified but always bound to equivocate, then we begin to detect a theoretical framework whose explicit textual determinism becomes a questionable substitute for historical understanding. All of Latin American textuality is thus reduced to a new periodicity, a free-floating epistemic big bang, according to which all writing since the conquest—including the texts produced by critics themselves—is rediscovered as a "raving polysemia." A sort of deconstructive master narrative begins to reveal itself.

In his *Myth and Archive,* a book that begins with an impressive charting of Latin America's discursive history, González Echevarría concludes with an analogous conflation of all of Latin America's textuality as an archive governed by a Borgesian master code of all possible fictions, "the major figure in modern Latin American fiction, or repository of stories and myths, one of which is the story about collecting those stories and myths."[50] As a "founding negativity," the archive is said to contain, at its core, the "heterogeneity of cultures, languages, sources, beginnings," a totalizing figure of narrative recombinations meant to stand for Latin American history as such, including earlier archives organized along legal, scientific, and anthropological discursive formations.[51] Mirroring the reading/writing construction of *One Hundred Years of Solitude* set forth by Melquíades, myths of beginning are conflated with those of modern history into the ultimate archive of postmodern writing as literary celebration, a newly configured all-encompassing myth of writing that always already subsumes earlier forms of discursive formation—legal, scientific, and anthropological. Thus, colonial America is at one with postmodern Latin America, and history, particularly that which tells the story of independence and revolutionary wars, is integrated in this repository of literariness through deconstruction and critical performance. Writing about Latin America becomes particularly unproblematic once this pedagogy of designification has been mastered. The nitty-gritty nature of history is absorbed into tropes that compress, or dismiss, social specificity. Neither the virtual contestation implicit in Spivak's postcolonial predicament nor Dirlik's call for a historical account of ongoing structural inequalities between First and Third Worlds applies any longer.

One should also question a construct that conflates all of the linguistic extravagance and rhetorical errancy employed in the conquest and colonization of America into a strictly Latin American foundational precept. Would it not also inform the history and literature of North America? One can assume, for example, either that the formation of the United States was not an errant fiction, or that it was; but in either case, U.S. history is not caught up in the celebration of a discursive abyss imposed by the discovery, and reinforced thereafter. Through expansion, slavery, wars of independence, wars of consolidation, and subsequent modernizations of various sorts, the United States has managed to invest other historical moments with defining textual power, whether fictional or not. Its history may also be read as a repository of texts that is eminently subject to deconstruction, but one whose will to power is unlikely to yield a literary reification of colonial times as the prelude to postmodernism. Analogously, Western Europe must also have learned to resemanticize its histories of foundational conquests, epic equivocations, and epistemological clashes on the way to consolidation as nation-states through modernity whose authority, not errancy, we now must deconstruct.

The broad critique of logocentric premises and teleological projections of modernity as "master narrative" are obviously applicable to the history and future of the United States, Canada, and Europe, as well as of Latin America. But the way in which such premises are applied to areas that correspond to profoundly different histories of the modern narrative (in that still undeconstructed sense do I use the politically anachronic First World/ Third World splits) provides a telling contrast. Indeed, it could be said that the critique of modernity that guides postmodernism remains bound to epistemological refinement in the First World, but obtains political specificity in its approach to the Third World. This political shadow, or residue, may well constitute the grounds for postcolonial inflections. The significance of the Third World's peripherally modern histories, particularly its narratives of revolutions and insurrections, is placed under erasure for having failed to enter modernity, and for generating a sense of identity that is but a symptom of such failures. On the other hand, because their more central position in the world of capitalism, the modern histories of Europe, the United States, or even Japan—along with their concomitant identitarian bearings—would be deconstructed differently. A representative rehearsal of this selective critique is advanced by Carlos J. Alonso in *The Spanish American Regional Novel: Modernity and Autochthony:*

> Historical misfortune is not the outcome of Latin America's cultural errancy or self-ignorance, but the condition of its possibility. In this regard, Latin America's situation can be illuminated by comparing it to that of the United States. Born of modernity as well, the United States shared from the beginning the linguistic and historical difficulties attendant on the formulation of a cultural essence that have been identified in the case of Latin America. But in contrast to the latter, the ascendance of the United States to a position of historical hegemony has managed to invest with authority the myths of cultural identity that were generated by that country's intelligentsia.[52]

Of course, "ascendance to a position of historical hegemony" does not necessarily endow cultural identity with truth, nor exempt it from deconstruction, particularly by critics engaged in reading the culture of regions in which U.S. hegemony weighs uncomfortably. Moreover, if a dialectic between power and myth constitutes the contrasting variable for a historical understanding of modernity, the experience of Latin America, as well as that of other postcolonial societies, requires much more than a negative assignation within a binary logic that totalizes it as "the failed other," of value only in an undifferentiated literary history. Deconstructive thinking teaches us to avoid such neat divisions between winners and losers. Perhaps one way to look at the postcolonial attempt to alter the postmodern approach is an awareness that there is always the possibility of slippage. The necessary critique of modern traditions in postcolonial societies must perforce be radically different.

A more recent rehearsal of this problematic is found in Santiago Colás's attempts to chart all of Latin American modernity (a period beginning with the independence wars and roughly ending with the postboom literature in the 1970s) as a single modern narrative readily understood from a few literary texts. It is important to note that Colás wants to bring the political into a postmodern critique of that modern tradition. But that promise immediately lapses into a predictable foreclosure: Latin American modernity is reduced to mistakes and delusions—indeed, a series of symptoms easily diagnosed through Lacanian psychoanalysis and overcome through the advent of postmodern literature, whose radical rhetoric and links with mass culture will somehow conjure a new liberationist history.[53] Colás, perhaps sensing that the political framework he seeks for postmodernism is still not beyond the scope of discursive aestheticism, calls for a division of Latin Americanist modes of deconstruction into two camps: one hegemonic, poststructuralist, de Manian, aesthetically and politically modernist, and still bound by Latin American nationalist tendencies; the other postmodern, capable of rejecting master narratives, ostensibly postnational, and attending to marginality in ways that are antagonistic to hegemonic poststructural modes of critique.[54]

Colás's attempt to make this distinction is, in my view, an important register of inherent problems within the theoretical work I have attempted to describe thus far. Yet, it remains unclear just how the postmodern differs from the poststructural in Colás's own critique of the Latin American modern tradition as an unspecified legacy of failure that is best understood from the purview of aesthetic, albeit postmodern, deconstruction. Indeed, if the truly postmodern crossroads that Colás advocates is largely imbued by the notion that "Latin America seems to be emerging from its most recent cycle of revolution and counterrevolutionary repression to embrace U.S.-style democracy and the free market," it would seem to acquire definition in a rather undeconstructed journalistic plane in which postmodern constructs acquire a globalizing and neoliberal turn.[55] That turn, one should add, is what has brought the most accomplished deconstructive critics, including Derrida, Judith Butler, and Spivak herself, to argue in the opposite direction, that is, to question the hegemony of the postmodern construct at the expense of post-structuralist means of analysis.

Another important register of the Latin Americanist cartography evolving from deconstructive work is found in the debates on *testimonio* literature. Does *testimonio* constitute a literary, or antiliterary, mode of expression? Is it realist, modern, or postmodern? Is it a subaltern articulation or simply another expression of identity? These debates, often exclusively centered on *I, Rigoberta Menchú*, and the *Autobiography of a Runaway Slave*, include many critics and different positions, including, most notably, John Beverley, George Yúdice, Doris Sommer, Elsbieta Sklodowska, Nelly Richard, Fredric Jameson, Roberto González Echevarría, and Alberto Moreiras, among many others. What is still missing from the debate, in my view, is a comparative analysis, with perhaps some empirical work on reader reception, of how Rigoberta Menchú is read in the different parts of Latin America itself. As José Rabasa explains, "Both Menchú's testimonio and the communiqués of the EZLN (Ejército Zapatista de Liberación Nacional] are forms of subaltern discourse that should not be confused with what subaltern studies produces in the intellectual centers."[56] My aim here is not to attempt a comprehensive review of these debates, however, but to underline the symptoms that provide continuity to the problematics attendant to literary Latin Americanism that I have been describing, particularly the ways in which deconstruction constitutes a necessary yet insufficient level of analysis. I will therefore limit myself to delineating Beverley's ongoing attempt to privilege *testimonio* as a form of postmodern writing that goes against the grain of humanistic literariness, and Alberto Moreiras's methodical deconstruction of that notion as a pernicious form of identity politics made on behalf of Latin America by Latin Americanists from the distance.

Indeed, on one level, one could not help but question, with Moreiras as well as Nelly Richard and Neil Larson, whether Rigoberta Menchú's story has not been appropriated into a cause for a leftist politics of reading and a multicultural curricular reform in the Unites States. Although these are crucially important issues, they show precisely how Latin America turns into a codified object from the distance, or gets erased as a complex living culture with many other forms of discourse and politics. One can see how *testimonio* texts and the politics of reading they appear to invoke in the United States, can easily become a complete hermeneutical circle for a Latin Americanist literary left that, in Moreiras's view, is closer to an "aesthetic fix" than a form of solidarity, because *testimonio* only produces "a poetics of solidarity of a fallen and derivative kind."[57]

But this critique, acute as it is, does not really address two of Beverley's central contentions: that *testimonio* can be seen as an articulation of post-modern experiences in Latin America itself, and that *testimonio* as a form of writing constitutes a new, posthumanist, "antiliterary" form of writing. I hasten to add that these are controversial but crucial contentions often ignored by literary critics, even though they are inherent to postmodern culture on a global scale. Moreiras does address them, albeit in favor of Borgesian indeterminacy. He begins by recognizing the exhaustion of the boom/postboom literary models, and the importance of different aesthetic practices in late-capitalist globalization, besides those provided by "high literature." But he rushes to conclude that the way out of this contemporary bind is to observe that post–Cold War global conditions usher in a new age that will bring a new, postidentitarian way of conceiving sociopolitical and cultural practices. Hence, our task is to leave Latin America to those dynamic forces and return to Borges, to learn to read *testimonio* "as literature, beyond literature," as "the indexical reference to the singularity of a pain beyond any possibility of representation," and, above all, as the refusal to read any form of "identitarian construction."[58] Thus, we find the invocation of a postsymbolic terrain for a postmodern readerly and cultural praxis on Latin America that has been rendered into an either/or bind once again, a position thoroughly thematized by boom and postboom deconstruction. Is there a deconstructive aesthetic fix in which Latin America is neatly divided between identity seekers and a postmodern literary horizon always already able to deconstruct itself? The latter would then turn into a notion that Moreiras ontologizes as a "self-mourning" that "survives in an undecisive labor of translation whose precariousness, however, shelters the uncompromising joy of knowing itself faithful to itself, following its own law."[59]

In *The Logic of Disintegration*, Peter Dews explains that poststructuralist thought has been received in the United States and parts of Europe predominantly through literary criticism as a form of avant-garde consciousness. A "sense of invading unknown territory, exposing oneself to the dangers of sudden, shocking encounters, and conquering an as yet unoccupied future, has been taken at face value, with little attempt being made to enquire into possible philosophical antecedents of the positions discussed or adopted, or into their relations to other contemporary philosophical currents."[60] It is therefore highly ironic that, upon closer readings, the notion of Latin America as a model of nonrepresentational discursivity can be said to function as yet one more theory of chronic underdevelopment. Latin America's modern past, its history, becomes useless except for the literary merits of texts that exemplify such failures through rhetorical transgression. Accordingly, postmodernism will liberate Latin America through its literary prowess, a future safely ensconced within a radical critique that is already there within its theory of writing. The masses, or even the ruling classes of Latin America, will hopefully follow a set of precepts to be derived from criticism as literary transgression. Or not. By positing the literary as the matrix of all writing and hence all historical articulation, this form of deconstructionism substitutes the logic of signifieds it seeks to undermine with an equally privileged discourse accountable only to its own process of immanent inscription. In *La estratificación de los márgenes,* Nelly Richard points to how the logic of disintegration administers difference: "Postmodernism defends itself against the destabilizing threat of the 'other' by integrating it back into a framework which absorbs all differences and contradictions. The center, though claiming to be in disintegration, still operates as a center: filing away any divergences into a system of codes whose meanings, both semantically and territorially, it continues to administer by exclusive right."[61]

Feminism and the Social Text

One hastens to add, these criticisms notwithstanding, that poststructuralist textuality was profoundly influential, through the agency of deconstruction, for bringing much-needed scrutiny to the totalizing vocation inherent in earlier forms of literary analysis. That critical impulse shifted the ground from universal value schemes, fixity, and representation to an appreciation for slippages, indeterminacy, and dialogism. Both the social sciences and the humanities have been profoundly influenced by this new focus on the intransitive and self-reflexive aspects of writing. Yet, it could also be argued that much deconstructive practice in literary studies remains ambiguously ensconced within the institutionally shielded domains that New Criticism left behind. Saussurrean epistemology and academic high culture predominate in a practice of conflating all texts, social and artistic, under a generalized notion of discourse, or through an undifferentiated affinity with a loosely defined notion of postmodernism. With the new pressures of cultural studies on humanistic poststructuralism, the possibility of a redrawing of boundaries may not be far, as evident in the work of Harold Bloom and Richard Rorty.[62] Poststructuralist criticism may have initially challenged traditional humanism, but its search for disjunction from the Western paradigm ultimately called for internal compression rather than semiotic dispersal.[63] Its potential to engage in dialogue with other disciplines and with society at large has been considerably foreclosed by the narrow epistemological nature of its most predominant strands as well as the internal challenges of a new market logic that informs global capitalism.

As Dirlik reminds us, the humanist legacy is challenged, if not threatened, by the West's own economic, migratory, and mass cultural needs, and not just by theories that "resonate" with such contradictory transformations. An intertextuality held within the boundaries of a new aestheticism, even when invigorated by epistemological angst and a performative pedagogy of textual interplay, is not likely to meet such a challenge; hence, the current call for cultural studies as well as postcolonial and feminist mediations that invest and critique the powerful tools of poststructuralism, a possibility whose promise may well require both structural and deconstructive interpellations. In one of the most incisive pieces of writing on contemporary Latin American culture, José Rabasa indicates precisely how deconstructive and metanarrative work must overcome its blind spots. He acknowledges the standing debt of subaltern theory to postmodern theory, but still argues for a new epistemology that "curtails the appropriation of its findings by dominant discourse," and "does not limit itself to understandings of power that ignore oppositions such as dominant classes vis-à-vis the colonized. These oppositions tend to be dismissed as instances of Western binary thinking."[64]

As the postcolonialist turn of theoretical paradigms continues to unfold beyond the British intellectual tradition, Latin America's study of cultural transculturations, as well as Latin American feminist articulations of the First World/Third World junctures, may present avenues worthy of further exploration and debate. Transculturation, a corpus worthy of comparison with India's subaltern studies, forms an intertextual body of cultural production and critical reflection fully imbued with the intricate relationship between textuality and historical understanding, particularly as a register of the relationship between modernization and culture in Latin America.[65] Unfortunately, transculturation has been often confused with sociohistorical content analysis, or structuralist attempts to account for Latin American heterogeneity as a synthesis rather than an intricate web of dialogical relations with texts and other cultural forms.[66] A closer examination of transculturation in the context of postmodern performances will be found in chapter 3. Suffice it to say for now that key moments of Latin America's modern critical sources can be reread in the context of transcultural theoretical work, even if they themselves harbor blind spots and culs-de-sac. Examples include Juan Carlos Mariátegui, particularly his attempt to bridge Crocean aesthetics and Inca imagery; the prolific yet often forgotten novelist José María Arguedas, who fused the worlds of creative writing, linguistics, and social-scientific analysis—perhaps an early manifestation of some current anthropological methods—into a unique Andean Latin Americanism; Fer-

nando Ortiz, whose readings of the Caribbean's sugar and tobacco industries were creatively imbued with tropes from medieval literature; Ángel
Rama's unique and lifelong endeavor to bring structuralism's critique of the
humanistic tradition to Latin America's notions of literary modernism and
identity, along with an early critique of modernity through Theodor
Adorno's negative dialectic; and, more recently, Néstor García Canclini's attempt to provide a critique that is informed by, as well as critical of, postmodern precepts.[67]

Such a different construction of Latin America remains open to postmodern as well as postcolonial articulations without erasing their modern
past as a single, disposable narrative. It takes us beyond hermetic or lyrical
theoreticism and into the living experience of multiple cultural modernization with a sense of multitemporal and multicultural entanglements that
are worthy of both critique and historical discovery. José Rabasa again reminds us that "subaltern movements should be seen as cultural forms where
the modern and nonmodern are compatible."[68] He also warns that "subaltern studies would thus first have the task of elaborating an inventory of
the colonial legacy of modernity, before even beginning to conceptualize
'elsewheres' to dominant Western rationalities (to borrow Donna Haraway's
utopian phrase)."[69] Enrique Dussel, one of Latin America's leading philosophers of liberation theology, observes that "the 'realization' of modernity no
longer lies in the passage from its abstract potential to its 'real,' European,
embodiment. It lies today, rather, in a process that will transcend modernity as such, a trans-modernity, in which both modernity and its negated alterity co-realize themselves in a process of mutual creative fertilization."[70]

It must be emphasized that the broad, shifting, transcultural notion
that I am invoking aims to find a framework able to examine the modern
with the postmodern, with a vigilant eye to colonial residues. I should also
add that Latin American theories of transculturation have kept a deaf ear to
the crucial terrain of women's readings and writings, which today constitute
a space of extraordinary critical importance. Indeed, that may be a blind
spot shared by transculturation and postmodern Latin Americanism. It is
not by accident that it is in the work of Jean Franco, Beatriz Sarlo, Doris
Sommer, Josephine Ludmer, Nelly Richard, Gabriela Mora, and Sylvia Molloy, among others, that new theoretical modes are at once both employed
and deeply challenged. Lucía Guerra Cunningham, for instance, suggests an
array of discursive strategies for the "Latin American woman as subject/
object of writing" that includes "the aesthetic phenomena of silence and the
void," "the diglossia of the feminine," and "mimicry with a transgressive
value."[71] Debra Castillo, in *Talking Back,* speaks of a "parallel construction"

that assumes the difficulty of negotiating the Other from a First World institution: "I try to build an applicable feminist strategy based on an infrastruc-
ture of evolved and evolving Latin American theory, while taking from first-
world feminist theory that which seems pertinent and complementary."[72]
The importance of these voices, as Jean Franco declares, lies not in the discovery of feminist writing per se, nor in its inclusion in a consumer-bound
academic pluralism, but in the way that they advance a critique of power relations and preceding discourses.[73]

These voices also gather force from the very theories into which they
introduce unsuspected contradictions, thus their value for contemporary
approaches—postcolonial or other—to Latin American cultural and literary studies. Feminist claims on history derive from the pertinence of a here
and now that includes material consequences for existing world orders.
Through them, the immediacy of social criticism and the distance of literary history are compressed into a contemporary political tension that poststructural theories perhaps did not expect. The basis on which referential
claims could be made has been shaken, but such crucial insights can be invoked by voices pursuing quotidian discourses whose relevance will address
ongoing needs for social transformation.[74] Thus, their challenge to both
poststructuralism and postmodernism from within their own vast claims to
historical understanding.

It is often observed that the boundaries between discourses, genres,
and historical periodizations have been blurred, along with strict disciplinary criteria for legitimizing critical competence. The very definition of a
literary critic is no longer guarded by the traditional domain of literary
sedimentation, even though it remains unclear whether the new frontier of
visual cultural studies can recast the best of print culture to formulate new
modes of resistance. But whether poststructuralist literary critics can be
drawn to deconstruct social texts remains a question. Those who really test
these borders—often women and postcolonial voices—inevitably seek to
apply deconstructed notions of history and literature to their daily lives as
well. This in itself is a project that will likely lay its own claim to the past
not merely as an archive of critical liminality and epistemic abyss but as a
textual repository of antecedents with the potential to sustain hope, and
maybe even action. The claims of deconstruction are too vast and broad for
there to be any ultimate refuge in a new aestheticism. Beatriz Sarlo's analysis
of "electronic aesthetics" in political texts such as the Persian Gulf War and
Alberto Fujimori's Peruvian presidential campaign exemplifies such an approach.[75] Christopher Norris's *Uncritical Theory, Postmodernism, Intellectu-*

als and the Gulf War also substantiates the need to test epistemological extrapolations within the sphere of the political.

In his prominent essays on postmodernism, Fredric Jameson has argued convincingly that we should look on postmodernism as a late-capitalist cultural logic through which modes of reading and writing could still historicize a critical space, albeit with greater difficulty, amid the existing hierarchies that still divided the world in various spheres. But since then, with the advent of neoliberal regimes, global or hypercapitalism may have narrowed that critical space, a shift that is now clearly felt in Latin America with particular intensity. This predicament, one that awaits all postcolonial societies, brings a new set of challenges to critical theorists. In the words of Martin Hopenhayn:

> How can the postmodern debate be incorporated in order to reactivate the cultural base of development, without it leading to the postmodernism functionally inherent in the project of political-cultural hegemony of neoliberalism? How do we creatively confront our crisis of paradigms and projects, without this confrontation submerging us in a twilight "pathos" where the only option is the administration of entropy, the uncritical acceptance of a status quo that is critical of itself?[76]

Today, in the Americas, one finds the most concrete example of a cultural earthquake in NAFTA (North American Free Trade Agreement) as well as the Chiapas rebellion, possibly its "constitutive other." The Chiapas story may itself contain a complex pastiche of premodern, modern, and postmodern presuppositions. It comprises a number of indigenous cultures and ethnic groups who still communicate in non-European languages and cultivate oral traditions. It is also an area that was largely left behind by the Mexican Revolution's drive for agrarian reforms. And it is the center of attention for transnational investors whose sense of stability has been disturbed, as the Chase Manhattan Bank memo that was leaked to the Internet in April 1995 makes clear.[77] Is it possible, after several decades of metanarrative critique, that masquerading rebels invoking Zapata constitute the only available deconstruction of neoliberal developmentalism?[78]

Deciphering such a text will require a simultaneous glance at the North and the South and perhaps a more rigorous look at the political within postcolonial theories. This will obviously entail a challenging critique that must traverse the opposing discourses of celebratory dispersal and unburdened rationality, or the binary of identity fixation and self-deconstructive melancholy—a possible postcolonial mode of deconstruction capable of inscribing new discourses to frame still needed alternative economic and political modernizations. In "Chiapas: The Other Face of Mexican Modernity," Rossana Reguillo writes that "Chiapas reconfigures Mexican modernity in two meaningful ways: that which was not and that which might be."[79]

But then again, mapping the Chiapas text through other Latin American "postmodern" texts, such as those of Borges, or Manuel Puig, or Vargas Llosa, or even testimonial narratives, will likely call for distinctions regarding the nature of literary and political discourses. It remains unclear how or if literary critics will adjust to these changes in the expanded world of textuality. Indeed, though literary criticism flirts with disciplinary shifts, humanistic ordering ultimately prevails. On the other hand, if an overarching sense of Latin American history as postsymbolic errancy is to be drawn from the voice of such writers, spelling out its relevance to the present must begin by exploring the recuperative work forgotten by such a reading. That, in the long run, may be the most important task for a postcolonial approach to Latin Americanism. Otherwise we are only left with an aporetic quirk, an all-too-evident, though perhaps comfortable, blind spot for Latin America.

2

Postmodernism and Revolution
Borges, Che, and Other Slippages

The moral persuasion of the Zapatistas is founded on the character of their indige-
nous rebellion, which the government vainly tried to deny. More than 501 years
since the conquest, the indigenous theme/problem returns with vigor to a society that
thought it had buried it in the shadows of premodernity. Suddenly, the generalized
consciousness of racism in Mexico, the pride in the Indian sector of which we are a
part, the real or theatrical guilt toward the abandonment and marginality of more
than ten million people in the country, come together in one great question: Why
haven't we given greater importance to the brutal inequality and exploitation of our
brethren?

                                        Carlos Monsiváis, "Los milenarismos"

Metanarrative critique has taught us to look at the epistemic organizations
of history, to unhinge their discursive anchors, and to probe how power is
produced and reproduced through them. Revolution could be one of those
narratives. It has come under increasing scrutiny as a key chapter in the
postmodern reading of Latin America's modern history as a failed narrative.
It is also seen, often, as part of the Creole neocolonial order that has per-
petuated itself for nearly two centuries through chronic cycles of violence,
obsessive claims of national or ethnic identity, and deeply ingrained patri-
archical impulses that have stood in the way of liberal democratic republics.
In this context, as discussed in the last chapter, contemporary Latin American literature becomes a postmodern antidote of sorts, a discursive territory
that undermines and questions these social failures from within the purview
of a new aesthetic or epistemological domain. This chapter aims to probe
the depth of this reading, particularly in its relationship to literature. Is
there a literary or textual side to revolution that is shunned by metanarrative critique and postmodern readers? Is revolution the best example of
Latin America's failed modern legacy? Is the literature of Latin America a
distinctly separate discursive order? Can literature and revolution be read
in unison, how they feed each other into a broader sense of discourse that

encompasses texts as different as Borges's "Tlön, Uqbar, Orbis Tertius" and Che Guevara's life story? How might the recent fifteen-year Central American revolutionary period that ended in the early 1990s serve as a test case for such a reading?

In the spring of 1993, a United Nations-sponsored Truth Commission on El Salvador published a lengthy and carefully researched report. It documents the killing of seventy-five thousand men, women, and children during ten years of revolutionary and civil war. The story, thus far, remains largely ignored by print journalism, television, and even academic journals in the United States. Murray Kempton, an American journalist whose elaborate prose and heightened political sensitivities frequently adorn the pages of the *New York Review of Books,* wrote in 1993 that "the Commission's report is so far available only in Spanish and is hard going for the monolingual majority of Americans whose social standing qualifies them for opinions worth taking seriously."[1] He adds that "to defer the English translation may, of course, be an exercise of diplomatic tact, since it spares the feelings of those official Americans, past and present, who were at best guilty bystanders and at worst willing partners to these crimes."[2]

The conflict in El Salvador is but one of many that have sprung up in Central America and Mexico during a recent era that seems almost forgotten, even though its effects are still very much with us. It is an era of novel military and semiotic deployments: stealth bombers flattened El Chorrillo neighborhood in Panama, and the term *contras* inflicted considerable semantic attrition on Nicaragua's revolutionaries. It is therefore striking to find mainstream journalists focusing on texts with the word *Truth* in the title page, or sympathizing with claims of justice made by revolutionary movements. One could say that postmodern indifference still encounters some opposition in residues of liberalism. But what about the assumptions behind Kempton's conviction, that is, his call for a return to an almost natural nexus between educated readers, the national language as monolingual register, and a magnanimous foreign policy?

Aside from the question of whether Latin America was ever really a beneficiary of such largesse, one has to wonder about the proposition that an English version of the UN Truth Commission's report might mobilize clear and sensitive reporting by the global information networks centered in the United States. After all, few in the United States will have failed to notice the almost decade-long stream of English-only Iran-contra broadcasts on Ted Koppel's *Nightline.* Yet, it is clear that the American people could not be more unfamiliar with the Central American revolution that has so preoccupied this country's foreign policy since the early 1980s. Except for various writers and solidarity organizations, the text of Central America's revolution and its historical roots appear to have met with indifference or contempt, both among the masses and among the more educated sectors of the American population.[3]

A yearning for liberal values like Kempton's may be more symptomatic of an ongoing debate over national identity in Anglo-America than a sign of concern for the future of Central America. Intense culture wars now define U.S. national politics. Debates over ethnic identity, levels of immigration, and welfare eligibility dominate the political discourse of both parties. In 1994, the head of the National Endowment for the Humanities (NEH) issued a conciliatory call to redefine American pluralism through a series of sponsored conferences.[4] Indeed, Kempton's doubts about the future of journalism underscore a growing sense of uncertainty in the post–Cold War era about the impact of media teletechnology, particularly on language and how we understand history. Worldwide "technomediatic power" now constitutes a "dogmatic orchestration," observes Derrida in his essay, "Spectres of Marx," a power that at the same time, in a differentiated and contradictory fashion, *conditions and endangers* any democracy."[5]

As with many other contemporary revolutionary movements, Central America's has been translated into a political culture of neoliberalism that reads Third World claims of redress as nothing but chronic conflicts of underdevelopment, inexplicable civil wars, or irrational residues from outdated master narratives. But it would be inaccurate to simply hold mass culture responsible for such indifference. Impatience with underdevelopment, poverty, and subaltern claims from the Third World (or minority populations in the First World) is also found in academic culture, including that of postmodernism. In the context of a neoliberal economics and neoconservative politics, academic research has been absorbed by the "manic triumphalism" of a dominant discourse that basically preempts contestation.[6] Whether or not deconstruction can avoid becoming an unwitting contributor to this hegemony remains an open question. The answer may ultimately depend on whether its insights are in any way applicable to cultural and social projects that are politically engaged. It is rather evident, however, that the languages of humanistic understanding have become much more withdrawn and equivocal about their relationship to the world in the past few decades; and the social sciences appear to have turned in their claims to comprehensive explanatory power of the social realm for the wisdom of market forces.

Current theories of reading and writing bear witness to these historical tensions, a critical juncture that has solicited new ways of producing and understanding knowledge, particularly as defined by Euro-American research centers. Yet, it is Jorge Luis Borges—perhaps more than any other twentieth-century writer—who has come to exemplify a postliberal academic humanism, a paradigm committed to showing the artifice implicit in all historical constructs, particularly those that aspire to universal value or pretend to foundational truths. His undeniable influence on postmodern Western philosophy has been acknowledged by Paul de Man, Jacques Derrida, and Michel Foucault, for example, even though his specific Latin American cultural bearings are often discounted in the process—as if Borges were just another European author, or a Latin American author whose true value has no bearing on Latin American specificity.[7]

Indeed, many current First World philosophers and theorists have found an indispensable source of inspiration in stories written by Borges during the 1930s and 1940s. But they often ignore the relationship between his world, his texts, and those decades. His story of Tlön is not only an equivocating bibliographical ordering of the world experienced as an aesthetics of impossibility; it is also the representation of the social as absolute impossibility. One could argue that what best defines Borges's uniqueness is his Latin American provenance, a historical sense of political and intellectual liminality not devoid of a sense of epistemic violence that is now observed on a global scale. It is often said that one of the principal features of postmodern times is a global culture in which the First World can find relevance in authors that come from the Third World, or what used to be categorized as such. But what about Borges's specific alterity, that is, his links to the modes of historical experience characteristic of a hybrid modernity, the product in large measure of Argentina's rapid process of industrialization after the Great Depression? Does it come under erasure as a result of a global literary canon administered through English-only translations and criticism, and informed by inchoate multiculturalism, a new postmodern aesthetics, or a loosely defined sense of postcolonial multiple loci of enunciation?

A story about Borges during one of his visits to a U.S. campus has him asking a student if he had read the *Arabian Nights*. Without a second thought, the student responded that he had no need to study Arabic, to which Borges replied, in deadpan fashion, that he did not either, but that he had managed to read it in night school.[8] At first glance, this brief anecdote, whose truth-value is yet to be determined with absolute certainty, may seem like just a bit of Borgesian irony aimed at utilitarian and isolationist modes of education that place insufficient value on learning foreign languages. Borges, like Murray Kempton, could be said to yearn for a world governed by educated, if not refined, readers. But Borges, who is often portrayed in simplified form as an Argentinean aesthete with aristocratic European tastes, was a Latin American writer for whom the experience of Anglo-American liberalism was much more distant than the hybrid forms of academic and political cultures that characterize his part of the world. His work, in form and content, defies all existing discursive genres, except perhaps the standard Latin American experience with contradictory, and often foreign, teleologies. It is this culture, so laden with ludic uncertainty, that was masterfully "transcreated" by Borges into cerebral essays and detective narratives riddled with epistemological twists filled with their own sense of violence. In that light, Borges's *Arabian Nights* story could also remind us that successful acts of reading and understanding are not simply guaranteed by any given "natural" or "national" language, but by one's ability to sift through the layers of linguistic and ideological interplay always implicit in speech acts.

Reading Borges cannot fail to reveal that reading, whether literature or history, can become a treacherous and contentious undertaking from which one may gather both knowledge and pleasure. "Tlön, Uqbar, Orbis Tertius" posits that nations and even continents can originate out of bibliographical accidents, and defines reality not as a "concourse of objects in time and space but a series of independent acts" to be strung together at will by readers and writers.[9] But how is this insight employed when we look at what his literature portends for nonliterary modes of reading and writing, or when applied to war-torn areas like Central America, whose current experience would seem to require a distinction between the immediacy of historical agency and the sedimentation of literary appreciation? Does Borges necessarily stand, then, for reading as a figure of designification, bound to unmask all social constructs as impertinent pretenses?[10] Are his powerful insights into the verbal construction of discourses transferable to a world in which aesthetics and politics are much more synchronically intertwined? In short, how do contemporary theories of language and history based on writers such as Borges allow for an understanding of differences embodied in multiple and complex texts such as revolutions?

Revolution as Text

Contemporary theoretical wisdom holds that history's complicity with language disallows any attempt to look on the realm of experience as if it were free of emplotments. Texts beget more texts; thereby the importance of contesting the canon, for any as yet unrecognized experiences—or narratives—remain adrift, unread, and "uninscribed" in history, in a state of dispensable marginality or illegitimacy. I wonder if revolution could still qualify as such a text. By this I do not mean the possible impacts that political revolutions may have had on literature. I mean revolutionary inscriptions, revolution as a written experience that may or may not be seen in its direct impact on the political realm. I ask myself if it is possible to chart that narrative in today's post–Cold War climate of global capitalist triumphalism. We are now told, with the force of considerable authority, that revolutions belong to modernism and realism, a failed legacy best left behind by a postmodernist aesthetic.[11] Current and old revolutions, different though they may be, face this sort of discursive cul-de-sac. They perform, largely unclaimed, in the space vacated by great narratives and ideas. They have thus become, by definition, untenable or undecidable territory at a time when self-reflexive designification occupies the Western tradition. Given that juncture, it would seem crucial, if not strategic, to examine how contemporary revolutions continue to write themselves, that is, their textual nature; for they are, after all, thoroughly discursive manifestations.

Reading revolutions in this fashion could perhaps allow one to explore relationships between literature and politics in ways that are generally shunned by both modes of organizing knowledge. With this aim, assisted by the thought that revolutions are neither inevitable nor anachronistic, I took to rereading the biography of Ernesto Che Guevara, another renowned Argentine writer, albeit of different types of texts. I hasten to add that this chapter was begun prior to the current flurry of books and events regarding Che, including several biographies, important books of political reflection such as Carlos Castañeda's *Compañero,* the English translation of Che's own *Motorcycle Diaries,* and the moving of the remains of Che's body from an anonymous Bolivian grave to a Cuban monument.[12] These are important texts that add significantly to Che's bibliography, if not mythology, but they did not compel me to draft a different course or edit my earlier chart. As I read on Che, a series of unsuspected connections immediately caught my attention, particularly the fortuitous encounters experienced by this bohemian rebel, beginning in 1954 with the Jacobo Arbenz regime in Guatemala, where Che witnessed an elected social-democratic government suddenly overturned by a CIA-sponsored local general. Che had gone there as a political tourist for a stopover in a somewhat aimless journey of discovery as he hitchhiked northward all over that "other" America south of the Rio Grande. Partially politicized from this experience, he was forced to leave, but moved on to Mexico instead of returning to his native land.

What struck me most about this tale was not the obvious radicalization experienced by Che in Guatemala, but his subsequent encounter in Mexico with the Castro brothers, who had been released from Cuban prison by another CIA-sponsored local general. After that, it was not surprising to learn that Che ultimately joined the Cubans' mission in Mexico, a prelude to the 1956 insurrectionist invasion that would later become the Cuban Revolution. It did seem interesting, however, that all the knowledge and training in guerrilla warfare gathered by Che, the Castro brothers, and their comrades, came to them from a man named Alberto Bayo Giroud, a veteran of the Spanish Civil War who had fought in Africa and various parts of Spain in the 1930s and 1940s. An engaging story, I thought, with a widening field of references that suddenly crossed oceans and bounced naturally from the 1950s and 1960s back into the 1930s: Che's life, Guatemala, the Cuban Revolution, and the Spanish Civil War. Up to this point, tracing and documenting these links seemed like an almost self-referential plot, followed easily enough through Che's biographers, as well as through many academically established histories such as Hugh Thomas's volumes on the Spanish Civil War and the Cuban Revolution.[13]

Sometime later, however, while reading Donald C. Hodges's *Intellectual Foundations of the Nicaraguan Revolution* (1986), the story took a somewhat different path.[14] Hodges tells us that Colonel Alberto Bayo Giroud had also trained expeditionary forces against two other well-known generals during the 1940s: Nicaragua's Anastasio Somosa and Rafael Leónidas Trujillo of the Dominican Republic. One also learns that one of Bayo's books, *150 Questions for a Guerrilla,* was employed as a training manual for Che and the Castros in Mexico, and that it later inspired Che to write his own famous text titled *Guerrilla Warfare,* which the CIA has used to instruct guerrillas for invasions in Central America and the Caribbean ever since.[15] But of greatest importance is the revelation that Bayo's influential text was actually a transcription of Augusto César Sandino's political-military experience in Nicaragua, which Bayo gathered after leaving Spain in 1939 from veteran Sandinista legionnaires still alive after their leader's assassination.

On matters of literary history, Borges's story of Tlön and Uqbar concludes that critics often invent an author and then "determine most scrupulously the psychology of this interesting homme de lettres."[16] Thus, I asked myself if such a pursuit of bibliographical references could ultimately turn Sandino into the author of all Latin American guerrilla wars since the 1930s, with the Cuban (1959) and then the Nicaraguan (1979) victories as his major works, and with many other less successful attempts interspersed between. Had he, indeed, provided a textual force that has been read, chased, and fought over during half a century all over Central America and the Caribbean Basin? But what about the source of that oral tradition kept alive by his remaining soldiers spread throughout Central America, which Colonel Bayo ultimately gathered into a book that later begot all those other texts and revolutions? Was there an important, but missing, link to Sandino himself prior to Bayo's scriptural rendition of the oral tradition? Or should revolution be regarded as an experiential register of both oral and written discourse, a deeper structure that disseminates simultaneously through either code?

In time, I wondered if this intricate web of unsuspected permutations would deepen the implicit lesson in Borges's *Arabian Nights* reference. Could revolution claim the Latin American archive of fiction and history as limitlessly translatable narrative? Was that the legacy of Latin America's thwarted brushes with modernity? I even wondered if the story of Tlön and Uqbar, which was written in Argentina around the same time as Bayo's guerrilla manual, could in some allegorical way be read as Borges's own way of translating Sandino's historical concerns with nation building. Borges's story, after all, does formulate a response to the overt social realism predominant in Latin American literature at the time, albeit a deconstructive one.[17] His inventions of countries like Tlön have been commonly interpreted as an early (1940) manifestation of a postmodern disbelief in modernity's master narratives. In Latin America, however, such incredulity may not just inform a new literary frontier that negates dead-end political utopias, but also instance yet another attempt to construct or imagine autonomous communities. Deconstruction, Derrida reminds us, is a radicalization, and as such, "always indebted to the very thing it radicalizes."[18] Borges's entry in the Latin American anthology of national undoing, charted as it is through bibliographical mirrors, reflects on Sandino's.

The labyrinth of textual and experiential articulations involving Che, Bayo, and Sandino, among other writers and revolutionaries, suggests a new way to approach that famous last paragraph of Paul de Man's essay "Literary History and Literary Modernity," where de Man seems to claim that history is nothing but texts, "even if they masquerade in the guise of wars and revolutions."[19] For Latin America, as well as for other peripherally modern societies, this formulation becomes particularly significant when altered to read: "history reveals a propensity toward revolutions, even if its best articulations often masquerade in the guise of novels and short stories." To reorient de Man's thought in this direction also avoids a strictly literary definition of what constitutes "texts," a comprehensible, if not necessary, shift of emphasis for a postmodern recasting of literariness and a broader understanding of intertextuality.

Thus changed, this formulation may serve as a timely reminder of the ideological investment inherent in all definitions of textuality, including that which understands reading and writing as an exclusive testimony to literary dissemination or epistemological performativity. As death, hunger, persecution, structural inequalities, and sheer exploitation continue to enter the world of discourse and narratology, postmodern deconstructions of revolutionary events and contexts come under closer scrutiny.[20] Needless to say, in the process of emplotment into larger narrative units, experiences with revolutions are also prone to manipulation and the will to produce meaning for the sake of histories, literature, biographies, and constitutions. But even after the passage of time necessary for such encoding, with attention shifted to the verbal nature of generic features and authorial inscriptions, reading revolutions can still constitute considerable challenges, particularly for readers positioned in Euro-American research centers. Such readers are bound to encounter texts still calling for various forms of alterity hard to contain in rhetorical self-discovery, or for political programs still heavily invested in the needs for a modernization even if it no longer enjoys narratives of legitimation—precisely the features that postmodern exegesis eschews from afar. How, then, to critique the potential pitfalls of essentialism without trivializing such historical claims or acknowledging them as mere fictional ruses?

Travel Narrative and *Testimonio*

Borges, Che Guevara, Colonel Bayo, Sandino, and Farabundo Martí (leader of the Salvadoran revolution during the 1930s), despotic generals, death squads, U.S. interventions, and nationalist fervor—all are characters and episodes that accent a rich narrative constellation from the 1930s and 1940s. In typical Latin American style, this was a time when both politics and literature paved the way for a nonsynchronous brush with the avant-garde, a period often overshadowed by the emphasis on the area's "novelistic boom" since the 1960s. As the persistent fame of Borges and Sandino attests, those earlier decades await interested readers with unsuspected connections. Naturally, one could also search further back for intertextual relations, such as the earlier Mexican Revolution and its likely influence on the thought of Sandino, which Donald Hodges has explored in *Sandino's Communism*, a book on this Central American revolutionary. Followers and precursors are both susceptible to inscription and discovery, Borges would remind us in Tlön. One hastens to add, somewhat inspired by de Man, that this sort of fungible, open-ended intertextuality obtains for revolutionary as well as literary history.

Readings of Rubén Darío provide an interesting example. A turn-of-the-century Nicaraguan poet whose exquisite lyricism is often claimed as the bedrock of Spanish American modernism, Darío has been regarded as an apolitical, if not reactionary, aesthetic icon—an assessment somewhat reminiscent of the way Borges is often characterized. Heated debates about Darío's place in Latin American cultural history have raged for many decades, until the Sandinista revolution—armed with a forceful rereading of his work—claimed him as a primary source of inspiration. Suddenly, Darío became another precursor of the Sandinista movement and its love for poetry as a form of cultural revolution. Sergio Ramírez, a Sandinista military leader as well as an accomplished novelist, observes:

> The revolution rescues Darío, not from oblivion but from false idoliza-
> tion, because Darío has always been authentically present in the popu-
> lar imagination as the source of a pride more intuited than understood,
> as the figure of the "great poet," the genius of unknown acts who could
> triumph over any rival, over death itself: the poet of poets, the fabulous
> creator of impossible rhymes and images. Because poetry as such, and
> poetic inspiration, are values which the Nicaraguan people esteem
> without limit.[21]

This sort of rereading reintroduces the interplay of political and economic demands into the realm of literary history that deconstruction generally dissolves or invalidates. Such rereading, however, may also point to possible blind spots within deconstructive modes of thinking regarding the relationship between language and history, particularly in literary circles. If modernity's master narratives no longer obtain on a social or epistemological plane, perhaps the realm of relative autonomy granted to literature and the arts since the Enlightenment should also come under scrutiny. What, then, is the place for a readership that sees itself integrally linked to a process of revolution simultaneously driven by cultural and socioeconomic interests?

Central America's contemporary revolution configures an archive of stories with a northern point of origin that frames the century, as the early Mexican Revolution gathers its residual force in a new Chiapas chapter. This archive reveals an extraordinary intertextual range whose pertinence often goes unnoticed in postmodern renderings of literature, philosophy, or history. One need not privilege any of these revolutionary stories politically, present them as transcendent utopias, or fail to acknowledge the failures of regimes that have come into power under their aegis, but they nonetheless constitute a textual epicenter from which much writing issues. José Rabasa imputes the postmodern tendency of erasing this important narrative tradition:

One of the tasks of subaltern studies would consist of writing histories of Indian insurgencies in Mexico that would not be interpreted according to supposedly more advanced or developed political movements. These histories would practice what Guha calls writing in reverse, that is, against the grain of the documents that first recorded rebellions, but also against the counterinsurgent histories that sought to explain and contain insurrection. This would include tertiary histories that would privilege the wars of independence, the revolution or Marxist theory as providing categories to evaluate earlier movements as ineffectual.[22]

Indeed, when viewed from a cultural, rather than a purely political perspective, the multilayered text of the Central American revolution becomes specifically pertinent for what could be called "transmodern" configurations. It has responded to more than six decades of tremendous military and political upheavals, often augmented, if not induced, by direct external interventions. But its corresponding cultural history has left a legacy rich in aesthetics as much as politics, oral tradition, ethnic and religious transculturation, as well as elite and popular culture hybridization. Whether under neocolonial or postcolonial frameworks of understanding, such a cultural history marks a special instance of that nonsynchronous mixture that characterizes societies where peripherally modern and postmodern cultures coexist, often in the most difficult circumstances. That duality in time, a lapse as well as a continuity, contains a rich and varied textuality that betrays any attempt to reduce it to detectable forms of identity and essentialism.

With the advent of multiculturalist representation, a handful of Central American writers have obtained notoriety in Euro-American literary circles. New translated editions and anthologies often include Roque Dalton, Rigoberta Menchú, and Ernesto Cardenal, although, characteristically, they often present these authors as isolated individuals. Serious reflection on the common cultural history that binds them has been scarce, giving way instead to various modes of literary analysis all too readily predisposed to praise or condemn any context that links literary and revolutionary values. One notable exception, in the United States, is *Literature and Politics in the Central American Revolution* (1990), by John Beverley and Marc Zimmerman. This book offers a comprehensive look at the rich tradition of poetry, *testimonio* narratives, and other cultural forms from the region, but not for the sake of a loosely periodized panoramic survey. The authors argue that this literary core is a primary agent of revolutionary articulation, not just an expression or a representation of economic and political developments, as is generally understood by traditional bourgeois or Marxist aesthetics. Most important, Beverley and Zimmerman bring to light how reading revolution as cultural articulation presents a particular challenge for any attempt to understand postmodernism in Latin America, for it shows how precapitalism, neoliberalism, deconstruction, feminism, and ethnic identity struggles—among other integral elements of social reality—all simultaneously inform Central America's hybrid texts.

I should add that some of the central propositions in their book remain open for further analysis and debate. The notion of *testimonio* as a primary agent of revolutionary articulation is left wanting. Similarly, it is not clear to me how the authors come to understand the ingenious ways in which Rubén Darío's modernist poetry was incorporated into Nicaraguan revolutionary rhetoric, while insisting that contemporary classics such as García Márquez's narrative can only correspond to a fixed mode of literary reception. Both questions have to do with the notion of antiliterature that informs Beverley's recent work, which raises important questions regarding the foundational role of literature while focusing explicitly on alternative modes of writing such as *testimonio*. For these reasons, doubts included, this is a crucial book, perhaps the only one of its kind in contemporary Latin Americanist criticism, in that it brings to bear contemporary metropolitan theory as well as the area's difficult history.[23]

But perhaps there is another aspect of Beverley and Zimmerman's book that responds directly to the moving vantage point I have proposed as a way of reading Latin America's revolutionary textuality. Reading revolution as a cultural text, perhaps more than any other text, provides a mirror that shows oneself at work, reading oneself, as one approaches that disquieting and profoundly heterogeneous form of otherness. It is important to note, therefore, that Beverley's and Zimmerman's book is a composite of many texts: a literary critique of a few authors, a literary history, a detailed analysis of the area's cultural industries, and a travel narrative, for it is also a record of their experiences in the area witnessing an attempt to transform a society, as well as a record of the desires and disappointments that went along with that journey. As the most incisive forms of feminism have taught us, positionality is profoundly revealing. I would therefore propose to expand the genre of texts that began with Che, Borges, and Sandino to include readings such as these, to observe in these journeys a moment of deconstruction that refuses to leave the writerly agent in a state of distant bliss, that is, how the reader/writer encounters a point in which fictionalization and revolutionary emplotment disturb each other.

The texts I have in mind correspond to a wide array of literary critics, artists, journalists, and social scientists who have journeyed to the revolution through texts and other forms of representation. For a closer look at such readings, I have chosen three very influential travel narratives written by Latin and Anglo Americans since the 1960s. They focus on Guatemala, Nicaragua, and El Salvador, arguably the three primary sites of Central America's revolution since the 1920s. They are Eduardo Galeano's *Guatemala, Occupied Country* (1967), Julio Cortázar's "Apocalypse at Solentiname" (1976), and Joan Didion's *Salvador* (1983).[24] Each of these writers traveled to Central America and turned his or her experience into a text that traverses common barriers between the literary and the political. More specifically, each attempts to give artistic form to an encounter with revolution.

Galeano's Male Witness

Although not a professional historian, Uruguayan Eduardo Galeano has become one of the most prolific and comprehensive writers of Latin American history. His use of literary devices to dramatize key moments in the area's history has considerable appeal in Latin America itself. His texts, however, have eluded mainstream distribution channels in the U.S. academic market for Latin American literature and social science. In those circles, Galeano's work has been judged as neither history nor literature, perhaps too bound by unchanging ideological presuppositions and schematic economic outlines. His panoramic histories of Latin America often depict the role of Europe and the United States as motivated solely by imperialist interests. Nonetheless, his *Open Veins of Latin America* (1965) has probably reached a wider Latin American audience than any other historical account of the area. It articulates economic history since colonial times into a crafty narrative form that nonacademic readers appreciate as much for its literary as for its historical emplotments.

During 1967, after two months in Guatemala, Galeano's firsthand accounts of guerrilla camps were serialized in various Spanish American countries, Italy, and the United States, before being published in book form. *Guatemala, Occupied Country* tests the difficult balance of history, novel writing, and journalism characteristic of travel literature with questions about the relationship between intellectuals and revolution. Although written in the 1960s at a time when many of today's most recognized Latin American boom novelists were active sympathizers of Cuba's revolution, Galeano's text departs significantly from the more strictly existential explorations of political commitment then employed by Mario Vargas Llosa, Ernesto Sábato, and Edmundo Desnoes. What we see, instead, is an early version of a type of *testimonio* literature that has since become a proper genre in Latin America. Galeano's text privileges accounts of social histories and oral traditions emphasizing collective experiences of subjects and classes generally denied a voice.

Galeano's writing poses many of the interesting formal dilemmas that characterize this type of literature of the subaltern as well as some forms of anthropological writing. As with Rigoberta Menchú, whose experience was transcribed by Venezuelan Elisabeth Burgos in *I, Rigoberta Menchú: An Indian Woman in Guatemala,* or the *Autobiography of a Runaway Slave,* in which the Cuban novelist Miguel Barnet presents the experience of former slave Esteban Montejo, Galeano finds that he must give way to the Other. This is doubly difficult in his case, because he does not intend to camouflage the implicit privilege of his voice as that of a distant editor. He first presents the guerrillas as the primary subject of his study, and then attempts to earn the right to speak for them through his first-person narrative. His strategy would seem to challenge any simplified understanding of testimonial writing as nonliterature or as a genre through which the social can be transparently transmitted without textual complications.

The bulk of the material is a historical critique of socioeconomic conditions in Guatemala since the 1930s, a thorough discussion of imperialist and oligarchic collusion to exploit the land and the people, and a careful speculation on how the Mayan Indians might integrate themselves with the campesinos as a new subject of history to guide the guerrilla insurrection and ultimately the revolution. All of this extensive analytic work flows initially from the author's third-person omniscience. These are interspersed with various dialogues, interviews, and other first-person interventions that introduce the author and various guerrillas as individual speakers. Galeano's voice, however, remains in the background as a passive interlocutor. To accent this self-effacement, he casts himself as a weak and alien Other who must recognize his limitations and suffer in dangerous jungles before his voice can attempt to speak with proper credentials.

Galeano dramatizes his shortcomings on the very first page: "I am ashamed because I am cold," he writes as he travels through the mountains on his way to the guerrilla camp. "Walking, even if my leg muscles are as hard as fists, is better than any futile attempt to sleep on top of the foliage with nothing to cover myself and my sweat freezing over my body. By contrast, there is not an ounce of sweat in the bodies of my companions, and for them neither cold nor sleep matters."[25] It is important to observe the exclusive emphasis that Galeano places on his cosmopolitan condition. It is the one form of otherness that seems to concern him, as if bridging the world of intellectuals and revolutionaries were his sole object. Ethnic, national, and even linguistic elements of difference are ignored, even though they are crucial factors separating the Uruguayan writer from a Guatemalan guerrilla force. At this stage of Galeano's writing, one can detect an overarching identity that glosses over crucial differences imbued by a Latin American insurrectionist discourse and a 1960s male aesthetic. Later articulations, such as Che's 1967 experience with Bolivian Indians and the Sandinista struggles with ethnic and gender issues during the 1970s and 1980s, illustrate the need for a sobering corrective to this unilateral perspective. But Galeano's mode of self-legitimation as an intellectual in the guerrilla world is of particular interest because it deviates from the example set by Fidel Castro and Che Guevara—both intellectuals in their own right—who abandoned their professions, thereby symbolizing the sacrifice of privileged positions necessary to overcome class boundaries with campesinos and other insurrectionists. By joining the guerrillas as fighters, not as lawyers or medical doctors, Fidel and Che appear to forego their roles as professional intellectuals, a category whose value the Cuban Revolution has kept stigmatized, even after assuming power. One could always question whether leading a guerrilla band or institutionalizing a revolution does not incur a certain level of privilege, even an intellectual one, through which prerevolutionary or new class privileges are maintained. In any case, it is particularly instructive to see Galeano assert the role of professional writers in a revolutionary context during the sixties, even when he recasts himself as an organic intellectual whose legitimacy will be determined by his utility to the guerrilla cause.

In a later scene, Galeano outlines the profile of a politically committed writer in greater detail. The narrator's access to the city as a foreign journalist turns into an opportunity for urban spying. As his voice grows more familiar with the world of guerrillas, it suddenly reveals how he can aid their cause with crucial information from the city:

> The vice president of Guatemala, Don Clemente Marroquín Rojas, talked to me about napalm, in an informal interview. It wasn't hard to gain his confidence; it came to me effortlessly thanks to my extraordinary likeness to a friend of his, someone named Newbery, who'd been in exile with him in Honduras. . . . That's how I found out that a squadron of North American planes, with North American pilots, had dumped North American napalm over a Guatemalan mountain and returned to Panama without landing here.[26]

Ironically, Galeano's most available weapon derives from the power attendant upon his journalistic craft, in combination with his physical likeness to the enemy. This important note of self-reflection turns this scene into an interesting contradiction, for it reveals the limitations implicit in the author's project of self-denial. His usefulness derives particularly from his status as outsider, as cosmopolitan writer whose class and ethnic features allow him to pass unnoticed among the oligarchy. One could conclude that he has failed to bridge the worlds of writers and revolutionaries after all. On the other hand, one could also read this fact as Galeano's mode of traversing, rather than sacrificing, the way revolutions understand the roles of writers and intellectuals, after having incurred risks and put his commitment to various tests.

Cortázar's Tricks

In contrast to Galeano's attempt to bring art to the revolution, Julio Cortázar's "Apocalypse at Solentiname" could be seen as an experiment to bring revolution to the world of art. But the story is also a travel narrative that retells an exploratory visit by this Argentine-born writer to Solentiname, Nicaragua, in 1976, three years before the Sandinista victory. Cortázar, a world-renowned novelist and short-story writer, is best known for *Hopscotch* (1964), one of the most influential contemporary Latin American novels, notable for its experimental treatment of theory and jazz, and for its self-referential awareness of the reader's role in deciphering the text.

For Cortázar, who lived most of his adult life in Paris, the Nicaraguan revolution became a genuine passion, mostly because of its reliance on cultural and spiritual revival for political awakening. Neither surrealism, which significantly influenced his earlier work, nor the Cuban Revolution, to which he felt some attraction at first, intrigued him the way Nicaragua would in his later years. By the mid-1970s, his curiosity brought him to Solentiname, an archipelago of small islands that had acquired special significance for many Latin American writers. It was an artistic commune founded by Ernesto Cardenal, the Nicaraguan priest/poet/revolutionary whose earlier experience as a Trappist monk in Kentucky left a clear imprint in the artistic ideals of this beautiful and small island retreat. The story of Cortázar's first visit would eventually become part of an anthology, *Nicaragua, So Violently Sweet,* that gathers various accounts of trips he made to that country over a span of seven years before his death in 1984.

"Apocalypse at Solentiname," though brief, brilliantly engages the complex relationships among politics, literature, and the representation of otherness from within the realm of artistic form, a pursuit that informs nearly all of Cortázar's later works. But the story's considerable notoriety results largely from its prophetic value, for it can be said to forecast the apocalyptic end that came to Solentiname at the hands of the Somoza National Guard about

a year after its publication. Ernesto Cardenal and his aesthetic/religious collective had allowed training and military expeditions to take place from
their commune as a sign of solidarity with the Sandinista revolution during
the final stages of the insurrectionist struggle. Shortly after the first Sandinista guerrilla attack was launched from Solentiname, the Somosa National
Guard wiped out the entire commune. One of the few buildings left standing had housed an exceptional library of unpublished literary and religious
manuscripts. It was turned into the main barracks.

Barbara Harlow includes a detailed account of the story as prophecy in
her *Resistance Literature,* from which she goes on to draw definitive conclusions regarding its political meaning. This text, she writes, "presents in its
reading of the images of Solentiname the necessary conditions for subsequent resistance to the situation of repression and terror exercised by the
hegemonic powers of the First World and its collaborators in the Third
World."[27] Reading it only as a prophecy neatly fulfilled in history, however,
fails to account for many significant and problematic aspects of the story,
some of which are pertinent to the political conclusion preferred by Harlow. Linking the story to a subsequent and historically verifiable outcome
like the destruction of the commune at the hands of the National Guard is
not inapposite, but Cortázar's representation of the massacre at Solentiname turns out to be somewhat more polysemic than Harlow has allowed.

The narrative unfolds from pictures taken by Cortázar during his brief
and peaceful stay in Solentiname that are developed and viewed in a slide
projector after his return to Paris. Suddenly, as he studies them, they begin
to show more than the friendly and serene surroundings he had photo-
graphed. Government soldiers appear out of the blue. A young man is shot
through the head. As Cortázar proceeds with his private screening, images
of arrest and torture from his native Argentina also come into focus, and
the identity of the young man is revealed: it is Roque Dalton, the renowned
Salvadoran poet who had been brutally assassinated in El Salvador one year
earlier. When Cortázar's wife Claudine appears, he leaves the room and asks
her to view the slides. She, however, does not see any of these rather unusual revelations.

In Harlow's analysis of this story, we are told that "Claudine, who
comes in only at the end of the showing and repeats the sequence of slides
for herself, sees nothing of those events which the shocked narrator had dis-
cerned in the photographic images."[28] In her "blindness," adds Harlow,
"Claudine may resemble the naive reader for whom there is only the text."[29]
Such a reading understandably attempts to underline the importance of political awareness and contextualization when reading the Other, but in her

rush for political metaphors, Harlow appears to leave the text too soon. If Cortázar is the ideally informed reader, then we would need to explore all of what he sees, which includes not only Argentine and Nicaraguan right-wing soldiers, but a reflection on left-wing violence as well, represented by Roque Dalton's execution. Cortázar's clairvoyance, therefore, requires a broader political frame that can only issue from a closer analysis of the text. In that same light, Claudine's blindness or naïveté may also be subject to further textual scrutiny.

Cortazár's mode of fictionalizing lived experience is of particular interest, given that the story's self-awareness as art would seem to challenge from within how texts and revolutions read each other. The author's trip to the Solentiname archipelago in the south of Lake Nicaragua already carries a multitude of signifying elements that are intricately woven together in rather suggestive ways. From Paris, where he lives with his wife who will be left in the dark until the need for that "innocent" reader arises, we see that he travels to Havana—perhaps a necessary stopover in the contextualization of a political journey to meet the revolution. From there he goes on to San José, Costa Rica, the closest city from which to fly to the lake in a Piper Aztec—perhaps a coincidental reference to the world of Native Americans. While in Solentiname, Cortázar attends a Sandinista Mass, a mixture of spiritualism, oral tradition, and liberationist politics—perhaps the most autochthonous cultural form of that revolution. He then talks to a few campesinos about their application of the gospel to their lives and engages in friendly conversation with Cardenal, Ramírez, and other well-known writers. From the outset, the author/narrator openly assumes the profile of a visiting famous artist who values the revolution but is not about to nullify or camouflage his social bearings. On the contrary, in a fashion worthy of Walter Benjamin, his sense of politics is defined only by his zeal to bring his artistic means to the revolution.

Before leaving Solentiname, the customary farewell photographs are taken by hosts and guests alike, but here the story grows a bit more complicated, demanding further review of the political conclusions implicit in the prophecy already discussed. Before Cortázar takes the slides he will review in Paris later, one of the locals uses a Polaroid, a device the narrator claims to have never seen in action before. This becomes a crucial gesture with multiple implications, for it places Cortázar—a cosmopolitan Latino-Parisian artist with an international reputation—into a position of lesser technological sophistication than the campesino community. The scene functions as a cultural equalizer of sorts, analogous to Galeano's nullifying his body before meeting the guerrillas. The nature of this move is political to the extent that it is also textual, because it identifies a mode of artistic re-production and reception, again in Benjaminian fashion, that Cortázar will take from the campesinos and employ in the development of the story later on in Paris.

As he observes the Polaroid, Cortázar describes how this "celestial piece of paper, slowly and marvelously Polaroid, begins to fill itself with images, first disquieting ectoplasms and then, little by little, a nose, a curly hair, Ernesto's smile, Doña María and Don José, leaning against the veranda."[30] "They were all used to this," he says, "but I wasn't. . . . I remember asking Oscar what would happen if one day, after a family picture, this celestial paper were to begin filling itself with Napoleon on horseback, and Don José just laughed."[31] Pondering whether Napoleon could surface in the picture is, however, only a playful distraction from the image of Ernesto standing next to Joseph and Mary that has already been placed before us. The worlds of miracles and photographs have already fused.

The Polaroid photograph is thus transformed, before our very eyes, not into an image of the real but into a syncretized picture of the Holy Family, perhaps inspired by the Sandinista Mass that Cortázar had just witnessed. More important, the poetic depictions of Polaroid magic foreground and anticipate the transformations seen by Cortázar in Paris later on. This other reading, more textually bound, seems to indicate a particular investment in how technology and peripheral modernity come together as artwork. Ecto-plasms, spiritualism, Sandinista politics, and theology of liberation all come into play right there in Solentiname, through the Polaroid magic that Cor-tázar has supposedly never seen before.

The unexpected images of torture that Cortázar observes at the end of the story are undoubtedly meant to bring a Latin American context of po-litical and military repression into focus, including that which comes at the hand of left-wing guerrilla groups. Roque Dalton's death, after all, had re-sulted from a factional fight within the FMLN (Frente Farabundo Martí de Liberación Nacional). It is therefore important to resist the rush to enclose this story within a framework that pans out in a historical interpretation without attending to the broader critique of violence inscribed in it. Reality effects can overwhelm the reading of a story like this one, given its almost irresistible prophetic content. The slippery relationship between reality and literature that it indicates reminds me of one of Tlön's most severe precepts, which holds that "manuals, anthologies, summaries, literal versions, autho-rized re-editions and pirated editions of the Greatest Work of Man flooded and still flood the earth. Almost immediately, reality yielded on more than one account. The truth is that it longed to yield."[32]

A closer reading of this story, therefore, calls for a different and much more specific understanding of literature and revolution in contemporary Latin America than those that derive their impetus from the too-simple category of resistance literature. In contrast to Galeano's concern with social history, Cortázar's text seems much more fictionalized. It reveals a much greater control of how his writing will accommodate the few days spent in that special, almost mystical, Solentiname in 1976, during the insurgency stage of the Nicaraguan revolution. Indeed, Cortázar's artistic design overwhelms any attempt to throw himself into the story with some degree of spontaneity, as one might otherwise expect of a travel narrative. The story's impact thus depends radically on its literary form, on its immanent approach to the notion of revolution as a text that can beget other texts, crisscrossing from the literary to the nonliterary and back. Through these creative impulses, Cortázar forges a self-reflexive fusion of technological novelty, Sandinista spiritualism, and his own memory of politically motivated violence in Latin American liberation movements. Through this unusual mix of texts and chronologies, it could be said that his art and the early phases of the Nicaraguan revolution transform a snapshot into a disturbing mirror, thereby giving a new meaning to the idea of revelation.

Didion's Literary Model

By the beginning of the 1980s, after Nicaragua's revolutionary government took power and the insurrection in El Salvador grew stronger, Central America became a focal point of U.S. foreign policy. Mainstream American television and journalism, perhaps responding to a new post-Vietnam rigor, closely reflected the alarmist discourse of political figures from both parties. In time, writers and filmmakers became more directly acquainted with ongoing events in the area, not only to provide a more balanced or complex panorama than the mainstream media, but as a personal and artistic exploration as well. Joan Didion's *Salvador* can be said to respond to this context in the United States. As such, it constitutes yet a different turn of the relationship between textuality and revolution explored in this chapter. Didion, well known for combining journalism and fiction, has authored more than ten books since the late sixties, including *Run River, After Henry, Democracy, Miami,* and *Salvador.*

Before publication in 1983, most of the various vignettes that later became *Salvador* were serialized in the *New York Review of Books.* But the most striking early reception of this book is to be found in the blurbs awaiting the reader on the cover of its first edition, promising "a surrealist docudrama," "a poetic exploration in fear," "a muted outrage that appalls the mind and stiffens the spine," "bodies found everywhere—in vacant lots, in garbage, in rest rooms, in bus stations . . . bodies, bodies—and vultures to feed on them wherever they lie."[33] This litany concludes with the observation (suggested by the epigraph Didion supplies for the book): "El Salvador has truly become the Heart of Darkness."[34] As with the advent of music videos that superimpose a visual narrative structure on the listener, the reader must here confront not simply a reading but a thoroughly constructed cultural reference point, be it Joseph Conrad's masterful story or Francis Ford Coppola's contemporary film *Apocalypse Now*. Africa and Vietnam come immediately to mind, as well as images of violence, intervention, and misrepresentation of the Other. Readers are being asked to transfer these time-honored Western reference points, entirely uncritically, to a new Latin American setting.

George Yúdice, a Salvadoran-born critic who lives in the United States, has commented on these promotional campaigns in the text's margins: "One has to trust the 'wisdom' of the marketing industry to understand the prurient taste for horror that links desire to read this book with the desire to see the *Texas Chainsaw Massacre, The Terminator, Angel Heart,* and other displays of mutilation."[35] He is led to conclude that, "like pornographic representations of violence against women, works such as *Salvador* draw much of their fascination from the violation of 'marginal' Others, the oppressed."[36] As with Harlow's reading of Cortázar, this take on *Salvador* is surely pertinent, but it leaves much of the text behind, including elements that bear on the question of Didion's representation of violence in El Salvador, and whether, like the publisher's blurbs, it simply caters to a need for presenting revolution in a sensationalist light.

Salvador narrates Didion's two-week trip to that war-torn country in 1982, accompanied by her husband, John Gregory Dunne, who remains anonymous whenever he appears in the story but is identified in the book's prefatory note acknowledgments. In Cortázar's story, it may be recalled, Claudine only surfaces at the end when her husband, the author/narrator, stereotypes her as a naive reader. In Didion's, the husband plays no discernible role, yet he frequently appears in her daily references to the ongoing plot. One is led to infer that this anonymous "husband" character is also a device within the story, standing for the need of trust and security an investigative reporter requires in a truly dangerous setting, where neither the Salvadoran government nor the American embassy inspires any degree of confidence. Similarly, one could also surmise that his cultural and linguistic sameness provides a respite for the author/narrator/protagonist during an exploration of otherness from which she feels a different sort of threat.

Unlike Galeano and Cortázar, Didion never travels to any guerrilla camp, alone or accompanied. Her reportage focuses exclusively on the violent life of the capital city, San Salvador—its sights, sounds, and, most particularly, the language that sustains such a world. Her story describes what happens in a first-person account that is not quite ready to inscribe the Other as either a new historical subject, like Galeano's, or an incursion within artistic form, like Cortázar's. Instead, Didion seems to pursue an experience of otherness as a loss in itself, as a bewildering experience for an American journalist lodged in downtown San Salvador, caught in the cross fire of bullets and conflicting claims from the guerrillas, the U.S. embassy, and the Salvadoran government. On the very first page, she observes that "in the general absence of tourists these hotels have since been abandoned, ghost resorts on the empty Pacific beaches, and to land at this airport built to service them is to plunge directly into a state in which no ground is solid, no depth of field reliable, no perception so definite that it might not dissolve into its reverse."[37]

One can almost hear echoes of Borges's main aesthetic precepts here, which exhort one not to "seek for the truth or even for verisimilitude, but rather for the astounding."[38] It is important to notice, however, that Didion does examine, sporadically, the concrete elements of power that traverse this uncanny world. By the third page, we read about police cars, roadblocks, and unidentified bodies of dead men, women, and children, as well as how these are reported by the local media, from which, she adds, "the United States embassy compiles its body counts which are transmitted to Washington in a weekly dispatch referred to by embassy people as 'the grimgram,' . . . a kind of tortured code that fails to obscure what is taken for granted in El Salvador, that government forces do most of the killing."[39]

Indeed, *Salvador* does feed on the collusion between the United States and the Salvadoran government, underlining a political concern that is not likely to be advertised in the publisher's blurbs. In this sense, it bears some analogy to Galeano's story, except that its primary interest is not causal, historical, or accusatory, but a more ambivalent and synchronic presentation of how it feels to be in a culture that can seem so foreign to the protagonist's sensitivities. What we get, then, is a fairly detailed grammar of terror: the daily grimgram of body counts, how *to disappear* is often used as a transitive verb in El Salvador, how agrarian reform can be promoted and its desirability precluded at the same time, how asking people for the truth is interpreted as a test of what the government means—in short, how an elaborate code of dissimulation underlies the pretense of democratic rule. In this strange world, Didion begins to question how her writing will respond. This apparent loss of confidence, if not identity, is carefully outlined when

she visits an exclusive Americanized shopping mall filled with Sergio Va-
lente jeans, big towels with maps of Manhattan, and all the trappings of
U.S. upper-middle-class suburbia. As she gets set to depict the apparent in-
congruity of such a scene in San Salvador at the time, she turns on herself:

> I wrote it down dutifully, this being the kind of "color" I know how to
> interpret, the kind of inductive irony, the detail that was supposed to
> illuminate the story. As I wrote it down I realized I was no longer
> much interested in this kind of irony, that this was a story that would
> not be illuminated by such details, that this was perhaps less a "story"
> than a true noche obscura.[40]

Whereas Galeano's text required a self-inscribed nullification, and Cortázar's a quasi-religious revelation of Polaroid magic (for their respective en-
tries into the world of the Other), Didion's predicament is considerably different, because her interest lies in that *noche obscura* itself. By denying
herself recourse to irony, she allows her writing to drift about without a
clear subject to affirm and, more important, without a familiar textual
form. Thus, what the story pursues is a model for writing El Salvador as a
loss, one it seeks to discover as it writes it. With that aim in view, we learn
one night that Didion has met Victor Barriere, a well-to-do Salvadoran
painter who has volunteered to give her a quick but personalized rundown
of his country's history. As it turns out, this man is history himself, since he
is the grandson of the late General Maximiliano Hernández Martínez,
whose thirteen-year-long dictatorship in El Salvador was built on the massacre of Farabundo Martí, his followers, and thirty thousand other Salva-
dorans in 1932.

As fate would have it, Didion also discovers that this most ruthless of
dictators has literary relevance, for he is said to have directly informed
Gabriel García Márquez's well-known *The Autumn of the Patriarch,* one of
the most celebrated of the "dictator novels" that have become a special Latin
American subgenre. Didion's search for a different voice is thus claimed by
Central America's own textual traditions, as she discovers the significance of
the 1930s in the voice of General Maximiliano Hernández Martínez, recalled amid the echoes of revolutionary wars, the memory of living relatives,
and current literary masterpieces. All of them appear as surreal to her as the
world she has been trying to describe in 1982. The general was, she says, "a
sinister visionary," who "held séances in the Presidential Palace" and "conducted the country's affairs along lines dictated by eccentric insights, which
he sometimes shared by radio with the remaining citizens."[41] She goes on to
sample two of his most uncanny postulates:

It is good that children go barefoot. That way they can better receive the beneficial effluvia of the planet, the vibrations of the earth. Plants and animals don't use shoes.

Biologists have discovered only five senses. But in reality there are ten. Hunger, thirst, procreation, urination, and bowel movements are the senses not included in the lists of biologists.[42]

At this moment, Didion's willingness to drift without a clue as to the form her writing will finally take comes to a sudden halt under the weight of Latin American fiction. The intertextual relations between García Márquez's *The Autumn of the Patriarch* and General Martínez's eccentric musings from the 1930s suddenly translate the author's search into a direct encounter with magic realism, as if it were the only possible form for such a world after all. One could surmise from this conclusion, in a manner inspired by a narrow interpretation of Borgesian principles, that history reveals itself to Didion as literary form, ultimately the only way to rewrite the past, particularly in Latin America. Conversely, one could judge that Didion's attempt to write about a problematic and ongoing revolution ultimately gives way to a contemplative, and somewhat reductive, exercise in literary appreciation. But it could also be argued that Didion's text thwarts such clear-cut enclosures, given that what informs her approach to the language of magic realism is a brush with revolution as a lived, and not just read, threatening experience.

After dining with the general's grandson and suffering through an earthquake at midnight, Didion concludes a most difficult day with an awakening: she now understands García Márquez in a new light, that is, "as a social realist."[43] Later on, she adds that

language has always been used a little differently in this part of the world (an apparent statement of fact often expresses something only wished for, or something that might be true, a story, as in García Márquez's *many years later, as he faced the firing squad, Colonel Aureliano Buendía was to remember that distant afternoon when his father took him to discover ice*).[44]

Like Galeano and Cortázar, Didion delves into the world of revolution through a self-reflective progression that incorporates an initial loss and then a transformation. Her story does not attempt a direct contact with a guerrilla camp and it appears to hover on the surface of events, constantly drawing information from readily accessible U.S. embassy contacts and colorful oligarchical figures. A San Salvadoran cityscape filled with demeaning violent images of the Other is ever-present, as Yúdice suggests. But *Salvador* also permits a different and more complex reading. It flows from Didion's need to reach beyond the language of ironic depictions into a dialogue with two other forms of writing, both foreign to her: the grammar of terror and magic realism. The first allows her to move about between episodes of violence in descriptive fashion, drifting along without a sense of structure, other than the ever-present U.S. embassy and its clients, the local generals, and their offspring. The second brings her to read García Márquez as many Latin Americans do, as an effect of the real that includes but complicates the practice of reading and writing with ongoing experiential exigencies.

Didion goes to El Salvador to explore the revolution and comes back a better reader of García Márquez. Unquestionably, such a turn constitutes as much of a device as Cortázar's discovery of Polaroids and Galeano's accidental experience as an urban spy. These travel stories conjure up the image of a diary, where living and writing are supposedly closely linked, as if they mirrored each other in some simplified way to bring an experience with "the real" to a text. But that may be just another literary conceit implicit in the intensive act of editing and rewriting obviously present in these narratives. Some readers of Borges, not to be denied, would probably see them as just literary permutations of one basic story, and perhaps even a further reflection on the *Arabian Nights,* his model for the ultimate sense of historical reality. Yet, there is more than an immanent reflection on writing that defines otherness in these texts. A chronologically inscribed community of demographically constitutive others is also present, claiming its place in that sense of loss from within that each writer experiences.

The historical value of the stories discussed here will obviously remain open to debate. This is not to suggest, however, that they are open to any form of manipulation. Placing them neatly into this or that model of representing or deconstructing Latin America will probably become a transparent imposition for the sake of another text or experience. They respond to a century-old constellation of texts and revolution, to the grammar of terror supported from within and without, to local generals and the fiction they inspire, and, most important, to a rich cultural experience performed through narratives such as these and through readings complex enough to do them justice.

Hybridity, an image frequently invoked in postmodern aesthetics, is operative in these texts only as a dually inscribed property where both writing and revolution bring otherness into a dialogue with what Enrique Dussel calls "the Reason of the Other."[45] Dussel, an Argentine-born professor of philosophy and theology at the Universidad Nacional Autónoma Metropolitana (UNAM) in Mexico City, argues that modernity and postmodernity have a different meaning for those who have been historically "excluded, dominated, or compelled" to an asymmetrical position in history and epistemology. He adds:

> Unlike the postmodernists, we do not propose a critique of reason as such; but we do accept their critique of a violent, coercive, genocidal reason. We do not deny the rational kernel of the universalist rationalism of the Enlightenment, only its irrational moment as sacrificial myth. We do not negate reason, in other words, but the irrationality of the violence generated by the myth of modernity. Against postmodernist irrationalism, we affirm the "reason of the Other."[46]

Traces of such a reason can perhaps be observed in the Zapatista revolt, arguably the most recent chapter in the Latin American revolutionary text. To many observers it signals a postmodern conflict. Others have seen it as a classic seventeenth- or eighteenth-century claim for equality justified under Mexican and international law. Zapatista subcommander Marcos has indeed toyed with the question of his "real identity," and his group's manifestos subscribe to a local more than a national definition of community. But the Zapatista rebellion has from the outset also laid claim to article 39 of the Mexican constitution. It reads: "All public power emanates from the people and is established for the benefit of the people. The people have, at all times, the inalienable right to alter or modify the form of their government."[47] That provision, derived from John Locke's 1690 *Treatise on Government*, can also be traced to the English and American Revolutions. Undoubtedly, it is still to be read for more than its literary values.

3

Of Border Artists and Transculturation
Toward a Politics of Transmodern Performances

At the end of the century, Latin America finds itself forced to burn years of its own history to enter into a different order and rhythm, into a transnational temporality. This leap would leave behind a historical remainder, a national future that wasn't. Culture will transform that residue into a lost temporality because it jumps to another future, which is the present of the transnational temporality.
    Josefina Ludmer, "El coloquio de Yale: máquinas de leer 'fin de siglo'"

The twentieth century's fascination with the problems of signification and representation could well be its most stable narrative. Since the discovery of Saussurean epistemology, the allure of the sign has only intensified. We have grown accustomed to its multiple turns as part of a largely Western legacy, less concerned or aware of the ways in which the same legacy has been read or introduced in other parts of the world. The growing body of metacriticism and its authorial corpus—Michel Foucault, Julia Kristeva, Jean-François Lyotard, and Jacques Derrida, for instance—are now part of a new indispensable body of theory. Yet, it is also well known that this contemporary flurry of extraordinary epistemic paradigms resists any sense of cumulative scale. Postmodernism—as period, style, or logic—is polysemic in the most equivocal sense: it absorbs a capricious array of methods and theories that can simultaneously signify difference and sameness, the old and the new, the self and the other, the radical and the conservative. My interest in this chapter is to reread Latin American theories of transculturation as a different chapter of this same theoretical legacy, which I understand as century-long search for the nexus between knowledge and language, a quest that discovers, in different ways and at different times, the performative aspects of its object of study.

Before moving on to transculturation, I want to underline the ambivalence of contemporary theory, which is exemplified in the practice of reclaiming authors as various as Giambattista Vico, Friedrich Nietzsche, Mikhail

Bakhtin, and Jorge Luis Borges as contemporaries—to us and to each other. Although this practice may be an important attempt to debunk linear and generational modes of periodization by positing a proto-postmodern angst throughout the history of modernity, it also entails a somewhat conventional mode of literary history. Postmodern periodization, particularly in the sphere of literary studies, manifests itself whenever writerly transgression becomes apparent to the trained eye, thereby reasserting its primacy over all other forms of history. For example, Antonio Benítez-Rojo's *Repeating Island,* an influential text on Caribbean postmodernism, carefully argues that the sixteenth-century theologian Bartolomé de Las Casas is best understood in a postmodern light. Such assertions become less surprising if one considers their premise: that semiological self-reflection willingly cultivates a fervor for ambiguity and contradiction. Turning to thinkers and writers from disparate periods is the necessary leap of a history content with being able to invent its own precursors—evoking a Borgesian sense of time strictly bound to a radical presentism.

As this epistemic horizon continues to extend, the century draws to a close with an unusual paradox. The accretion of methods and theories of knowledge that paved the way for today's sophisticated modes of textual analysis has steadily shifted from more systemic pursuits to the exigencies of creation. Elaborate semiotic presuppositions of earlier periods have given way to a deconstructive praxis whose discipline invokes scriptural invention as much as conceptual argumentation, or a mixture of the two as *episthetics*: that uncertain interplay between epistemology as aesthetics. The deeper the look into the constitution of the sign, the greater the role of rhetoric and metafiction in the production of critical discourses. But this should not be understood simply as a triumph of art and literature over critical thinking. The art world itself is not exempt from foundational slippage. Texts, performances, and other imprecise flows have also interfered with the very definition of art and literature. Writing and discourse now celebrate rhetorical spaces in which the specificity of art and literature are conflated with that of culture, history, ideology, or the shifty ground of theory, constituting a new culturalist horizon that often fuels its own critical markets, such as multiculturalism.

None of this is new for the postmodern scene, except perhaps the longevity of its seeming novelty. Its most brilliant and elaborate precursor is still found in the early and paradigmatic figure of Borges, whose cerebral narratives—many written during the 1930s and 1940s—have made an indelible imprint on theory and fiction over the last two decades of the twentieth century. A discussion of how Borges was translated into a quintessential figure of the postmodern 1990s is an interesting and difficult question touched on at other times in this book. What I wish to explore for now is the intensity that sustains and renews the nexus between discursivity and semiological doubt in two different moments and two different sites during the twentieth century, one very contemporary and largely Euro-American, the other a bit older and more Latin American. The first is the notion of *performativity*, a prevailing strand of this nexus in the United States. The second is *transculturation*, a much less known Latin American theoretical articulation that, despite its unquestionable flaws, retains considerable relevance for contemporary Latin American theoretical debates, particularly as postcolonialism, cultural studies, and hybridity attempt to chart new territories within the postmodern to accommodate rhetorical residues of Third World histories.

An important point of departure is the work of Judith Butler, now widely read by a new generation of scholars across the entire spectrum of humanities and social sciences. Her book *Gender Trouble: Feminism and the Subversion of Identity* argues for the centrality of "performance," a concept best understood as putting into play an impulse that decodes various key notions of the modern logos, particularly the relations between identity, sex, and gender. Butler amply demonstrates how politics is complicit with semiology by showing how languages and discourses construct identity, be it masculine or feminine. Transgression—through writing, dressing, or other means of expression—takes place through contestation and designification of such codes. In this early but still widely quoted book, there is the implication that transformations in the social sphere also evolve from such transgressions. That leap, however, not only remains unclear in *Gender Trouble*, but one might even question whether "the performative" unwittingly invokes a reified concept of avant-garde aesthetics.[1]

Performance should be understood here as a deconstructive/creative act capable of unpacking the Western humanistic tradition with critical operations that draw their force largely from discursive self-awareness. Performativity thus invokes transgression of roles codified in discourses—a semiotic insight deployed by way of writing, dressing, and other forms of self-representation. For Butler, gender construction is the most important terrain for performing such work, a site from which models of sexual conduct are questioned and traversed. It is important to note, however, that the critical function is here relegated to a textual praxis in which the writing subject remains always at work in the creative designification of the Western paradigm as a floating state of vigilance. The political is to be exclusively derived from potential discursive rearrangements whose capacity to reorganize the social from within is a given. More precise questions about the social and political impact of such a project are turned back on themselves, into their naïveté regarding rhetorical power: the political is sustained by the underlying structures of language that can only be unearthed through epistemological awareness. There are no more imaginative and incisive articulations of gender performativity than Butler's, but, as one would expect, not all contemporary theorists find the implications of her work sufficiently thought through. Nancy Fraser, for example, though persuaded by Butler's "claim that the self-deconstructing tendencies within feminism are endemic to identity movements and cannot be eliminated by fiat," argues:

> The idea of "women" as the sign of an untotalizable field of differences is susceptible to two interpretations, one strong and indefensible, the other weak and defensible, but hardly the cause for celebration. The strong thesis is the one associated with "New French Feminist" theory, according to which "woman" cannot be defined but signifies difference and nonidentity. This, of course, is a paradoxical claim, since to make the term "woman" the sign of the undefinable is thereby precisely to define it. Moreover, this (anti)definition is mystifying. Why should "woman" or "women" be the sign of the nonidentical? Isn't everything Butler says about "women" also true of "men", "workers", "people of color", "Chicanos", or any collective nomination. A more defensible interpretation [of Butler's suggestion] would follow [that] generalizing claims about "women" are inescapable but always subject to revision; they should be advanced nonfoundationally and fallibilistically. Further, the assumptions underlying such claims should be genealogized, framed by contextualizing narrative and rendered culturally and historically specific.[2]

Another significant source of performative theory is found in the postcolonial work of Homi Bhabha.[3] Although discussed in chapter 1 in terms of Gayatri Chakravorty Spivak's work and Latin Americanism, I will make here just a few observations that flow specifically from Bhabha's work. Postcolonialism here is understood as a deconstructive look at the culturalist theory of the Third World in opposition to the First, or of the culture of Third World diasporas within the First. Indeed, the aims of postcolonial criticism could be understood as an attempt to critique both modern Third Worldism and postmodern First Worldism. It includes, among other things, the need to question, or even nullify, developmental terms and schemes, and the ideologies they imply. It also recognizes that the world of postmodern globalization must still face its colonial and neocolonial legacies. Postcolonialism, according to this definition, was first associated with the work of English-writing diasporic intellectuals living in England and the United States, even though it has since caught the attention of critics in Australia, Africa, the Caribbean, and Latin America.[4] Besides Bhabha, Spivak and Edward Said are some of the principal exponents of postcolonial thinking and writing, though there are significant differences among them, particularly in Said's case. Latin American critics now working within this paradigm include Walter Mignolo, Fernando Coronil, and José Rabasa.[5]

The postcolonial intellectual, according to Bhabha, is inscribed in a postmodern hybridity whose "performance" comes from the attempt to problematize what is usually termed "otherness." Such writing feeds from the tension of being in a liminal subject position, an epistemological exile, without possible referent, willing to remain in a state of constant writerly vigilance, placed before the contradictory impulses that define the "Other" (Third World, minority) as the antithesis of the colonizing center. Awareness of this tension and the way it manifests itself in equivocal and transgressive ways allows the subject to subvert the processes of slow self-negation (assimilation). Such an intellectual turns cultural hybridity into a more critical position that transforms the rhetoric of otherness into a discourse of suspicion, thereby shaking loose the binary logic of identity/otherness. As in Butler's notion of performance, there is here a profound sense of revolution through language as master metaphor, and praxis as the work of immanent designification as individualized but symbolic critical creativity. "My revolt," declares Bhabha, "is to face the Life of literature and history with the scraps and fragments that constitute its double, which is living as surviving, meaning as melancholia."[6]

Deconstructive practice, arguably the most rigorous form of postmodern thought, obtains a highly sophisticated elaboration in the work of Butler and Bhabha. They bring the rigors of deconstruction to feminism and postcolonial referentiality as specific sites of contestation that often lie outside the boundaries of a more general understanding of literary postmodernism. The search for the uncanny and the desire to abound in the "unsayable" are still central to their theoretical work, but they come closer to specific contemporary referential points, such as women and the former Third World, thereby approaching the political realm in their own ways. They also share an opposition to pedagogical or sentential discourses that aim to teach, totalize, or enclose rather than perform by unhinging set patterns of meaning. Nonetheless, one could argue that the iteration of certain precepts and themes in the work of Butler and Bhabha at times betrays a pedagogical will of its own. Conceptual unpacking becomes the sole province of a "performative" discourse whose "truth" is always found in a notion of "writing" or "rhetoric" that takes on the role of a master code sufficient unto itself. The uncanny and the aporetic, imbued as they are by simultaneous interplay of writerly creativity and the negation of modern metanarratives, are thought to be intrinsically transgressive and liberationist. Pedagogical and scientific discourses, on the other hand, regardless of their aim and sphere of application, are identified with stale traditions because they lack awareness of their complicity with language, thereby incurring a semiological naïveté that is, by fiat, the site where negative power and authority are reconstituted. Lastly, unmasking essentialism assumes the force of an inexhaustible truth-value, and the critique of identities through language somehow accounts for the totality of social construction.[7]

Seen as such, deconstruction alludes to a potentially liberating purpose, but its praxis is also constrained by the philosophical and literary terrain enclosing it. For many intellectuals, the work of performative designification spells a new political frontier defined as a radicalism devoid of a concrete political program, or a redefinition of political program defined by the "language metaphor," perhaps the only way of conceiving emancipation within the increasingly hegemonic conjuncture of global capitalism. But this project also constitutes a new aesthetic vanguard prone to privilege discursive free play at times closer to Adornian hibernation, at other times bound to a new aestheticism that bespeaks a conservative paradigm now controlling access to many academic positions, particularly in the United States. As Peter Dews explains, there is a glaring lack of proportion between the far-reaching ambition of deconstructivist work—its radical critique of history, rationality, identity, and modernity as a whole—and the academic hermeticism to which it adheres.[8]

Public support for the academy's traditional role in liberal education has waned considerably in the past decades. The need for institutional stability and philanthropic investments is particularly acute in a culture whose growing reliance on markets as the ultimate arbiter of social policy goes unabated. In that context, the most radical elements of humanistic theory have been absorbed by a new generation of intellectuals caught in a dubious predicament: they must witness, and in some cases participate in, academic downsizing, while aspiring to the comfort and privileges of earlier generations. Until the late 1980s, for example, postmodern positionality remained predictable. The radical call to deconstruct modernity's past was openly embraced, but its more threatening attempt to theorize a posthumanistic culture remained quite fuzzy and tame even though the postcapitalist transformations felt outside the academy were momentous, if not revolutionary. Indeed, the neoliberal fusion of culture, markets, and politics during the

1990s left much less room to engage in a postmodern celebration of free-floating signifiers as theory. Such dispersion is now lived more than theorized. The nation, the family, the private sphere, reproductive technologies, the body—indeed, life itself—have been recast beyond the wildest dreams of deconstructive speculation. Then again, the postcolonial turn of the 1990s, some forms of feminist practices, as well as cultural studies, attempted to maintain the promise of a new and different theoretical turn in their call for a less male-centered, traditionally Euro-American understanding of postmodern history and literature.

As instability within the social sphere exacerbates the need for truly interdisciplinary engagement with globalization, it is no wonder that contemporary theoretical work is subject to contradictory enunciations and equivocal understanding. Even the work of highly influential thinkers is likely to harbor many simultaneously disparate readings. The pedagogy of moves available to discursive critiques must now reassume a critical role within the context of other postmodern discourses, including those corresponding to neoliberal globalization.[9] Derrida's call for a rigorous reappraisal of the contemporary critical landscape is quite germane, even to his own contributions. It should be noted, however, that the need for such a call has been obvious to many feminists and Third World theorists for decades. The Chilean theorist Nelly Richard, author of an incisive book on postmodern thought, had already observed in 1989:

> Postmodernism defends itself against destabilizing effects of the "other," integrating its manifestations into an order perfectly trained to level differences and reabsorb contradictions. The Center, though it clothes itself as the object of disintegration, has not stopped operating as Center; it now archives the deviant under a repertoire of figures whose codes, semantic and territorial, it continues to administer with total exclusivity.[10]

As seen in chapter 1, Latin American literary studies perhaps constitutes a key new arena for examining how postmodern and postcolonial discursive communities articulate and administer conceptual disintegration. I attempted to chart there the parallel emergence of new contemporary theories and a Latin American literary corpus that reached the world stage since the 1960s.[11] Communities of Latin Americanism, I argued, have risen to constitute a new sense of discursive cartography from which the very meaning of Latin America, the postmodern, or now the postcolonial, evolves. Language and disciplinary boundaries also become a factor in theoretical codification between Latin American and U.S. Latin Americanism. The postmodern work of critics living and working in Latin America such as Enrique Dussel, Néstor García Canclini, Nelly Richard, and Martin Hopenhayn, among others, straddles the lines of demarcation between literature and the social sciences; furthermore, their work has only recently appeared in anthologies translated into English.[12] Even in Spanish, their work may be beyond the reach of those who do Latin America largely in Spanish from the United States and Canada, where various notions of postmodernism based on a few Latin American texts have circulated for decades.[13]

At stake is the crucial link between Latin America as an objective correlative of literary postmodernism and Latin America as a dynamic entity whose presence in the United States grows incrementally each day through migration, television, and increased commerce. It has been noted that in Latin America today, "soap operas are turning away from Cinderella stories and toward real-life issues, tackling corruption and drug traffickers, sexism and sadists (the latter being the U.S. Border Patrol)."[14] More than 50 percent of the people in Mexico watch *telenovelas* (televised soaps), and in Brazil it is close to 60 percent, compared to 20 percent in the United States. Women's issues, Mexican political assassinations, Venezuelan corruption— these topics are now portrayed, respectively, in *Mirada de mujer (*A woman's glance), *Nada personal* (Nothing personal), and *Por estas calles* (Through these streets), in ways that suggest the possibility of turning to *telenovelas* to observe a new type of commentary that invokes aesthetic and social change. It remains to be seen how metropolitan literary paradigms will approach these postmodern phenomena in Latin America, or if their forms of textual analysis will even acknowledge their cultural relevance.

For these reasons, I am interested in exploring a Latin American paradigm of transcultural production and reflection whose history reveals intersemiological processes within Latin America. This is not an attempt to ignore the undeniable blind spots of that critical tradition, or to privilege the local over the transnational, but rather to complicate the universalizing tendencies of use-value postmodern Latin Americanism often produced in the United States. I am referring to "transculturation," a key concept at play in the work of many important Latin American theorists throughout the twentieth century. My specific interest here lies in the different anthropological, literary, and cultural studies approaches to transmodernity in Latin America, as seen in the work of Fernando Ortiz, Ángel Rama, and Néstor García Canclini. By transmodernity, I am referring to an uncertain inbetween modern and postmodern that also carries colonial traces—a nonsynchronicity that is necessarily flattened when traditional First World metanarrative critiques approach Latin America. Through transculturation or cultural reconversion, these theorists offer a broad range of transmodern constructs for Latin America. They provide an intertextual look at literary, social, and even political hybridity often not available through literary deconstructivism that could very well offer—as Walter Mignolo's recent work on the work of Rodolfo Kusch suggests—a postcolonial corrective to postmodern immanence.[15] The reader will also find an attempt to signal a key blind spot in transculturation, most particularly its failure to engage Latin American feminism and women's writing, an indispensable discourse for rereading and contesting any strand of Latin Americanism.

There are, I hasten to add, differing views on the relative value of transculturation theory. For some critics, transculturation belongs to the modern totalizing paradigm that often yields a Latin American tradition of identitarian longings, a will to cultural or racial synthesis all too willing to erase difference, or a structuralist approach to Latin American hybridity. According to these critiques, transculturation is part of an ideology largely based in an understanding of *mestizaje* as a unifying force of cultural or even racial elements that is no longer tenable under postmodern dispersion and deconstructive scrutiny.[16] Transculturation thus necessarily becomes a failed discourse whose ultimate demise could not arrive soon enough.[17] There are, however, other postmodern readings that see transculturation in a more ambiguous deconstructive light. Some of these turn to the early work of figures such as Fernando Ortiz for a discourse that includes certain elements of literary free play. Here one finds a recuperation of sorts, albeit one that will only understand transculturation discourse as a form of writing that betrays its "scientific aspirations," giving way instead to the inherent contradictions of any attempt to theorize the social sphere.[18] Yet, other contemporary critics observe the possibility of new Latin Americanist theoretical engagements through transculturation, whether for a transnational cultural critique or in terms of a dialogue with Foucauldian metanarrative critique that complicates standard postmodernist approaches to cast literature as a deconstructive master code.[19]

My aim in the subsequent sections of this chapter will be to traverse and complement these differing views of Latin America's discourse on transculturation. This will entail an introduction of its central historic dimensions couched in an argument in favor of its strategic potential for contemporary cultural reception and for an understanding of Latin American modernity that is often flattened or erased by postmodern metanarrative critiques. As Lisa Lowe and David Lloyd explain in their anthology *The Politics of Culture in the Shadow of Capital*, alternative modernity is "not the 'other' outside, but the 'what-has-been-formed' in the conjunction with and

in differentiation from modernity over time."[20] That interplay of antago-
nism and adaptation "belies the homogenization of capitalist social relations
according to the Western model," and "it also contradicts the assumption of
a correspondence between the cultural and political domains."[21]

Cultural Hybridity

Given the current turn toward postcolonial and subaltern theoretical questions, it seems particularly fitting to consider the twentieth century's epistemic unfolding from the viewpoint of a critical tradition rooted in Latin
America. Transculturation permits this kind of exploration precisely because
it is a contested field that attracts and resists attempts to unhinge its presuppositions. Its story generally begins with the renowned anthropologist
Bronislaw Malinowski, a Polish scientist who emigrated first to England and
then to the United States at the turn of the century, where he established his
functionalist school of ethnology. In his 1940 prologue to the well-known
treatise *Contrapunteo cubano del tabaco y el azúcar* (Cuban counterpoint of
tobacco and sugar) of Cuban anthropologist Fernando Ortiz, Malinowski
expounds on the merits of "transculturation."[22] The new term avoids the
limitations of notions such as *deculturation* and *acculturation,* much in use at
the time to describe modernity's impact on non-Western cultures. Ortiz refuses to accept the cultural history of the Other as one of passive resistance
to modernizing forces. Moreover, he seeks to historicize the central importance of subaltern producers to the formation of national identity in settler
societies such as Cuba. To write a history of Caribbean culture, Ortiz finds it
indispensable to foreground the constant struggle among colonizers, colonized, Creoles, and subaltern ethnicities. He accounts for the Other not
only as contributor to future rhetorical traces, but as a decisive participant in
the formation of peripherally modern societies.

Some four decades later, the Uruguayan critic Ángel Rama redeployed
Ortiz's concept in his influential *Transculturación narrativa en América Latina,* with special focus on the Latin American novel of the Andean region.
Rama treats literature as an intertextual web much in the mode of Bakhtinian criticism. But, for Rama, transculturation makes possible a deeper account of the extraordinary world of ethnicities, cultures, languages, and
temporalities that give life to the modern Latin American novel. As a
heightened form of intertextuality, transculturation in Rama becomes a
mode of articulating and reading Latin America's specific form of cultural
hybridity in its multitemporal, multicultural dimensions, an arche-writing
or signifying that also includes literature. *Hybrid Cultures,* by the Mexico-

based Argentine theorist Néstor García Canclini, focuses on the work of urban artisans and the increasing fusion between popular and mass cultural formations in Latin America, including television, arguably bringing transculturation to a postmodern conjuncture, not only as a theory of textuality, but as a politics for everyday life.

Obviously, the generational chronology implicit in these three Latin American theorists may suggest a clear line of demarcation, a century-old uninterrupted teleology of sorts. But the practice of rereading (as I hope this chapter will show) demands a more asynchronical understanding. Regarding Malinowski, for example, it has become indispensable to consider the importance of his *Diary in the Strict Sense of the Term,* written between 1914 and 1918 but not published until 1967. This contradictory text has sparked a new interest in the way narrativity and subjectivity inform anthropological research, as evidenced in the work of Clifford Geertz and James Clifford. In their rereading, Malinowski becomes a contemporary of sorts. The diary unveils a less-guarded moment of profound subjectivity in his fieldwork among the Trobriands, an aspect absent from the original transcriptions of his experience in the Pacific, as published in 1922 under the title *Argonauts of the Western Pacific.* Today, we can read both of Malinowski's texts within and against each other, as James Clifford has done, thereby revealing the writerly aspects of transcription, its links to other forms of narration, and, above all, to ways of imagining the "other."

Current critical wisdom holds that presentism seeps into all historical formulations, as Borges's Pierre Menard demonstrates in his daring attempt to rewrite Cervantes's *Don Quixote* word for word. The question is not whether complicity with the present is avoidable, but how consciously one assumes it, in the hope of capturing its potential heuristic traps as well as its performative possibilities. I embark, therefore, from the end of my story, that is, from García Canclini's *Hybrid Cultures: Strategies for Entering and Leaving Modernity* (first published in Spanish 1990). The title itself sets forth an enigmatic proposal (for modernists and postmodernists) that places modernity within a liminal space often forgotten by postmodernism. Third World, peripherally modern, and postcolonial societies continue to face a modern/postmodern dilemma that often carries colonial residues: modernity is something that must still be entered, provided one is ready to leave it. This, I believe, could be understood as an ongoing need to register the desire for modernizing processes at a time when such processes are no longer sustained by constitutive or programmatic utopian narratives. García Canclini dramatizes this predicament through an anecdote that reveals his own performative strategies: a constant attempt to overcome theoretical barriers, and an intricate look at the growing bonds between popular culture and the media of mass communication in Latin America:

> Let me say that when I began to study these changes, my immediate reaction was to lament the subordination of the producers to the tastes of urban consumers and tourists. Then eight years ago I went into a shop in Teotitlán del Valle—a Oaxacan town dedicated to weaving— where a fifty-year-old man was watching television with his father while exchanging phrases in Zapotec. When I asked him about the tapestries with images by Picasso, Klee, and Miró that he had on display, he told me they started to make them in 1968, when some tourists visited who worked in the Museum of Modern Art in New York and proposed that they renovate their designs. He showed me an album of photos and newspaper clippings in English that analyzed the exhibitions this artisan had done in California. In a half hour I saw him move with ease from Zapotec to Spanish and to English, from art to crafts, from his ethnic group to the information and entertainment of mass culture, passing through the art criticism of a metropolis. I understood that my worries about the loss of their traditions [were] not shared by this man who moved without too many conflicts between three cultural systems.[23]

This lively scene of a border artist crossing languages, ethnicities, geographies, and modes of cultural production underpins García Canclini's central hypothesis regarding postmodernism. In many ways it resonates with Guillermo Gómez-Peña's own performative autobiographical accounts of life as a culturally nomadic subject in the United States. Most important, García Canclini refrains from both mourning the loss of traditional culture and celebrating a new horizon of floating identities. Instead, he underscores the necessary pilgrimage of creative interpellation, the nomadic experience of an artisan's involvement with a popular culture that in Latin America is also implicit in mass culture. It is also reminiscent of the film *El Mariachi* by the Mexican-American director Robert Rodríguez, in which border cultures are not just a geographic point of departure, but a site from which various transculturations take shape: Americanization, Mexicanization, narcotics industry, feminism, and video culture. García Canclini's postmodern protagonist, however, is not an academic intellectual, as is so often the case in literary and philosophical treatises on the subject. On the other hand, his frontier artisan has modernized his craft with a grade of confidence that bespeaks considerable acuity.

Border artistry or performativity challenges a postmodernity that is always caught within theory and distances itself from life, as the now customary methods of unpacking and critiquing metanarratives are wont to be. García Canclini is fully aware that his artisan is basically responding to market forces. But such concerns yield to the author's confidence in "cultural reconversion," which I see in light of transculturation theory as a new nexus between the subjectivity of popular culture producers and the hegemony of market economies. *Hybrid Cultures* turns this nexus into a site for new texts, products, and performances imbued by the producer's awareness of self-inscription, indeed, as a writing or performance in ways reminiscent of Butler's and Bhabha's concepts. In an epoch characterized by overdetermined mass cultural markets, the transformational potential in García Canclini's notion of border artistry thus comes close as well to almost autotelic value, albeit of a different sort: the popular producer in Latin America carries orality, traditions, and yet is open to individual transformations. In a certain sense, his search for *cultural reconversion* is much more anchored in the material relations of the cultural market than in the processes of troping. In a subsequent section titled "The Staging of the Popular" García Canclini derives a series of principles from the disjunctions between popular and elite cultures in the context of mass media. They include the following:

- Modern development by itself does not suppress traditional popular culture.
- Rural and traditional cultures no longer represent the majority of popular culture.
- The popular is not primarily a body of artifacts and objects.
- The popular is not a monopoly of the popular sectors.
- The popular is not lived by popular subjects as melancholic compliance with traditions.
- The pure preservation of traditions is not always the best resource for the reproduction and reelaboration of social conditions for popular sectors.[24]

It must be understood that popular traditions in Latin America are still revered, even by elites whose lives are much closer to Western metropolitan styles of consumption than the ranks of unemployed and barely employed sectors that generally constitute the popular sector. One finds in this contradictory constellation a profound difference between the United States and Latin America. Any contemporary attempt to periodize Latin American culture today—whether as postindustrial society, New World Order, postmodernity, globalization, or neoliberalism—runs into a strong domain of popular culture that is often held by elites as the ground of national identity, no matter how contradictory that seems in the face of the material conditions of popular classes. Ethnicity and multiculturalism there are not as immediately conflictual as multitemporality. The cultural debate in the United States, on the other hand, is usually confined to relations between mass and elite cultures, with profound concerns with ethnicity and multiculturalism. In Latin America, identity formation continues to rely on the popular as a reference point for the autochthonous, be it racial, agrarian, proletarian, or other forms of resistance that pitted tradition against modernity. García Canclini attempts to deconstruct this conception as ongoing transcultural forces, not as a narrative that can be simply discarded, by showing how the traditional survives through hybridization with markets, as a Latin American cultural economy that interpellates global capitalism driven by the constant production of new norms of appropriation and intertextualities.

Hybrid Cultures makes a special point of the growing number of artisans, dancers, and poets in Latin America. It is also aware that there are more cultural discourses in (and about) Latin America in general, that discursive and material hyperproduction continue to reflect on each other. It also shows how popular discourses now respond to redrawn boundaries and border zones: the links of traditionalism and populism have loosened considerably with the anarchic growth of Latin American cities, rural communities have been displaced by larger ungovernable enclaves surrounding urban centers, and new forms of cultural reconversion and transculturation have risen. If identity formation, consolidation, and critique are also evident in Latin American cultural studies, they obtain a difference in these particular elements; hence, García Canclini's emphasis on the multitemporal aspect of multiculturalism, given Latin America's inherently transmodern history, an ongoing criss-crossing of disrupted modernities, with its lingering colonialism alongside its intermittent imperialisms.

These new territories lie beyond the grasp of metanarrative critique as a standard set of universally sedimented modern precepts, a practice whose transgressive potential is readily reabsorbed into the aesthetic mainstream. Dissolving such traditions within the institutional safeguard of academic discourses is bound to find far less resistance than in other cultural spheres. The ongoing cultural wars in the United States are a case in point, particularly when seen as symptoms of a sense of loss—ethical, cultural, social— now felt in the public sphere. Within the literary realm, the new Latin American novel provides another interesting case study. This genre has become an integral part of the Western canon. During the 1960s and 1970s, a few prominent male writers, most notably García Márquez, Carlos Fuentes,

and Mario Vargas Llosa, acquired worldwide renown for their highly innovative narrative forms. But the celebration of their extraordinary achievements acquires a different dimension when we move from the terrain of
postmodern literary history—which emphasizes transgressive moments
within individual texts—to that of cultural theories and histories. An interesting example is found in John Barth's "discoveries." He claims to have discovered postmodern literature reading Borges, for example, and later claims
to have rediscovered it reading García Márquez. But he has little to say, beyond stylistic impressions, of what postmodern writing is about.[25] What
does it mean for Latin America's novels to become part of the U.S. canon?
Who is being read through whose texts? Are there different readings of the
same texts in Latin America, where national literature and alternative tests
respond to and resonate with everyday cultural experiences?[26] How do different postmodern performances approach texts whose aesthetic and historical import are doubly coded? *Hybrid Cultures* offers novel responses to such
questions as it aims to fuse discursive theory and empirical reception studies
into a new cultural studies paradigm. It begins with a detailed account of
how working-class and middle-class Mexicans consume televised images of
traditionally high-culture territory, including museums and great literary
stars. Televised interviews with Octavio Paz and Jorge Luis Borges on national programs, for example, are reviewed as instruments through which
the lines of demarcation between cultural spheres are broken down. Suddenly, sacred literary figures are seen, or consumed, by the video mind-set of
new interpretive communities asking how literature can still work in their
imaginaries. A shift in the relation between Latin American literature and
postmodernity from the primacy of Continental theory and hypercritical
troping to an unsuspected interface with the everyday emphasis of mass culture, much like the 1997 readings of Pablo Neruda's poetry on U.S. television, were sparked by the success of the Italian film *Il Postino*. Literature is
suddenly asked to speak to the construction of meaning in people's lives,
even if only at the affective surface level of television audiences. García Canclini thus submits theory and criticism to a new interplay of diverse discursive practices, which may still store many questions and contradictions, but
which are nonetheless much less prone to evade contemporary daily life.

The contrast between this type of performance as registered in a living
audience and the more hermetic forms of literary or performative postmodernism is dramatic. Deconstructive work targeted for strict academic
circulation often claims to transgress modern aesthetics, but in general it remains embedded in traditional structures of aestheticism, self-enclosed discourses of appreciation, and a vast distance from social life. Writing as such

becomes a space of perennial negation that is adverse to advancing any sort of counterproposals and much less of speaking to the quotidian.[27] One could argue that such a critical stance allows for intellectual freedom—perhaps more necessary than ever in a global culture without opposition—but it also risks adhering to writing as an imprecise form of utopian thinking, devoid of links to a broader cultural terrain. The realm of literature or philosophy becomes reified once again by the privilege of institutionalized postmodern aesthetics, the same logic it sought to undermine through metanarrative critique. This possible aporia, internal to literary postmodernity, often slips away from deconstructive rigor. Derrida seems to have sensed this when he affirmed that "to break with the 'party form' or with some form of the State or with the International does not mean one should give up every form of practical or effective organization."[28]

Although deeply informed by contemporary theory, particularly its critique of the modern Western tradition, *Hybrid Cultures* calls for a different approach to Latin American postmodernism. Its reach goes beyond Latin American literary texts, recognizing perhaps that an exclusive emphasis on writerly transgression ends up as yet another form of reverence. *Hybrid Cultures* moves beyond deconstruction as well, turning instead to an array of cultural texts that are not ready-made, focusing, as discussed, on programs for mass participation in Mexican museums as well as painting, literature, and sculpture, or by looking at the constellation of artisans (producers, sellers, and buyers) whose presence in Latin American cities—a space that now contains 70 percent of the population—has become ubiquitous. García Canclini's approach to these new avenues of research includes a considerable investment in various strands of postmodern theory. He borrows eclectically from sources as diverse as Theodor Adorno, Jean-François Lyotard, and Jürgen Habermas. He combines a deep awareness of the ongoing need for modernization during postmodern reconfigurations, while recognizing the absence of utopian discourses, particularly for collective agency.

Hybrid Cultures presents a way of doing cultural studies in Latin America that begins by acknowledging the now prevalent nexus of cultural production under globalization and neoliberalism. In that sense, transculturation obtains through García Canclini a much more contemporary range than many of its critics usually expect. It is not merely a descriptive device for the give-and-take of cultures in contact, nor a sociological content analysis of Latin American history, but rather a complex strategy in which deconstruction is not left in a state of epistemological arrest, but is driven to ongoing construction of social and intellectual challenges that position the critic as producer as well. It should be pointed out, however, that

García Canclini's strategies of reconversion have so far failed to account for women's roles and women's issues in particular. It remains to be seen how this integral element will find its way in his work, how a woman reader, consumer, or border artist transforms the way he understands those subjectivities. Other questions requiring further attention include the following: Does reconversion turn into a mostly descriptive rather than critical register of Latin American cultural identities under global capitalism? Does it envision any sites of legitimation and codification other than the abstract negative notion described by the author as a lack of a "stable author or text"? Does it respond to any principle other than the constant movement between market, cultural producers, and modernizations? García Canclini's text does not propose definitive or immediate answers to these questions, although it explores them at various moments and problematizes them at others. If there is a suggestion, it would be found in his ample and defiant engagement with postmodern performances, which includes, of course, an acute awareness of the ideological apparatus supporting them.

Between Literature and Culture

Ángel Rama's *Transculturación narrativa en América Latina* (1982) blends his most widely read essays of the early and mid-1970s with later theoretical formulations. That book foregrounds one of Rama's main concerns: the scant attention paid to Andean literature by Latin American critics, particularly those working in the United States. When viewed from this perspective, one could argue that Rama prefigures postcolonial studies of Latin American literature that became prominent nearly twenty years later. Indeed, there is a growing recognition of the Latin Americanist blind spot for the rich archive of texts in which pre-Columbian oral traditions figure prominently. Recent attempts to fill this void include Amaryll Chanady's anthology *Latin American Identity and Constructions of Difference* and two special issues of *Poetics Today* edited by Walter Mignolo.[29] Rama's main interest is the Peruvian novelist José María Arguedas, but his book calls for a much broader reorientation of Latin American literary criticism. It scrutinizes many of the central premises of the so-called *boom* of the 1960s and 1970s, a period when Latin American narrative assumed a preeminent position in world literature.

Rama is more than a prolific essayist. He blends a wide-ranging knowledge of modern Latin American literary history with a richly informed theoretical framework. This fertile work of consolidation, even after Rama's death in 1983, continues to challenge many scholars. His last book, *La ciudad letrada* (The lettered city), for instance, offers a historical account of

Latin American intellectuals since colonial times, and is the central topic of chapter 5 in this book. It is a very heretical view by today's standards. Suffice it to say that in *La ciudad letrada* Rama historicizes writing and state interests in tandem: the lust for power cohabits with isolated acts of literary transgression. Far from an inherently liberationist practice, writing is rendered complicit with a much deeper and complex web of entanglements. Hence, *La ciudad letrada* provides an exacting test to many key deconstructive premises.[30]

There is a growing sense that, for Latin Americanists interested in the interconnections between culture and literature, Rama's work is indispensable. Jean Franco, Saúl Sosnowski, Jorge Ruffilleni, Jesús Díaz Caballero, and Neil Larsen, among others, have drawn significantly from his approach to Latin American literary culture.[31] The anthology *Ángel Rama y los estudios latinoamericanos* (Ángel Rama and Latin American studies), edited by Mabel Moraña, engages a significant number in that list in a debate that will undoubtedly make a considerable impact in how we view both Rama and the field.

Rama, it must be stated, takes pains to distance himself from transculturation as an impressionistic form of ethnic history. When taken as such, transculturation can summon greater affective than critical force and evoke an imprecise but generalized sense of Latin American authenticity, somewhat analogous to other commonly abused terms such as *mestizaje,* "marvelous realism," and "magical realism." But Rama is precise on this point. He makes it clear from the first chapter that his preference for the term *transculturation* draws from the work of Fernando Ortiz, but he is less interested in the latter's scientific methods than in his creative understanding of the way transmission occurs between different cultures, particularly those in dissimilar positions of power. Like Ortiz, Rama sees in transculturation a metaphor for inclusion and perhaps revindication, in contrast with *acculturation,* which emphasizes the acquisition of the new. But what appears to explain his attention to a discourse of the 1940s is not so much the term as the general mode in which Ortiz articulates it: Rama finds in Ortiz an approach to cultural analysis that moves from scientific to narrative flows. In that sense, Rama comes close to Foucauldian genealogies of power relations, an analysis that Edward Said also performed around the same time in his well-known *Orientalism.* What interests Rama, in the end, is transculturation as form, something that allowed him to reread Arguedas and other exceptionally hybrid writers in a more meaningful light: "In favor of the proposition by Fernando Ortiz," writes Rama, "militates his expressive joy. Ortiz's sensibility for the spirit of language, in contrast to what happens

with many texts of Latin American anthropologists and sociologists, turn his books into a creative linguistic experience."[32]

Rama first became known for his wide-ranging work on Latin American modernism. Unlike Octavio Paz, whose *Children of the Mire* addresses this modernist corpus exclusively as a poetic phenomenon without a single mention of Latin American narrative, political, or epistemological discourses, Rama carefully constructs modernity's relation to social as well as literary realms, avoiding mechanical derivations along the way. His texts on Rubén Darío and José Martí, the two great Latin American modernist poets, remain highly influential. His later work on contemporary narrative and transculturation is but a natural extension of that earlier focus on cultural history. It could be argued that Rama's capacity to theorize from within Latin America's traditions and transgressions is what makes his work unique to a critical landscape in which the most influential Latin American theory is now increasingly done by academics trained or anchored in Europe and the United States. To this new corps of critics, Rama's deeply rooted but yet decentered knowledge of the area constitutes either a refreshing alternative, a heavy burden, or both.

The lines of development in Rama's framework are evident: from his reappraisal of Latin American modernism, to his groundbreaking work on Latin American narrative, and ultimately to larger questions regarding Latin America's hybrid modernity. But what interests me here is Rama's assignation of a border zone for literary studies, a point where literature continues to figure prominently but is not given an a priori position of privilege in cultural history. Indeed, this zone operates instead as a critical limit that persistently challenges postmodern theory with particular intensity.[33] Literature, for Rama, is a plurality not just of voices but of cultural forms, which are in constant relation with markets of production and consumption—a notion somewhat reminiscent of García Canclini's border artisan, although Rama's main interest is the culture of writing. Rama articulates the possibility of redrawing lines of cultural vindication in Andean regions, and the critique of national boundaries this redrawing implies. In this regard, he comes much closer to the postcolonial writing of the 1990s than to the structuralist paradigm of the 1970s. Although analogies between Rama and García Canclini, or other more contemporary theorists, are relevant, there are also important differences. *Transculturación narrativa* is concerned with loss as much as change in popular cultures, that is, with the possible negative impact resulting from continuous exposure to modernizing markets. Rama does not lament these losses, but he highlights the value of resistance implicit in the oral traditions for providing a buffer zone—a localizing imprint—that can balance or perhaps reclaim such losses:

> this is not a new conflict, to the extent that it calls for a continuation of the ultimate conflict, which was the imposition of Hispanic culture on the indigenous cultures which then led to the Creole and regional extensions of that conflict, particularly as represented by the urban, liberal oligarchy that the Republic imposed on rural communities. It is a conflict that may find some resolution when brazen domination does not take place, when different regions can express and affirm themselves in spite of the unifying forces that confront them. Viewed from this perspective, one can conclude that there is a strengthening of cultures that are understood as interior to the continent, not in the sense that they have rigidly entrenched themselves in their traditions, but in the measure that they continue to experience transculturations without renouncing their soul.[34]

Rama's theoretical project has the marks of a Benjaminian cultural critic, at home in his travel through the field of Latin American discourses, who can accommodate various conflicting approaches at once. His essays combine an eclectic use of structuralism, critical theory, and early poststructuralism, among other elements. His complete works fill many volumes, but he was less concerned with publishing academic books than with the classic Latin American performance of writing essays. His insightful dialogue with the work of Claude Lévi-Strauss, for example, in many ways parallels V. Y. Mudimbe's engagement with the same body of work in *The Invention of Africa*. Rama's frequent incursions into Theodor Adorno's deconstructive practices deserve attention, as do the brief but interesting critiques of Derrida's definition of orality in Rama's *La ciudad letrada*. Yet, the crucial feature remains his proximity to Latin American cultural texts, which provides a wealth of Latin American sources, from anthropology, literature, and criticism to the history of writing as a Latin American institution since colonial times. These are all simultaneously inscribed in a continuous interplay between the regional and the global on the one hand, and between the social and the creative on the other.

Rama viewed the work of Peruvian novelist José María Arguedas as the most dramatic example of literary transculturation. Arguedas's originality is at once a force and an enigma that lies, according to Rama,

> in the association tended with a cultural configuration that *is not proper to us*. We perceive them as "literary values," that is, incorporat-

ing them into our habitual cultural text, but we can suspect that they only reach their plenitude of signification if they are related to the component elements of another cultural text, somewhat in the way Lévi-Strauss imagines the function of myths, seeing in them a "matrix of signification" that always refers to another matrix, incessantly.[35]

Obviously, Rama's reference to an incessant yet anonymous matrix of meaning can only be understood as a purely semiological construct, a chain of signifiers invoking the constant and unstable dissemination of knowledge that postmodern theory often underscores. But Rama, positioned as he is on the border between modernity and postmodernity, remains attentive to the void implicit in such a formulation. He is troubled with the potential loss of cultural definition in the Andean region (not so much as nations), and how its peoples will find ways of reproducing their culture under global capitalism. Rama's formulation here operates within dialogic tension that reaches beyond the general and often sterile lines of debate between tradition and postmodernity: autochthonous claims to identity become unsustainable because of constant exchanges between markets and cultural forms; on the other hand, such instability becomes a creative tension, and at times a struggle, not just a mere fiction that celebrates literary dissemination while disclaiming all relevance to social and political cultural formations.

The notion of border artists or critics applies to Rama's project as well as his life. He lived, worked, and traveled in many Latin American countries besides his native Uruguay. More important, he is one of the few Latin Americanists who has written extensively on all the main cultural strands that make up Latin America: Andean, Caribbean, Southern Cone, Brazilian, and Mesoamerican. With the notable exception of feminist theory and women's writing, which Rama did not study directly, and which he only began to articulate in his posthumous *Las máscaras democráticas del modernismo* (The democratic masks of modernism), it is difficult to find another body of work simultaneously informed by the key sites of Latin Americanist discursive production: Latin America, Europe, and the United States. *Transculturación narrativa* is the product of such an inclusive project. It is a rich and hybrid combination of critical material whose value extends beyond Latin America. Given its emphasis on global theories and local histories, it also has particular significance for postcolonial criticism.

Rama moves from Ortiz's socioeconomic accent on transculturation to a literary appreciation of the term. As stated earlier, he also combines a critical reading of Lévi-Strauss with his interest in the critique of the cultural industry and the negative dialectics of Adorno and Max Horkheimer. In *La ciudad letrada,* his last book, he began to engage with the work of Foucault and Derrida as well. This heterogeneous mix of French and German schools of theory allows Rama to draw crucial insights from both, while maintaining the implicit tension between the cultural framework of one and the more literary orientations of the other. One of the key moments in *Transculturación narrativa* derives directly from this theoretical interplay. It is a moment when Rama attempts to clarify the difference between Alejo Carpentier's notion of marvelous realism and magical realism, which is often associated with the work of Borges. Rama takes a rather critical position on both. On marvelous realism he is more directly dismissive: "a sui generis mix of sociological schemes [and a combination of] internal contents and external meanings."[36] On magical realism and its cosmopolitan-universalist perspective Rama issues a cryptic yet illuminating commentary that indicates his awareness of the irony implicit in the postmodern conception of modernity:

> Since "Tlön, Uqbar, Orbis Tertius" (1938), "myth" has become a bibliographic dream made from the books that composed the Library of Babel. This ultimately fulfilled the symmetrical inversion detected by Horkheimer-Adorno: once Enlightenment was transmuted into the dominant irrationalism of the twentieth century, the original transmutation of myth into Enlightenment that sustained bourgeois civilization was overturned.[37]

This intriguing paraphrase of an apparent Adornian syllogism is nothing but a very skeptical rendition of the now familiar view that modernity's master narratives have lost their epistemological bearings. In fact, this "symmetrical inversion" is far from celebratory: the project of Enlightenment may indeed have turned into a myth, but a bibliographic myth has replaced it. Early on, Rama seems to have detected a central postmodern dilemma: rationality and its foundational utopias may end up deconstructed but they also still remain caught in a cycle of symmetrical ironies prone to scholastic remythification. It is evidence of his theoretical insightfulness that he came upon this critique in the 1970s.

A close reading of Rama shows how his combination of Andean transculturation, French structuralism, German negative dialectics, and a very eclectic reading of Borges can lead to a new and complex understanding of postmodern contexts. Like García Canclini, he arrives at this juncture through an in-depth study of Latin American modernizations as a cultural logic that transmutates different strands of modernity and postmodernity.

This particular focus circumvents the futile debate regarding the relevance of postmodern thinking in relation to Third World and postcolonial societies. *Transculturación narrativa* accounts for the immediacy of global capitalism in cultural and literary analysis, a position that Derrida makes central in his *Spectres of Marx*.[38] That bond, so generalized today with the proliferation of cultural production as merchandise, is always central to Rama's research: his work on the relation beween marketing and writing in the narrative boom of the 1960s; his study of José María Arguedas's deployment of ethnology and writing as performances; and his rereading Fernando Ortiz's *Contrapunteo cubano del tabaco y el azúcar,* which accentuates its narrative qualities and the inventiveness of its approach to postcolonial modernizing.

Troping Otherness

The 1930s evidences a Latin American epistemological avant-garde that has been overshadowed by its literary counterpart. Fernando Ortiz belongs to the former, as does the Peruvian theorist Juan Carlos Mariátegui. Literary specialists often ignore their work, focusing exclusively on the towering figure of Jorge Luis Borges, whose work begins during the same period. Ortiz's *Contrapunteo cubano del tabaco y el azúcar,* published in 1940, consists of 540 pages filled with a challenging heterogeneity that Rama and other more recent readers have since discovered.[39] From the outset one can sense the potential aridity of a narrative attempting a history of sugar and tobacco. Quickly, however, Ortiz's talent as a writer becomes apparent. He intones his counterpoint invoking first the allegorical rhythm of Juan Ruiz's *Libro de buen amor* (Book of good love), a classic medieval Spanish text that parodies moral rigidity.

Ortiz brings Cuba's two main modes of cultural and economic production—sugar and tobacco—into a spiritual fight reminiscent of Juan Ruiz's suggestive squabble between Don Carnal and Doña Cuaresma. The force of transculturation as form becomes immediately apparent as a type of intertextuality not exclusively bound to aesthetic norms. More important, however, Ortiz provides a direct contrast to the nineteenth-century type of upper-class impressionistic observer that lingered on well into the twentieth century in Latin America. Instead, one finds a theorist whose dialectic and dialogic tensions evoke Marx's own creativity: his attention to every paragraph, particularly when leaping, unexpectedly, from familiar grounds into new semantic territories through sheer performative force: "In agriculture: tobacco brings mini-estates and sugar creates latifundia. In industry: tobacco is bound to the city and sugar to the fields. In commerce: the whole world becomes a market for our tobacco, and for our sugar only one market

in the whole world. Centripetism and centrifugation. Cubanness and for-
eignness. Sovereignty and colonialism. Haute crown and humble sack."[40]

Contrapunteo goes far beyond prevailing discourses of Latin American
social scientists during the 1940s and 1950s.[41] It leaves behind positivistic
accounts of Cuba's social formations to turn toward a cultural critique of
modernizing structures. One can readily understand how a prominent
scholar such as Malinowski could become so intrigued by Ortiz's originality, which transcends in many ways the protostructuralist precepts of functionalist ethnography, and perhaps even some of the tendencies of stylistics
and New Criticism that were on the way. Indeed, the lasting influence of
Ortiz's work is not limited to transculturation as a form of critical analysis.
Miguel Barnet, the renowned *testimonio* novelist, began his career as a student of Ortiz. Barnet's first novel, *Autobiography of a Runaway Slave,* was
initially conceived and researched as ethnographic fieldwork. Later, the influence of an enthusiastic popular readership and favorable market conditions turned that piece of anthropological research into a new narrative
form in which fiction, biography, and history converge and begin to complicate the story and the marketing of Latin American boom narrative with
works such as Rigoberta Menchú's autobiographical account. This link
brings the dawn of testimonial narrative to a noteworthy collusion with
transculturation theory that is still largely unexplored in Latin American
letters. In some ways, it is the story of a Latin American social-science discourse evolving into a literary genre that now seems to resist both traditional and postmodern arrests. Its texts transcreate voices and experiences of the
Latin American "Other," and most particularly the voice of women such as
Rigoberta Menchú, Domitila Barrios de Chungara, and María Teresa Tula.
Testimonio narratives may well constitute an alternative postmodern discourse to the boom and postboom novel, as some critics claim.[42] Undoubtedly, *testimonio*'s closer proximity to cultural and political history provides
significant challenges to traditional forms of Latin American postmodernism, even though *testimonio* is also prone to appropriation as the key site
of the multicultural canon in the United States.[43]

For an empirical study written in the first half of the twentieth century,
Contrapunteo already avoids many of structuralism's later pitfalls. Ortiz's
conceptual apparatus is never far from verbal play. His detailed morphological account of the characteristics of sugar and tobacco as plants, for example, is brilliantly rendered as an appraisal of their value, not only as ex-
changeable products through monetary abstraction, but more important as
discursive production: "sugar was always a business of writing: promissory
notes, export bills, and litigious documents for the Cuban courts, whereas

tobacco was a business done on the sounds of gold ounces, paid in hand, and through leased arrangements through a simple rural overseer. The business of sugar was written on paper, that of tobacco was left to the word."[44]

Ortiz's subjectivity as writer-scientist defines the intertextual nature of transculturation from the start. His life included many passions besides science. He began publishing around 1894 in Minorca, where he lived until his teens before returning to his native Cuba: a short story based on the siege of Paris during the Franco-Prussian War of 1872. He then wrote a novel, *Principi y prostes* (Beginnings and Endings; 1895), in Minorcan dialect and inspired by his readings about Paris, its mysteries, and its catacombs. In 1910, he published an edition of a novel by Benito Pérez Galdós, Spain's foremost novelist in the nineteenth century, and in the course of his many subsequent titles—literally hundreds—he conducted many studies on music and ethnography that correspond to a profoundly humanistic and creative passion. His readers have often neglected this writerly dimension, even though it accompanies—or perhaps I should say sustains—the prolific career of a social scientist initially inclined toward positivist criminology, and later preoccupied with aspects of Weberian sociology, functional anthropology, and historical materialism.

Ortiz accentuates the discursive aspects of oral narratives and his own position as subject in fieldwork research, features common in cultural anthropology today. After the publication of Malinowski's personal experience with the Trobriand people at the beginning of the century, much more attention was paid to the production of such texts. These are, in good measure, products of writing, of translation, and even invention, as one can perceive when comparing the official text of Malinowski (*Argonauts*) with his personal diary. From the differential reading of these two texts, James Clifford has concluded that "ethrographic comprehension (a combination of sympathy and hermeneutic engagement) is better seen as a creation of ethnographic *writing* than a consistent quality of ethnographic *experience*."[45]

Ortiz's understanding of otherness gains even more significance if one considers the crucial role this concept has played in the twentieth century's epistemological zest. Needless to say, the grounds for defining otherness have steadily shifted in the past few decades. The Other is no longer understood in binary terms, that is, through dialectical opposition to an external someone or something. But there are different aspects to this important shift. Some postmodern constructs, for example, have moved all the way into a strictly immanent definition of otherness, to reconfigure it only as a problem of the self, particularly the individual self, or the self within writing. Otherness thus turns into a rhetorical space that is much less relational, particularly to social and political contexts.[46] Contrary to this view, Edward Said has reclaimed otherness for subaltern, or subordinate experiences. He emphasizes the presence of a constitutive Other who continues to occupy an asymmetrical position in geopolitical power relations.[47] The Latin American philosopher Enrique Dussel has also affirmed the need to seek "the reason of the other," which he defines as the product of experiences of modernities that are different from the West.[48]

This demographically constitutive otherness, understood as ongoing formations of inequality, is no longer just an external Third World construct, but also a growing presence in Western cities. Its discursive position has become precarious with the decline of modernity's liberating projects and with the growing absence of discourses willing to address the social deficits created by globalization and neoliberalism. For postmodern writing, the Other may well have shifted to the Other-within, a space largely defined by an absence or an epistemological crisis. Like myth, Otherness is thus transmuted to the internal edge of a Western hegemony that remains powerful even while feeling the threat of dissemination through globalization. To that space of rhetorical introspection belongs a new and imaginative intellectuality, but one all too willing to forego the theoretical voids within the social text, a site in which numerous "others" and "subalterns" neither speak nor are spoken for.[49]

Ortiz's approach to otherness, conceived more than half a century ago, is particularly instructive in this regard. His position is situated in the space of an intellectual engaged in a collective conflict: Cuba's ruling white-Creole society had always denied the formative role of Afro-Cuban culture in constructions of national identity. Ortiz contested this view with his systematic and well-researched body of work. He studied the African foundations of Cuban society in an attempt to question official Cubanness—an act of defiance, not just transgression—with all the setbacks and uncertainties that entailed for him and his project, because he came from the very social and racial group that scorned his efforts. His discourse, at once empirical and creative, interpellates "reality" and becomes part of it. Otherness here is not an external object of study, nor is it only an internal disjuncture; it also assumes the contradictory force of a lifelong struggle, with both intellectual and political forces unwilling to support, and much less applaud, his transgressions.

In many respects, Ortiz's work is a prelude to a Latin American reflection on transmodernity that includes Ángel Rama and García Canclini. Together they constitute a genealogy of Latin American critical thought whose key formulations on history, culture, literature, modernization, discursive subjectivity, and the Other could still speak to some of the blind spots inherent in postmodern performances. Even though, as advanced earlier, the work of transculturation has failed to read women, it is important to see that the voids it does address are of primary concern to Latin American feminists. Indeed, one could argue that this body of writing brings an even more acute articulation of such voids in metropolitan theories. A crucial example is found in the work of Nelly Richard, who asks: "How does one revoke totalitarian projects (dictatorships) or totalitarian metanarratives (orthodox Marxism) without consenting to counterdiscourses whose negativity—satisfied by the now quasi-official value of marginality—exempts subjects from the responsibility of mobilizing forces that will link with and interpellate the social sphere?"[50] It is also not surprising to see, given the historical multidisciplinarity of transcultural theory, that key voices of contemporary anthropology raise similar questions. James Clifford, for example, whose work on Malinowski was so instrumental in scrutinizing anthropological research, proposes the following clarification:

> To reject a single progressive or entropic metanarrative is not to deny the existence of pervasive global processes unevenly at work. The world is increasingly connected, though not unified, economically and culturally. Indeed, modern ethnographic histories are perhaps condemned to oscillate between two metanarratives: one of homogenization, the other of emergence; one of loss, the other of invention."[51]

Oscillating between two metanarratives that deconstruct and reconstruct continuously, as Clifford suggests, affords a different notion of postmodern history. Like transculturation, this double coding comes close to Dussel's notion of different modernities and Ortiz's convergence of multiple forms of otherness. Transculturation, therefore, should be understood as a mode, not a method, particularly relevant for the study of the nonsynchronous development of peripherally modern and postcolonial societies. Such a construct is conceivably more heterogeneous and dialogic than both traditional identitarian readings of Latin American culture and recent frameworks of literary and epistemic immanence. The three writers discussed here, together with other contemporary critics provide an enriching and plural definition of critical theory and hybridity. Whether or not it is called transculturation matters much less than its account of the fluid transmission within various competing cultural discourses: narrativization, performativity, cultural marketing, and theoretical work. Transculturation thus

marks the ever-growing relation between Latin American cultural production and modernizations at different moments of the twentieth century, be
it modern, postmodern, or, more important, ambiguous moments of in-
betweenness. It incorporates the performative acts of critics, creators, and
scientists—border artists all—in their inevitable encounter between cultures
and economies.

4
Mimicry and the Uncanny in Caribbean Discourse

The only theory worth having is that which you have to fight off.
Stuart Hall, *"Cultural Studies and Its Theoretical Legacies"*

Mapping Caribbean culture has always conjured images of hybridity, mimicry, syncretism, and transculturation. Long before the advent of post-modern troping, the names Frantz Fanon, Aimé Césaire, Nicolás Guillén, C. L. R. James, and Fernando Ortiz gave meaning to such categories. But these very terms are now used to designate an imploded sense of otherness in a late-capitalist culture seeking to understand itself amid the cultural shifts of globalization, mass migrations, and a generalized condition of diaspora. Contemporary Euro-American discourses of self-critique, deconstruction, and epistemological unfixity display a tantalizing ambiguity. Unsure whether to celebrate the end of the Cold War or mourn the twilight of its modern legacy, these discourses now inform a grammar of globalized difference whose main tropes encode such concepts as liminality, in-betweenness, and otherness as rhetorical space. Yet, it is not altogether clear how such a grammar speaks to the Caribbean and other sites of colonial legacies. Whose image is reflected, or doubled, in the mirror of this transposed lexicon? Will it still recognize the voices and images of a Caribbean that is clinging to the need for "opacity" in order for "anxiety to have a full existence"?[1] Will the new grammar of difference speak to a culture that must now "confront the ideal of transparent universality, imposed by the West, with secretive and multiple manifestations of Diversity"?[2] Are there various Caribbeans, one Spanish, closer to postmodern Latin Americanism, the others English and French, closer to diasporic, postcolonial theorizing?

Fissures, aporias, chaos, and epistemic contradictions—these are now the primary foci of a critical paradigm that has gained considerable prominence in humanistic research during the past several decades. Paramount in such work is the argument that history, as either experience or discursive flow, undermines the pretense of teleological certainty. For Third World or postcolonial societies whose histories defy homogeneous definitions of modernity, rethinking the world through the lens of indeterminacy and disruptions seems apt, at least at the level of theory. But such insights become more pertinent still when distinguishing between Third World cultural production and the globalizing machinery of conceptual dissemination, a "techno-mediatic power that threatens any democracy," according to Jacques Derrida.[3] Postmodernism in the 1990s, particularly in the hegemonic neoliberal formation that concerns Derrida, seemed to move farther away from the late-capitalist but still somewhat open cultural logic that Fredric Jameson observed a decade earlier, to a more distinctly set of self-enclosed marketing features.[4] Can postmodern writing distinguish itself from the avant-garde cultural effects of late capitalism and focus on lingering structural hierarchies? Is this the terrain, or the promise, of postcolonialism? Are the two "posts" mutually intelligible?

Shifts in critical thought are generally thought to assume a central position in Western capitals first, only later being consigned to peripheral areas such as Latin America and the Caribbean. The avant-garde does not seize epistemological status so readily at the margins. Indeed, the rate of production and dissemination of critical work stemming from Euro-American academic institutions, and the disciplinary boundaries that speak through them, imposes a commanding presence. In peripheral sites, often devoid of well-financed research universities, conceptual newness tends to attach more to the artistic and literary domains. Such stratified relations between codification and performativity have often placed Caribbean culture on a secondary or derivative plane of signification—bespeaking perhaps a fissure inherent in the constitution of peripherally modern societies, a characteristic indelibly marked by legacies of struggle, including revolutions, in the arts and in politics. The effects of this peripheral status have also been implicit in various forms homogenizing programs throughout the area's history, such as the constant pursuit of cultural identity, nationhood, and other familiar modes of imagining modern societies. They all continue both to elude and to inform the Caribbean, in ambiguous yet enriching ways, constituting perhaps one of those "stubborn shadows where repetition leads to perpetual concealment."[5]

How, then, does one read Third World stories with lingering claims on the universalizing discourses of modernity? Are they mostly national allegories, a form of mimesis somehow bound to older and aesthetically simpler Western models? Are they exotic and nostalgic narratives prone to a magic realism that mystifies identitarian longings for multicultural mass marketing? Or should we look on such stories as cultural objects whose only value lies in their need for deconstructive demystification of foundational pretenses? Is there a postmodern way of reading that avoids modern and postmodern forms of reductionism and trivialization, an approach that does not resist the complex double coding of continuity and rupture implicit in postcolonial textuality?

One can no longer ignore the fact that shifting from a structural understanding of history, culture, and literature to an emphasis on postmodern discursivity avoids many pitfalls, particularly the tendency to impose an enclosing system on the texts and phenomena under study. But this theoretical turn deserves some scrutiny as well, especially insofar as it claims to speak in the name of both diversity and heterogeneity. Arif Dirlik, for instance, argues for the need to understand how neoliberal capitalism still structures postmodern logic. Although nations have been largely displaced by markets in the new global configuration, its boundaries are still structurally defined.[6] Yet, whether one insists on the structural category of *Third World* or opts for the discursive notion implicit in *postcolonial,* large regions of the world, including some within the industrialized West, still cling to the fallen utopian discourses of democratization, modernization, and national renovation. Postmodernity has not yet managed to bridge the gap between an absolute First World critique of such utopias and the ongoing hierarchy of material differences within the global village construct.

Signification, like investing, can be absorbed too loosely by the portfolio of floating metaphors and postmodern dissemination, thereby resulting in a critical space where undifferentiated abstractions take up the space of diversity. Debate over the meaning of Frantz Fanon's work today provides a telling example. For Homi Bhabha, Fanon's exceptional moments of rhetorical excess embody an exhilarating ambiguity, splitting, and rhetorical transgression that betray his otherwise banal propensity to existential humanism.[7] For Henry Louis Gates Jr., Fanon has become an object of appropriation for postmodern and postcolonial theorists bent on escalating a process of "epistemological hygiene" that dismisses the historical value of his colonial discourse.[8] Stuart Hall strikes a somewhat intermediate position in what is perhaps one of the most important essays on the topic of identity, and argues that Fanon calls for a double coding, a reading through both continuity and rupture, a dialogism that still informs the Caribbean and other postcolonial societies.[9]

Another telling instance of loosely absorbed theoretical insights—perhaps the central one for postmodernism—is the debate surrounding the figure of Jorge Luis Borges. How should one historicize the epistemological twists woven within Borges's masterful fiction? His direct influence on Euro-American writers and philosophers has been widely and openly acknowledged during the later stages of this century, most particularly by John Barth, Michel Foucault, Jacques Derrida, Italo Calvino, and Hans Robert Jauss.[10] Yet, Borges wrote much of his best work in the thirties and forties, decades prior to the rise of postmodern epochal constructs. If some of his stories have become essential to postmodernism today, among them "Pierre Menard, Author of the *Quixote*," all the more reason to question the logic of identity implicit in readings interested only in forging undisturbed similarities and analogies between the onset of the avant-garde period in the other Americas and contemporary First World postmodernity.[11]

Pierre Menard's often-cited attempt to rewrite Cervantes's *Don Quixote,* for example, reveals that time always inscribes a radical presentism on texts, to the point that texts are transformed through the force of the differential readings imposed by each epoch. Borges's irony toward a literary history tightly bound by philological reconstructions of the past is enacted by the fiction of Menard's authorship. Menard's *Quixote* manages to rewrite Cervantes's original masterpiece verbatim and yet claims to have constructed a radically different text, thereby dramatizing how acts of reading and rereading become synchronizing agents. Yet, Borges goes only so far in this process of demystifying canonical texts. He insists on an *original* writing by a reader who pretends to be beyond the influence of Cervantes's text. Borges also shuns any idea of copying, glossing, appropriating, or transcribing Cervantes's masterpiece, even though one could easily understand that Menard's contemporary readers—the ones who ultimately transform the horizon in which the text is understood—would hardly notice or care.

The force of Walter Benjamin's critique of artistic aura in the age of mechanical reproduction is sorely missed here as Menard sets out to reproduce the *Quixote* word for word with near fetishistic fervor. Thus, Borges appears to place the act of rewriting within the shrine previously reserved for original writing. More important, the radical change suggested by the practice of rereading remains at arm's length, a mere cryptic abstraction of temporal difference unable to account for a variety of simultaneous readings. Glissant writes that Borges "reconstructs a historical pattern in which abstract (and often hidden) connections are more important than the absurdities of the here and now. He faced the often ordinary hazards of cultural diversity and chose to transcend them through a universal absolute. . . . But this transcendence 'from above' demands the dramatization of an irretrievable solitude."[12]

It seems possible, if not necessary, for a clearer understanding of difference to place a greater emphasis on the stimuli of multiple textual and experiential horizons, particularly if it is to aspire to greater historical complexity. This other Menard, marked by difference in a broader and perhaps more radical sense, could conceivably become a symbol of simultaneous different responses to the *Quixote* as well, thereby responding to a variegated sense of otherness capable of reading difference differently. Needless to say, a single master transcription of the *Quixote* would no longer suffice if one were to acknowledge other readings from one another in a nonsynchronous and aesthetically multifarious present. Only then could one conceive Menard-like readers capable of reading difference into the *Quixote* in the cross-cultural and cross-gendered fashion that postmodernism claims as its own.

An emerging concept of world literature (or culture) is often implicit in the globalization of the literary marketplace. It offers evidence of an interesting but contradictory market of literariness, mostly codified through the English language, which encompasses discursive communities that no longer depend on their most immediate point of referential enunciation. To speak of "Caribbean literature," for example, is to conjure an object of study that is more than ever before free from local entanglements. This splitting from immediate referentiality allows such texts to circulate as signifiers suddenly capable of floating in multiple contexts. But an absence of boundaries also begins to codify the Other's world of lived experiences according to the expectations of a new and somewhat distanced readership. Texts, images, and discursive communities inevitably respond to the greater logic of marketable forms, a referential force field of force that inscribes itself into the work of writers and critics. Imagined communities written largely from abroad can indeed amount to sameness. Yet, Caribbeanness still designates a difference, that certain cultural quality Glissant calls "our hesitant clairvoyance," derived from a long history of creolization that has yet to be globally embraced.[13]

These and other problems implicit in cultural globalization still lie beyond the grasp of standard deconstructive insights. A nonidentitarian cultural politics is not as easily attained as one would like to think from First World academic positions of relative wealth, stability, and inchoate pluralism. Specificity in time and space must be constitutive in any valuation of writing from the Third World, lest we impose on it a cultural logic of exchange lacking any trace of resistance or claims on the world of life experiences. Obviously, the First World/Third World binarism often fails to account for many positions in between, but global structures retain certain hierarchies that are often left unattended by cultural theorization from afar. One could argue that Euro-America's postmodern investment in declaring an end to modernity holds crucial insights for societies still striving for new ways of modernizing, but the two predicaments could not be more distinct:

Euro-American postmodernism reflects on a legacy of abundance no longer taken for granted and searches for a new horizon within a position of prominence, not to mention privilege, while Third World or postcolonial societies struggle in a new void still fraught with a history of material necessities and modernizing entanglements. Even if one accounts for various intermediary positions between these two poles, it seems clear that postmodernism, globalization, and neoliberalism must necessarily entail substantially different strategies, particularly as these apply to literature, history, and the politics of identity.

The central aim of this chapter is to unearth these differences within contemporary Caribbean theoretical discourse. The work of Sylvia Wynter, Stuart Hall, Wilson Harris, C. L. R. James, Benita Parry, Neil Lazarus, Franklin Knight, Roberto Márquez, J. Michael Dash, and A. James Arnold, among others, has been of particular interest and value in this pursuit. Collectively, they offer a Caribbean purchase on the line between structural and poststructural epistemologies that cannot be denied, as evidenced by the increasing attention their work commands from the postcolonial and postmodern readership. Each of these writers or critics merits individual attention, but my main focus in this essay will be Antonio Benítez-Rojo's *The Repeating Island* and Édouard Glissant's *Carribbean Discourse,* two ambitious attempts to encompass the cultural history of the Caribbean primarily as discourse. My specific interest is not to locate these two established writers in conformity with new conceptual paradigms, nor with each other, but rather to probe how the difficulty within their work itself reveals surprising degrees of problematization, counterarguments, and specifically Caribbean modes of responding to current theoretical junctures. Benítez-Rojo's and Glissant's differing discourses reveal different Caribbean claims on signification as well as performance, and thus offer a concrete interpellation of the globalizing tendencies implicit in poststructural understanding.[14]

Antonio Benítez-Rojo

The Repeating Island, published in 1992, is the English version of *La isla que se repite* (1989), which Antonio Benítez-Rojo wrote after migrating to the United States from Cuba in 1980. James Maraniss's translation also contains some substantive changes with respect to the original. The book's explicit attempt to rewrite Caribbean culture as a postmodern performance had an immediate impact in the fields of Latin American and Caribbean literary and cultural studies. Of Benítez-Rojo's earlier short narratives in Spanish, *Tute de Reyes* (Royal flush; 1968) and *Heroica* (Heroic; 1977) have been widely acknowledged; but the novel *Mar de las lentejas,* published in

1979 and translated in 1985 as *Sea of Lentils*, is undoubtedly his most important title prior to *La isla que se repite*. *The Magic Dog and Other Stories* (1990) brings together various translated short stories representing a career that began in the late 1960s.

Though not quite a cultural history of the Caribbean, *The Repeating Island* composes a rich and at times daring combination of literary criticism, theory, and creative writing. Nearly all of these essays were published earlier in various U.S. journals throughout the 1980s, but their presence in this volume follows a well-devised logic of presentation and argumentation. Among its most innovative critical essays are those addressing the work of Nicolás Guillén, Fernando Ortiz, and Bartolomé de Las Casas. The latter deserves special commentary because it is arguably Benítez-Rojo's most original and far-reaching attempt to mix creative writing and textual analysis.

Interspersed among these critical pieces, however, one also finds large sections of traditional historicism that, although quite informative in their own right, evidently betray the author's commitment to novel modes of narration. (See chapter 1 in particular.) Such a historicist voice reappears with much greater force and frequency than Benítez-Rojo's narrative voice is willing to acknowledge. In one of the paragraphs excluded from the English translation of the book, he does state: "Without wanting to, I have drifted toward the inculpating and vertical rhetoric of my first readings of the Caribbean. It won't happen again."[15] The introductory essay, in turn, showcases the author's talents as a creative writer, despite its tendency toward speculative, and at times impressionistic, theoreticism. It nevertheless conjoins the book's plurality of forms, tones, and historical ranges in a somewhat daring, suggestive, and equivocal attempt to engage the Caribbean as an island always bound to repeat itself.

Benítez-Rojo's discourse on the Caribbean emerges from a postmodern perspective that he loosely constructs through a string of metasignifiers such as chaos, free play, supersyncretism, and polyrhythms, leading to his ultimate category of "performance"—which he portrays as a Caribbean cultural disposition, an ontology of sorts that is always already postmodern, particularly when viewed from the vantage point of a reader already fully versed in deconstructive insights. Although Benítez-Rojo calls on the force of well-known theorists such as Jean-François Lyotard, Gilles Deleuze, Félix Guattari, and various specialists in chaos theory, his understanding of the Caribbean comes largely—if not solely—from a critique of literary history, a theoretical framework much more closely bound to the work of Paul de Man.[16] Furthermore, it is evident that Benítez-Rojo's most important rhetorical devices are his vast knowledge of Caribbean syncretism (particularly religious myths and iconography), his use of philological skills to retrace the colonial history of such syncretism, and, most important, his narrative techniques. His mastery of narrative was already quite evident in his earlier fiction.

One should not conclude, however, that Cuba does not hold a central place in *The Repeating Island.* But it appears mainly as the author's inevitable point of reference in an attempt to deconstruct the modern legacy implicit in the Cuban literary canon, and as a site from which to extrapolate a broader engagement with the entire Caribbean. Nor is there an absence of political import in the book's main articulations, although it never drifts far from an epistemological/aesthetic understanding of politics. Benítez-Rojo's ultimate aim is to retrace the history of modern teleologies and developmental strategies in the Caribbean, both capitalist and socialist, revealing them as ineffective but violent projects prone to fail a culture whose virtuosity and resilience might best be described as *postmodern sublime.*

Unlike the work of other exiled Cuban writers, *The Repeating Island* is neither immediately political nor a clear testimony of dissidence. What drives the book is not an account of life in a country ruled by one party and the same leader since 1959 but rather the newly gathered critical insights of an author whose reputation as a novelist and short-story writer had been well established in Cuba by the time he moved to the United States. Indeed, Benítez-Rojo's enthusiasm for critical frontiers constitutes an unbridled celebration of new intellectual horizons that should provide the basis for our own critique, for it is that pursuit of theoretical insights that circumscribes the book and the author in various significant ways.

The Repeating Island contains the story of a novelist turned theorist; it evidences the dramatic adjustment of a writing career that suddenly attempts to absorb the postmodernist theoretical canon of U.S. research universities after twenty years of writing literature from within Cuba's paradigm of nationalist and historical realisms; and it reveals a continued, albeit radically transformed, reflection on Caribbean culture for a writer whose narrative work since the late sixties already manifested a deep interest in the area's colonial discourse. Finally, the book proclaims Benítez-Rojo's discovery of deconstructive writing, a performance imbued with a mixture of theoretical exploration and ludic textuality that is sometimes lost in the otherwise faithful English translation.

As one would expect, *The Repeating Island* also draws substantially on various strands of contemporary Cuban writing, not only novels but also critical sources of particular prominence within the U.S. poststructuralist and postmodern paradigm. At first glance, a reader may be tempted to explore just a few possible intertextual entanglements that are strictly from the strictly Cuban novelistic tradition. One could, for example, trace Benítez-Rojo's passion for Cuba's colonial past to his keen interest in Alejo Carpentier's influential oeuvre; or one could pursue the connections between ludic dimension of Benítez-Rojo's language and Guillermo Cabrera Infante's playful mastery of Cuban discourse. Or, again, one might explore the explicit link between literature and epistemology in Benítez-Rojo's book, in the context of Severo Sarduy's novels and essays (*Barroco* [Baroque] or *Escrito sobre un cuerpo* [Bodily scriptures], for example). An even more important source may be found, however, in the work of Roberto González Echevarría, Enrico Mario Santí, and Gustavo Pérez Firmat, a school of Cuban-American academic critics working in the United States whose deconstructive work on the Cuban canon precedes, informs, and codifies many of Benítez-Rojo's central propositions.[17]

These traces do not aim to underestimate the undeniable originality of Benítez-Rojo's text. Rather, they represent an attempt to examine whether *The Repeating Island*'s claims to a postmodern articulation of the entire Caribbean culture go beyond those found in earlier works of deconstructive literary criticism devoted mainly to Cuban literature. One could ask, for example, how postmodernity and the Caribbean are inscribed or defined by Benítez-Rojo in light of an increasingly contradictory constellation of New Critical discourses that take postmodernism beyond the literary precepts of Paul de Man or the philosophical immanence of Jacques Derrida. More specifically, one might ask: Is there space in Benítez-Rojo's "flaming paradigm" for the postnationalist, feminist, technocapitalist, and other concerns exhibited by contemporary theories of postmodernism, particularly those that pertain to the Caribbean diaspora?[18] These questions are now emerging with considerable clarity, as evidenced in various special editions of key academic journals dedicated to debating Latin American and Caribbean postmodernism in a broad interdisciplinary context: *Nueva Revista de Crítica Literaria* (1992), *Nuevo Texto Crítico* (1993), *LARR* (1993), *Social Text* (1994), *PMLA* (1995), *Poetics Today* (1995), and *Revista Iberoamericana* (1997), among others.

It is therefore important to probe whether *The Repeating Island* manages to forego Cuban-centeredness and how the critical tools it deploys allow it to encompass the Caribbean at large. In its immediate scope, in terms of which texts it submits to exegetical rigor, the book appears limited to the established corpus of a mostly Hispanic and largely Cuban configuration of the Caribbean (half of one essay out of nine is devoted to Wilson Harris, none to the French or Dutch-language Caribbean). The work does contain, however, various philological incursions into a pan-Caribbean syncretism that entails a broader, albeit undifferentiated, reading of the Caribbean constrained by an emphasis on premodern and colonial textuality. Equally important is the need to test the relationship between the practice of textual deconstruction deployed by Benítez-Rojo, and the claims it makes on a historical understanding of the Caribbean as a living cultural entity.

Modernity and the Cuban Canon

The main body of textual analysis offered by Benítez-Rojo centers on the figures of Nicolás Guillén, Fernando Ortiz, and Bartolomé de Las Casas. The remaining pieces on Alejo Carpentier, Edgardo Rodríguez Juliá, Wilson Harris, and Fanny Buitrago are substantially shorter and sketchier by comparison. Each of the three main essays attempts to counter the readings of traditional Hispanism, Latin Americanism, and, most important, the Cuban canon. The essay on Guillén, for instance, argues for a much more critical look at his work after the Cuban Revolution, a view that would retrace the history of a major literary figure whose work has been often read in terms of a thematic continuum. It therefore aims to defamiliarize readings of Guillén made canonical by the Cuban Revolution. It does so primarily by unearthing the suppressed sense of distance, if not alienation, that continued to inform Guillén's work beyond the moment of the revolutionary takeover in 1959, a rebelliousness that is best understood as antiracist rather than anti-imperialist. Benítez-Rojo suggests that Guillén's poetry should be reread carefully to detect moments of silence and implicit estrangement from a society that recites him but does not really read him, and argues that Guillén's critical and artistic voice must be rescued from attempts to idolize him or chisel his image into a political monument.

It is surprising that Benítez-Rojo's deconstruction of the Cuban canon does not encompass a regional reception of that literary tradition. He thus appears to forego an exploration of the broader intertextual field of contemporary Caribbean literature and criticism, filled as it is with debates on cultural identity informed by Cuban literature. One also wonders at the absence of any reference to a figure such as Glissant, given that the Martinican writer visited Cuba a number of times throughout the 1970s, wrote on the crucial relevance of Carpentier and many other Cuban writers and artists for contemporary Caribbean discourse, and earned a prominent place among Caribbean novelists and theoreticians before Benítez-Rojo's major works were published.

While providing close readings of Guillén, Carpentier, and Ortiz, *The Repeating Island* thus appears to evade a thorough consideration of how

these writers continue to inform various contemporary national and regional debates on Caribbean cultural understanding. In stark contrast to other
contemporary Cuban writers and artists, even those such as Tomás Gutiérrez Alea (see, for example, Alea's film *Strawberry and Chocolate* [1994]) who
have remained working within Cuba's more limited space for artistic exploration. Benítez-Rojo seems unwilling to look on Caribbean culture as an
ongoing set of social, political, and economic problems in any way affected
by his postmodern literary appreciation. His Caribbean remains always distant, always sedimented in canonical texts that become the object of a form
of literary history seeking to free the reader from afar.

Benítez-Rojo's depiction of the Cuban Revolution in broad, sketchy,
strictly epistemological strokes is a telling example of a postmodern view
that tends to evade contemporary history. He defines the socialist regime as
a modernizing force equally as incapable of forming an organic bond with
Caribbean culture as the capitalist regimes that preceded it. Both socialist
and capitalist socioeconomic programs are seen as part of a failed modernity, a series of plantation systems or machines, one substituting for the other,
tending toward the imposition of violence without hope for change under
any conceivable political definition. Such a broad form of historical periodization may provide some insights, allowing one to seize upon the epistemic features of the entire modern period, but its pitfalls soon become apparent when so many centuries are indiscriminately conflated. One is led to
ask whether the entire world is trapped in the dead-end flows of violent machines, or has this malaise affected only the peripheral areas that failed to
modernize according to Western precepts?

The author's investment in postmodern theory seems to fail him precisely at this crucial juncture, because his postmodern understanding seems
bound only to a literary appreciation of the negative socioeconomic out-
comes of Third World or postcolonial societies such as the Caribbean.
Nowhere does Benítez-Rojo draw any links between postmodernism and
global capitalism as an ongoing process; nor does he show how the reading
of modernity differs when it focuses on the history of more highly modernized societies. This becomes an important omission, for Jean-François Lyotard, the theorist whose work informs Benítez-Rojo's work most prominently, has engaged closely with postcapitalist culture as a living entity
through concepts such as "differends" and "phrase-regimes."[19]

The anthropological work of Fernando Ortiz, for example, particularly
his *Contrapunteo cubano del tabaco y el azúcar,* is given special value because
it allows itself to be read against the sweeping critique of modernity and its
sociopolitical discourses. What interests Benítez-Rojo is Ortiz's literariness,

his creativity as a narrator, a quality that is particularly exemplified in the use of medieval texts such as Juan Ruiz's *Libro de buen amor* (Book of good love), through which Ortiz structures his "scientific" narratives. Accordingly, Ortiz's slippage toward literary discourse at a time when anthropology was dominated by strictly positivistic prose styles becomes tantamount to an incipient postmodern literary quality that Benítez-Rojo sees as its definitive trait.

Since its publication, Ortiz's *Contrapunteo* has been widely acknowledged as the major work of Cuban social science, at least until the publication of Manuel Moreno Fraginals's more recent studies of the sugar plantation system. The narrative qualities of Ortiz's work have been a subject of interest for some time, although not always leading to the same conclusions.[20] Ortiz remains a complex writer whose extraordinary theoretical range is likely to continue to command new and different contestations. As Fernando Coronil has shown, even deconstructive readings that emphasize the literariness in Ortiz are likely to face a challenge, for *Contrapunteo* is a text "in which the fetishistic character of commodities is developed as a poetic means to understand the society that produces them. By treating tobacco and sugar not as things but as social actors, Ortiz in effect brings them back to the social world that creates them, resocializes them as it were."[21]

Choteo and the Uncanny

The Repeating Island fashions a Caribbean culture as an aggregate of rhetorical notions such as polyrhythms, chaos, and performativity, which together aim to display a primary form of resistance to modernization processes. The entire book evolves according to this performative principle. But it should be noted that rhetorical figures such as polyrhythms also seem to correspond, in this book, to modes of coping with reality that are portrayed as instinctive, in the sense that they invoke cultural experiences dating back to premodern times. An enactment of this ambiguity comes about at a crucial passage of ludic transparency in which the author, while reminiscing about the imminent danger of the Cuban missile crisis in 1962, explains how he came to dispel his own fears that a nuclear catastrophe would engulf the Caribbean:

> While the state bureaucracy searched for news off the shortwave or hid behind official speeches and communiqués, two old black women passed "in a certain way" beneath my balcony. I cannot describe this "certain kind of way"; I will say only that there was a kind of ancient and golden powder between their gnarled legs, a scent of basil and

mint in their dress, a symbolic, ritual wisdom in their gesture and their gay chatter. I knew then at once that there would be no apocalypse. The words and the archangels and the beasts and the trumpets and the breaking of the last seal were not going to come, for the simple reason that the Caribbean is not an apocalyptic world; it is not a phallic world in pursuit of the vertical desires of ejaculation and castration."[22]

It is not clear exactly how or why the author felt liberated from apocalyptic doom upon witnessing the swagger of the two black women, unless racial and sexual stereotypes can be turned into postmodern literary exorcism. Benítez-Rojo's use of the postmodern seems here less inflected by the thought of Lyotard, Guattari, or other theorists of the postmodern than by de Man's conflation of history and textuality. The passage does not seek an example of culture as a dynamic entity, but rather an understanding of history as a series of tropes against which close readings of a few chosen texts stand for all of history as a distant text.[23] But there is yet another aspect of this vignette that presents a notion of Cuban *choteo* as a playful narrative technique, an interesting and potentially innovative form of mimicry whose relation to Homi K. Bhabha's postcolonial troping and Glissant's notion of "diversion" are discussed in detail in the last section of this chapter.

Choteo, a tendency to joke around, a dismissal of all that pretends to be profound, or simply a failure to take seriously serious matters, has been historically seen as an inherent defect of Cuba's national culture first articulated by Jorge Mañach in his well-known *Indagación del choteo* (On Cuban wit). But in this street scene Benítez-Rojo attempts to deploy *choteo* as a posture of indifference struck by the two black women, that is, as contestation rather than resignation. They—or rather, their attitude—become a figure of *choteo* as wisdom or resistance before the menacing gaze of a history governed by East–West conflicts. A form of mimicry or "diversion," as Glissant would call it, is turned over, as it were, into a literary device. Apocalypse is thus rendered harmless and disarmed, albeit somewhat simplistically, by the mere swagger of two otherwise unimpressed Cubans. Mimicry is thus also shown as a form of disdain, not just imitation or intimidation. Yet, one must still wonder if and how this particular use of *choteo* as deep instinctive wisdom accrues value as a figure of postmodern writing. It would seem that fantasizing about black women, vaginal fluids, and gastronomic delights draws directly from a phallic racialist tradition well entrenched in the Caribbean, most particularly during the modern history that Benítez-Rojo aims to leave behind.

But the most challenging and emblematic articulation of *The Repeating*

Island's governing hypothesis must be found in the essay on Bartolomé de Las Casas; indeed, it is an elaborate and systematic instance of Benítez-Rojo's deconstructive enterprise. Slowly and very methodically, the author suggests how a contemporary reader should understand the (proto-)postmodern qualities of a sixteenth-century text such as *Historia de las Indias* (History of the Indies). Las Casas's lengthy and unruly text is submitted to a series of interesting sleuthing maneuvers, which are then juxtaposed to the way this historic chronicle was read during Cuba's abolitionist epoch in the nineteenth century. From there, Benítez-Rojo reconstructs a passage filled with complex and suggestive ambiguity. It begins by underscoring why the *Historia de las Indias* was outwardly repressed or dismissed as digressive by Spanish colonialist historiography up to and during the nineteenth century. From there, the author walks the contemporary reader through a carefully woven process of textual reconstruction and decipherment that is both a discovery and a performance.

Crucial elements of this unearthing surround the advent of a series of plagues on the island of Hispaniola as chronicled by Las Casas. Reference to smallpox is first made and understood as divine intervention: a plan to put an end to the torment suffered by the Indians forced to do slave labor. Later, after Las Casas has also acknowledged the error of African slavery, he writes of another "plague," a symbol of punishment also available from within his own discourse: rebellious slaves begin to descend on the colonizers with untold fury. But Benítez-Rojo's interest lies in a brief reference to another inscription of a plague narrated by Las Casas in such a way as to require a literary, rather than a historical or theological, unpacking. An "uncanny" story thus unfolds from *Historia de las Indias*—a sort of fable that encodes repressed contents of personal, political, and historical import for Las Casas's chronicle and our understanding of colonialism. It is the plague of the ants and the *solimán* stone, a rock made of mercuric chloride intended to attract and exterminate the ants even as it magically decreases in size with each ant bite. This image, in Benítez-Rojo's carefully crafted essay, becomes an in-between moment of extreme complexity in Las Casas's writing, in which the priest ciphers his misgivings about African slavery and his own guilt about having supported it for the sake of liberating the Indians. More important, in the process Benítez-Rojo also unearths the relationship between slavery and the sugar plantation system symbolized by the *solimán* stone, an allegory of exploitation bound to repeat itself over and over throughout the subsequent centuries. Ants/slaves are drawn to the stone/plantation that attracts/exterminates: in this allegory, a foundational tale of the plantation machine, a mythological combat of modernity finds origination.

For Benítez-Rojo, Caribbeanness is best understood through such un-canny articulations as conjuring violence with artistry, unearthing the am-biguity of repressed forms and contents, and demarcating the extraordinary value of writing as the originary site of Caribbean performative culture, from the time of the colonial chronicles to our own day. Las Casas's writing is thus given a new voice by exhuming, as in an archaeological expedition, its self-referential inscriptions: his confessional guilt, his ambiguity toward African slavery, his fear of monarchical rule, his symbolic fable. All of these elements become emblematic of much more, according to Benítez-Rojo. They constitute a mode of writing that has epistemic value as chaos; that is, as a mode that encompasses both literary transgressions of history's repres-sive iterations, etched in the colonial chronicle, and our equivocal attempts to reread and rewrite ourselves against the grain of such forces. Chaos un-folds into an agonistic celebration in Benítez-Rojo's pursuit of textual processes that always already affirm literariness as a special place of discov-ery. Las Casas thus becomes proto-postmodernist and proto-Caribbean at once, in the panhistoric logic of *The Repeating Island*:

> Las Casas's tale, in the tenacious ambiguity that places it between fic-tion and history, between transgression and the law, is a very good ex-ample of writing as "pharmacon," whose ability to mean anything—everything and nothing—Derrida observes in his analysis of the Phaedrus. . . . It is no more than a paradoxical signifier within whose limits a mineral from the pharmacopoeia is simultaneously reality and fiction, acrid and sweet, curative and poisonous, body and soul, tech-nology and metaphysic, life and death, monument and mutila-tion. . . . That's all there is on the other side of Las Casas's uncanny tale, or, if you like, before and beyond the soft, sticky chaos of the writing that organized it."[24]

The Postmodern as Caribbean Destiny

There should be no question that Benítez-Rojo's reading of Las Casas holds considerable heuristic value for a closer examination of the relationship be-tween literary deconstruction and postmodernity, a nexus that is not always as clear or direct as one might assume.[25] But behind the textual sleuthing and the interest in chaos or historical uncertainty as new modes of looking at writing in *The Repeating Island,* there lies a narrative and a conceptual strategy bound to certain repetitions of somewhat lesser reach. As narrative, Benítez-Rojo's deconstructive work seeks to become a performance—a goal substantially accomplished through a literary talent that shows how to complicate critical discoveries into an unfolding tale of ambiguity and textual decipherment. As conceptual or theoretical strategy, on the other hand, Benítez-Rojo's deconstruction is perhaps more prone to a general pattern whose steps, if not its outcome, become rather predictable: (1) identifying key moments of excess, aporia and contradiction within the texts that have been privileged or repressed by modernity becomes the index that problematizes it; (2) exegetical work or close readings on such texts or fragments provides a basis for a different pattern of anticanonical generalization that privileges indeterminacy; (3) substantive epistemic refutations can be made on the basis of designification once these counterreadings are carefully crafted to show history as an ongoing discursive battle prone to scrutiny as literary prowess. Needless to say, this is but a rough sketch of the presuppositions underlying the type of theoretical writing deployed by Benítez-Rojo, which, as stated earlier, appear to follow de Man's literary deconstructionism much closer than postmodernist precepts as such. Only a closer look at the historical and cultural boundaries drawn by *The Repeating Island* will illuminate the specific claims it makes on Caribbean postmodernity.

Benítez-Rojo's understanding of the "uncanny" as specially constitutive of literary dissemination finds a special moment in Bartolomé de Las Casas's text. Yet, such fragments of symbolic repression are hardly absent from other texts, societies, and historical times. Defining its presence in *Historia de las Indias* as a specifically postmodern quality, and then linking it to contemporary Caribbean culture, would seem to require a more precise and extended explanation than Benítez-Rojo is prepared to offer. Yet, such a claim is precisely the central idea of his book: postmodernism becomes the panhistoric shadow of modernity, a witness to the latter's repressive legacy, which is given a voice through the work of deconstruction in such a way as to allow any text since the colonial chronicles to understand itself as postmodern and, by extension, Caribbean.

If we understand Benítez-Rojo along these lines, it remains somewhat obscure how the Caribbean becomes the only heir to this method of reading against the grain of modernity. Moreover, one immediately wonders if medieval, pre-Columbian, and classical texts will conform to the ever-expansive category of Caribbean postmodernity conjured by Benítez-Rojo. His version of Caribbean postmodernity appears as an all-encompassing aquatic essence capable of drifting toward all ages and places, through open-ended metaphors such as chaos, meta-archipelagos, "the semipagan hagiography of the Middle Ages and African beliefs," and the "turbulent and erratic rhythms" of the entire Third World ("copper, black and yellow rhythms") that belong to the "Peoples of the Sea."[26]

This newly essentialized Caribbean is ultimately understood as nothing but literary dissemination, a dual process of seduction between reader and text that reaches its maximum intensity in what Benítez-Rojo calls "a certain kind of way" in which "both the text and the reader will transcend their statistical limits and will drift toward the decentered center of the paradoxical":

> Caribbean discourse is in many respects prestructuralist and preindustrial, and to make matters worse, a contrapuntal discourse that when seen à la Caribbean would look like a *rumba,* and when seen à la Europe like a perpetually moving baroque fugue, in which the voices meet once never to meet again. I mean by this that the space of "a certain kind of way" is explained by poststructuralist thought as episteme—for example, Derrida's notion of *différance*—while Caribbean discourse, as well as being capable of occupying it in theoretical terms, floods it with a poetic and vital stream navigated by Eros and Dionysus, by Oshun and Elegua, by the Great Mother of the Arawaks and the Virgen de la Caridad del Cobre, all of them defusing violence, the blind violence with which the Caribbean social dynamics collide, the violence organized by slavery, despotic colonialism, and the Plantation.[27]

This somewhat imprecise strategy of leaping back and forth from oral, preindustrial temporalities to postmodern discursivity is specifically aimed at erasing the cultural legacy of modernity as historically specific or variegated. Modernity is thus deconstructed in three related ways: as the repository of pain and violence implicit in exploitative regimes (plantation machines) that failed to produce modern industrialized states; as the root of disillusionment and historical failure to which premodern rituals, rhythms, and performativity become the antidote; and as the archive of texts whose major, if not only, remaining value lies in the possibility of unearthing their rhetorical and literary excess.

Accordingly, the flow of Caribbeanness in *The Repeating Island* swings back and forth from colonial to postmodern times—from Las Casas to Benítez-Rojo. In the process, this flow engulfs the modern explicitness of Guillén and Ortiz, slipping above and beyond the narratives of state formation, anticolonialism, anti-imperialism, socialist and capitalist dependency, literacy campaigns, and other traces of social textuality that still pertain to modernizing needs in the Caribbean, even if they are now devoid of modernity's utopian legacy. The specificity of all such historical traces comes under erasure in *The Repeating Island.* One could counter that these narratives are quite worthy of deconstructive work in their own right, and that Benítez-Rojo aims to do just that in a very general sense. But a post-modern reading of the Caribbean would need to resist the tendency to lump the rich and multifarious history of modernity into an undifferenti-ated chronology encompassing four hundred years. For the Caribbean, as well as other postcolonial societies, the narratives implicit in modernization remain rich in the dialogic entanglements of postmodern sociopolitical as well as literary textualization.

Needless to say, cultural mapping can no longer simply rely on designa-tors such as nation, patriarchy, party, class, race, and ethnicity, particularly in their now standard definitions as modern foundational narratives, with their concomitant notions of fixed identities and subject positions. The need to disturb these resting places of traditionalism remains paramount, even if calling for such work sometimes takes the form of an obligatory ritual aim-ing no further than to exorcise the easily found demons of essentialism. Yet, a certain utopian impulse also lurks behind a postmodernism that is strictly bound to a new celebration of literariness. Does not such a celebration also implicate certain identitarian tendencies in its complacent aestheticism, un-perturbed as it is by the grave distance between its radical epistemological claims and its general indifference toward the contemporary social world?

Benítez-Rojo never raises this doubt in *The Repeating Island,* where the contemporary social fabric of Caribbeanness remains largely absent from theoretical insights, and where cultural mapping relies considerably on a rather antiquarian gaze that essentializes the premodern and erases the modern in its literary pursuit of the postmodern. This utopian impulse is perhaps the only way to explain Benítez-Rojo's predominant emphasis on a religious syncretism whose transcendent value he never questions, most particularly the cult of the Virgin as a predominant signifier in Caribbean history. Its function in *The Repeating Island* is to create a privileged moment of cultural origination, whose symbolic value will be transferred from the field of religion to that of postmodern writing.

We should note, moreover, that within the protocol of religiosity, the author's position is quite different from that of the people whose culture he describes in *The Repeating Island.* For these people, religion seems to consti-tute an unconscious animistic behavior meant to exorcise the demons of modernity, much like the swagger of the two black women recalled at the time of the missile crisis. For the author, however, access to such a protocol of popular religious images is always presented as a finished intellectual product of historicism, a newly gathered critical consciousness. Benítez-Rojo deploys ethnological, philological, and literary research to reconstruct a colonial, and even precolonial, origination point for Caribbean culture and its religious rituals (see chapter 1 in particular). He often presents this information as incontestable facts of historiography, not as religious rituals that he himself practices, although one could surmise that for Benítez-Rojo there is a certain exorcism at work in a literary articulation that aims to link premodern animism with literary free play. Thus, postmodernity and premodernity come together through the power of traditional historicism and creative performance to constitute a new horizon of intertextuality.

Against this fusion of vastly dissimilar temporalities, cosmologies, and disciplines, the Caribbean's equivocal but rich experience with modernity is reduced to a literary archive, or to a selection of texts awaiting deconstructive appreciation. The narratives of emancipation, nationalism, cultural identity, developmentalism, political reform, educational campaigns, and revolutions, among others, all turn into profound errors. Benítez-Rojo prefers a historical void to the failed discourses of the past, and calls on postmodernity only to unearth the literary or rhetorical value left behind by such failures. In the meantime, conjuring the idea of a living community from this theoretical cul-de-sac becomes unlikely, if not irrelevant. The people of the Caribbean engaged in ongoing life experiences are left with an invitation to levitate from the coffin of their modern struggles, to leave their bodies behind as relics of a sad case of mistaken identity, and to join the celebration of a newly found and largely premodern indeterminacy.

Édouard Glissant

It is only in the past decade or so that Édouard Glissant's theoretical work has been felt beyond France and the Francophone world of the Caribbean and Canada. The appearance of the English translation of *Le discours antillais* (*Caribbean Discourse;* 1989), his most ambitious theoretical treatise, was perhaps the turning point. That same year, *World Literature Today* dedicated an entire issue to Glissant's work, some ten essays incorporating intricate references to his poetic and narrative art, though largely concentrating on the theoretical import of his writing for contemporary Caribbeanness, a subject his own essays tend to highlight. In that issue, Sylvia Wynter stated that Glissant's discourse constituted "performative acts of countermeaning" and "a new mode of revolt," in a line of filiation that includes Aimé Césaire and Frantz Fanon, as well as newer postcolonial discursive articulations in the Caribbean.[28] More recently, the international review *Transition* published a full-length essay on Glissant's *Caribbean Discourse* underlining the importance of Glissant's ambitious treatise for contemporary theoretical discourses in the Anglo-American academic environment.[29] Most significant in raising awareness of Glissant's importance, however, is J. Michael Dash's

Édouard Glissant (1995) in the Cambridge Studies in African and Caribbean Literature series. Dash, whose previous work on Glissant includes a
translation of and Introduction to *Caribbean Discourse,* here offers a comprehensive overview of the author's entire oeuvre, addressing the many rich
intertextual links between his novels, poetry, and theoretical essays, as well
as including an extensive bibliography and crucial biographical material.

Glissant's preeminence as a writer is now widely acknowledged in the
Caribbean, and is rapidly gaining in the United States and Latin America.
In any case, Glissant's artistry and his prolific output in nearly all narrative
genres are extraordinary achievements. A simple look at his oeuvre reveals a
commitment to all forms of writing over a career spanning more than thirty
years. As a novelist, Glissant's work begins with *La lézarde* (The ripening;
1958) and includes, among other titles, *Le quatrième siècle* (The fourth century; 1964), *Malemort* (Evil death; 1975), *La case du commandeur* (The dri-
ver's cabin; 1981), *Mahagony* (1987), and *Tout-monde* (All-world; 1993).
His poetry also begins with a flurry in the 1950s with *Un champ d'îles*
(A field of islands; 1953), *La terre inquiète* (The anxious land; 1954), *Les
Indes* (The Indies; 1956), and *Le sel noir* (Black salt; 1959). More recently,
one finds *Pays rêvé, pays réel* (Dream country, real country; 1985) and his
book of poems, *Fastes* (Splendors; 1992). *Monsieur Toussaint,* Glissant's first
published play, appeared in 1961. Two years later he wrote *Rêve de ce qui fut
la tragédie d'Askia* (Dream of the tragedy that was Askia's), and the appearance of his *Parabole d'un moulin de la Martinique* (Parable of a Martinican
windmill) was announced at a Carifesta celebration in 1976.[30] His most important theoretical essays include *Soleil de la conscience* (Sun of consciousness; 1956), *L'intention poétique* (The poetic intention; 1969), *Le discours
antillais* (Caribbean discourse; 1981), and *Poétique de la relation* (The poetics of relating; 1990).

It has been said that *Caribbean Discourse* constitutes an attempt to
"read the Caribbean and the New World Experience, not as a response to a
fixed, univocal meaning imposed by the past, but as an infinitely varied,
dauntingly inexhaustible text."[31] *Caribbean Discourse* has also been considered a "fascinating but frustrating read" that, like Benítez-Rojo's *The
Repeating Island,* requires the reader to engage the Caribbean in the context
of current theoretical discourses, and vice versa.[32] My aim here is to probe
further into *Caribbean Discourse,* this ambitious, difficult, and comprehensive text that continues to command so much attention in Caribbean studies. More specifically, I will focus on the ways in which Glissant's writing on
the Caribbean intersects with the work of Benítez-Rojo and cultural global-

ization, as well as with the postcolonial work of Homi Bhabha and certain Derridean aspects of postmodern writing.

It is significant to the question of reception that *Le discours antillais,* although available in English only since 1989, was first published in French in 1981, and was written largely during the middle and late 1970s. Benítez-Rojo's *La isla que se repite,* in contrast, was largely written during the 1980s. The availability of *Caribbean Discourse* in English—it is Glissant's only collection of essays translated into English to date—does not exhaust the book's claim to relevance, although this translation has undoubtedly become the instrument through which the English-speaking world has begun to appreciate Glissant's scope as a theorist. As Lucien Taylor and Dash attest, *Le discours antillais* remains a puzzling book whose theoretical import has only increased in light of the new emphasis on postcolonial discourses, even though it was published at the beginning of the 1980s. Dash explains Glissant's newfound importance as follows:

> It would [however] be impossible to derive a systematic politics from Glissant's poetic and generously open-ended ideal of irreducible plurality and diversity for the Caribbean. This at once explains his having been somewhat neglected in the past, as well as his present importance. His vision of opacity, disorder, chaos and infinite profusion, so confusing before, now seems to offer new insights into the elusive complexity of Caribbean experience.[33]

Indeed, Glissant's novelistic, poetic, and theoretical work during the late 1980s and early 1990s continues to augment, in a process he calls spiral repetition, the massive body of writing that was ultimately abridged for publication in English as *Caribbean Discourse.* His latest collection of essays, *Poétique de la relation* (1990), places greater emphasis on chaos as a category of particular theoretical value for the Caribbean. This book also expresses a much greater concern with the role and history of women in the formation of mimicry, camouflage, and other forms of what Glissant calls cultural *diversion.* Yet, *Poétique de la relation* continues to draw mainly on the notions developed in *Caribbean Discourse,* particularly those of cross-cultural poetics, opacity, baroque, and Creoleness, figures that Glissant extends beyond the context of the Caribbean itself to seek an understanding of globalization as chaos. His writing on women, though less prominent in his earlier theoretical essays than in his novels,[34] nonetheless includes the following passage in *Caribbean Discourse*: "No theory of cultural contact is conducive to generalization. Its operation is further intensified by the emergence of minorities that identify themselves as such and of which the most influential is undoubtedly the feminist movement."[35]

Diasporic Cartography and Street Theater

Caribbean Discourse presents a hybrid compilation of writerly forms imbued by a deep but fluid understanding of contemporary French theory and by repeated excursions into Caribbean literature and history. Although many contemporary philosophers and theorists have brought to the world of discourse an aesthetic awareness, Glissant has managed to distinguish himself as a creative writer who laces his art with epistemological acumen. The Cuban writer Severo Sarduy comes to mind as an analogous example. Interestingly, both Sarduy and Glissant drew significantly on the work of Roland Barthes, whose understanding of the relationship between art and theory attained a balance perhaps unequaled in the very influential field of contemporary French theory. Glissant, however, seems less deferential to semiological insights in his theoretical essays than Sarduy. This provides an intriguing tension, for Glissant's language and performativity constitute attempts to occupy the space of contemporary theory derived from life experiences and popular Caribbean art forms.

Glissant's discourse is thus, to a large extent, the reverse of what one finds in much contemporary theoretical work on postcolonial culture, which is more directly, if not solely, informed by the language and constructs of European and North American theorists. Glissant's construction of the Caribbean also attempts to link theory with historical experience through terms such as *opacity, otherness,* and *diversion,* categories that invoke neither identitarian complacency nor an easily deconstructed play on differences. These terms are read against the background of historical entanglements whose potential complicity with language and representation Glissant does not take for granted. *Caribbean Discourse* also calls on the writing and rewriting of history through complex imbrications absent from much postmodern theorizing, such as the continuous play of memory on orality, the need for a "prophetic vision of the past," and the refusal to relinquish the desire for imagining a community.[36]

A closer examination of the U. S. edition of *Caribbean Discourse* must account for an infinitude of splittings, the clear markers of a labyrinthine text in which each chapter unfolds into many other smaller and independent units of various length, many of which seem interchangeable and almost arbitrary in their order. This quality is not the result of abridgment for the English edition. On the contrary, as Debra L. Anderson observes, the English version is less faithful to Glissant's organizing principle of desultoriness: "Gone are the empty spaces in the text; the introductory pages to each 'book'—pages left deliberately blank except for the titles, subtitles and *repères* (landmarks, points of reference), all of which serve as guides to the reader—have been collapsed into one page."[37]

What Glissant offers is a coiled text made of nothing but fragments, a spiraling spring of scatterings in which *Caribbean Discourse* looks on itself as fragmentation incarnate. Content becomes secondary to a formal obsession with naming, splitting, and tidbits of "stubborn shadows where repetition leads to perpetual concealment."[38] A poetics of fragmentation comes into being, a process of nominalization that labels, or titles, each item as a species of discourse in need of preservation: litanies, interludes, fragments, aphorisms, graffiti, graphs, mappings, riddles, feigned dialogues, juxtaposed voices, historical overtures, tables, news reports, anonymous voices, events, dates, land, landscapes, outlines, a theatrical proposition, and so forth. This naming is neither a collage nor a pastiche, but rather an enactment of supplementarity and marginality, fused with an obsession for historical consciousness. *Caribbean Discourse* is a riddle that aims to frustrate and fascinate, or perhaps a form of historicized mimicry, that seeks to complicate our understanding of colonial history during postmodern times.

A decisive moment is found in a section titled "The Table of the Diaspora." At first glance it looks like a simple map of the Caribbean's cultural geography since colonial times, structured along a horizontal axis that includes continental America, the Caribbean, and Africa. Yet, the map has no visible vertical axis as such, though there are many cultural (music, poetry, and religion) signifiers spread about on different levels and planes. Political and economic categories (Plantation America, names of countries) occupy the lower strata of this cultural spacing, but its predominant element is a series of arrows and lines suggesting multiple ways of connecting to myriad cultural, economic, and even geographic signifiers. For example, Plantation America, Marcus Garvey, and salsa music occupy, in ascending order, the borderline between continental America and the Caribbean.

The map's most important features are uncertain zones filled with a dizzying array of crisscrossing lines and other indicators of potential interconnections. The table thus becomes an aesthetic representation of Glissant's theoretical poetics. It comes close to Benítez-Rojo's literary postmodernism in that it resists linearity, base–superstructure ordering, and other forms of historical and geographic representation as such, yet it contrasts with his postmodernism in that Glissant's formulation also resists relinquishing historical circumscription altogether. Glissant presents critical elements of the Caribbean's historical experience in nonsynchronous (or polyrhythmic, in Benítez-Rojo's terms) fashion, but unlike the Cuban writer, he gives the modern period of history a crucial role in determining the future. Contemporary cultural mapping for Glissant assumes its role as an act of discourse along the lines generally associated with the poststructuralist thinking that also informs Benítez-Rojo, but this does not lead Glissant to posit an exclusive emphasis on the premodern or colonial archive of Caribbean texts. Glissant's cartography revolts against both identitarian myths of origin and deconstructive dismissals of the Caribbean's stories of dispossession, decolonization, and other brushes with modernity.

Glissant's aesthetics of fragmentation always begins by calling on the cultural history of Martinique, his motherland, followed by the French Caribbean, the greater Caribbean, Latin America, and ultimately the world at large. He manages to keep this broad horizon within range at all times. Such a framework reveals a global awareness that is richly informed by specific international contrasts, not merely by synchronizing abstractions. The role of the West appears prominently in the brutal colonial legacy implicit in this story, but Glissant is equally incisive, if not harsh, in his views on the participation of Martinican society in this process. He warns that "the West is not in the West. It is a project, not a place."[39] He also devotes numerous passages to Martinique's own ruling cast of *bekés* and their role in shaping various forms of mimetic culture; and he is nothing less than scathing about any attempt to romanticize or mystify certain forms of popular culture, particularly folklore. A section titled "An Exploded Discourse" speaks to the relationship between the history of theater in the West and the Martinican "street scene":

> But the simple "street scene" does not provide us with the vital mechanism of the popular consciousness; in it energy intensifies in nothing but an everyday delirium. The street scene as a rule *does not create* popular consciousness but reinforces it and contributes to structuring it in those places where it already exists—that is, really, for a community already secure in its history and its traditions.
>
> Or else it is also an everyday manifestation of the *theatralization* that in the street feeds on our impulses . . .
>
> Community theater, on the other hand, diverts energy from the individual manifestation of delirium or from the collective tendency to the theatrical so as to orient it towards the shaping of a popular consciousness.
>
> But individual delirium and collective theatralization, as forms of cultural resistance, are the first "catalysts" of this consciousness.[40]

Theatricalization, delirium, community, consciousness, and resistance—these are some of the salient terms through which Glissant pursues the interplay between theoretical opacity and clairvoyance, a specular movement of ambivalence that runs from the street to his discourse, interspersed with critical pronouncements. For this, Glissant offers, as historical background, a carefully crafted outline of the formative relationship between theater and nationhood in Western culture. He then emphasizes that this history has been always already absent, thwarted, or diverted from taking place in Martinique and in the Caribbean as a whole:

> Our drama (which is not tragedy) is that we have collectively denied or forgotten the hero who in our true history *has taken unto himself* the cause of our resistance: the maroon. This historical lapse leads to the absence of tragedy.
>
> Therefore we have not exploited these gaps either—the feverish nature of the sacred—which are the links between the tragic and the political. Neither the systematic release of Cyrano, nor the tortured obsessiveness of Artaud. In this area we know nothing but the folkloric debasement of self-expression.[41]

The focus on Western theater as a cultural model of universal value, however, must be seen as part of Glissant's own ambivalent performance. The passage bemoans Martinique's failure to have traveled the Western road to national or collective consciousness through theatrical forms, but it is also a pretext for Glissant's own theoretical dramaturgy. The enactment of a developmental cultural reference that has become an impossibility in the Caribbean turns into a script with deconstructive potential. From the precepts of Greek tragedy, through Hegelian aesthetics, to Brechtian principles of modern alienation, Glissant's review turns into an invocation of the performative, by taking the tone of stage directions for a future Caribbean dramaturgy: "(Let us therefore leave History and go down into the gully course that is our future—our difficult becoming. Hegel does not enter with us.) The rupture of the slave trade, then the experience of slavery, introduces between blind belief and clear consciousness a gap that we have never finished filling."[42]

In an apparent attempt to fill that gap, Glissant turns to a neighboring cultural formation: the Latin American theater of collective creation, a different dramaturgy that flourished during the late seventies and early eighties. This is a theatrical form that forgoes the need for tragedy and alienated heroes, but reconfirms Glissant's investment in the value of collective performativity as resistance and awareness: "A theater springing from a 'collective politics' would banish such debasement. It is emerging everywhere in South America with the same provisional characteristics: a schematic conception of 'character' (there is no 'profound' psychological examination), exemplary situations, historical implications, audience participation, elementary decor and costume, importance of physical gesture."[43]

Latin American theater of collective creation, like *testimonio* literature, constitutes an innovative form of cultural engagement that incorporates but also goes beyond deconstructive precepts to posit new ways of understanding subjectivity within subalternity. Yet, because of the confinement of postmodern articulations of the Caribbean and Latin America almost exclusively to the literary domain, collective creation theater has never received much critical attention in U.S. research universities where Latin Americanism is largely codified today. Collective creation theater clings to notions of social agency that postmodernity proper tends to find naive or too closely bound to modern metanarratives; this trait may well have contributed to academic disinterest. Although collective creation theater, like *testimonio,* has waned considerably, it was contemporaneous with the emergence of postmodernity as an epochal construct in the 1970s.[44]

Glissant's interest in popular theater points to a series of crucial questions regarding the articulation of "collective consciousness" through artistic means. It foregrounds the question of whether deconstructive modes of configuring postcolonial subjectivity recognize the value of collective empowerment in any concrete way. Can Foucault's notions of self-care as self-knowledge, for example, or various forms of deconstruction inspired by Derrida's work, call upon individuals to act on the social text from a set of shared and generalizable principles? If so, do such theoretical constructs constitute forms of awareness that approach the notion of resistance beyond individual acts or the pursuit of collective goals? These and similar questions are defining the difference between postmodernism proper and postcolonialism.[45]

Glissant's reaffirmation of the quest for national and regional Caribbean models invokes the need to account for the ways in which Caribbean societies continue to conceive and imagine themselves at a time when all metanarratives have become suspect. One could ask, nonetheless, whether his continuous use of the idea of consciousness itself corresponds to a lingering vestige of Western metaphysics, which Glissant has failed to sufficiently examine. More specifically, does *Caribbean Discourse* fail to acknowledge individual ways of cohabiting with neocolonization in its call for a collective consciousness as a prelude to a liberating collective will? Are delirium, folklore, the street scene, impulsive theatricalization, as well as other forms of diversion or mimicry described by Glissant, something more than the unconscious and submissive mimetic devaluations of a utopian Martinican culture conceived out of modern fantasies? Finally, does Glissant's notion of "diversion," like Benítez-Rojo's *choteo,* come close to more ambiguous strategies of survival and resistance, or does it only suggest the absence of more totalizing programs for a distant or absolute liberation?

Diversion, Mimicry, and Mimesis

The practice of diversion, writes Glissant,

> is not a systematic refusal to see. No, it is not a kind of self-inflicted blindness nor a conscious strategy of flight in the face of reality. Rather, we would say that it is formed, like a habit, from an interweaving of negative forces that go unchallenged. . . . Diversion is the ultimate resort of a population whose domination by an Other is concealed: it then must search *elsewhere* for the principle of domination, which is not evident in the country itself. Diversion is the parallactic displacement of this strategy. Its deception is not therefore systematic, just as the *other world* that is frequented can indeed be on the "inside." It is an "attitude of collective release."[46]

For Glissant, the possibility of resistance is always already present in the complex notion of "diversion" (*détour*), which composes the central construct in his understanding of Caribbean cultural formations. In time, he expands the notion of diversion to include Creole, syncretism, orality, cross-cultural poetics, the Caribbean folktale—indeed, all the major aspects of his discourse—as creative forms of diversion. Most important, Glissant distinguishes diversion from mimeticism in a considerably different way than Bhabha, Achille Mbembe, and other established postcolonial critics draw distinctions between mimicry and mimesis.

This is unquestionably the crucial point in which *Caribbean Discourse* intervenes and contends with the constellation of postmodern and postcolonial discourses on the Caribbean. The distinction between diversion and mimeticism forces the reader into a theoretical territory that is often equivocal, and itself not devoid of its own opacity. In his review essay, for instance, Lucien Taylor states, on the one hand, that Bhabha's notion of "splitting" largely parallels Glissant's concept of creolization, but he then declares that Glissant "makes no distinction between mimesis and mimicry, failing to acknowledge how the latter has the potential to destabilize relations of power, that it may be as much an aspect of colonial resistance as colonial domination."[47]

Diversion, like the lines in Glissant's "Table of the Diaspora," points in various directions at once. Its possibilities include resistance, but only in terms of a broader historical inscription of Caribbean history (*retour*). Taylor's ambivalence toward Glissant's notion of creolization reveals the difficulty of locating Glissant's thought within the boundaries of contemporary deconstructive theory, but still finds no other frame of comparison than the highly deconstructive writing of Homi Bhabha. J. Michael Dash is much more categorical in his assessment of the theoretical value of *Caribbean Discourse*: "With these ideas on creolisation and *Antillanité* Glissant fully enters the arena of post-colonial theory."[48] Yet, Dash does not revisit his understanding of diversion itself in this new appraisal. His understanding of the term remains somewhat cryptic and closely bound to Glissant's notion of "reversion" (*rétour*), in a movement Dash understands as "the dialectic of withdrawal and return."[49] This connection is no doubt important, but one needs to look more closely at the inner side of diversion, its puzzling interplay with mimesis, its ambiguously productive nature, and its possible inscription of mimicry, which is precisely the arena of contemporary debates within postcolonial theory.

A brief reference to my earlier discussion of Benítez-Rojo's own use of mimicry seems fitting at this point—that crucial moment when the reader is asked to observe a magnificent gesture of indifference on the part of two anonymous black women walking past the author during the darkest moments of the Cuban missile crisis. Benítez-Rojo clearly presents this gesture as a form of popular disdain toward the very source of apocalyptic power from which such dangers derive, a sort of native wisdom understood as a mocking or an exorcism. Yet, it is not clear whether the author's appropriation of this form of mimicry as writing also constitutes a strategy of resistance on the part of the two women he portrays. They do not speak, but their bodies are written into the author's construction of performativity as mockery. One wonders, however, if they are as conscious of the implicit power of indifference as the writer is of its discursive subversion. Is the body language of these two women not different from a critical discourse that reads them into a complex theoretical construct? Must they be black, women, and anonymous? Does this scene constitute a form of passive mimesis (or *choteo,* in the discourse of Jorge Mañach), or is it a form mimicry that entails a more active participation in a regime of power?

The most elaborate and influential theorization of mimicry as an active strategy of postcolonial engagement is found in the work of Homi Bhabha. In his deconstructive formulation, he calls it "a writing, a mode of representation that marginalizes the monumentality of history."[50] Bhabha warns that it is not the "familiar exercise of *dependent* colonial relations" but rather the figures of a doubling, the part-objects of a metonymy of colonial desire which alienates the modality and normality of those dominant discourses in which they emerge as "inappropriate" colonial subjects. A desire that, through the repetition of *partial presence,* which is the basis of mimicry, articulates those disturbances of cultural, racial and historical difference that menace the narcissistic demand of colonial authority. It is a desire that reverses "in part" the colonial appropriation by now producing a partial vision of the colonizer's presence. A gaze of otherness, that shares the acuity of the genealogical gaze which, as Foucault describes it, liberates marginal elements and shatters the unity of man's being through which he extends his sovereignty.[51]

In addition to his own commitment to creative theoretical discourse, Bhabha brings an array of contemporary theoretical insights to bear on this construct, especially Foucauldian notions of power as an ascending order that always implies individual subjects, Derridean observance of slippage and supplementarity in the critique of totalizing ontologies, and Lacanian troping of desire, splitting, and imaging. Bhabha finds in mimicry a deconstructive potential that goes far beyond the idea of resistance: "A strategy of subversion emerges. It is a mode of negation that seeks not to unveil the fullness of Man but to manipulate his representation. It is a form of power that is exercised at the very limits of identity and authority, in the mocking spirit of mask and image."[52]

Glissant's notion of diversion, on the other hand, straddles the line between mimesis and mimicry. Individual acts of diversion may indeed be seen as being nothing more than floating signifiers awaiting some form of inscription into narrative engagements. In this sense, diversion comes close to Bhabha's concept of mimicry in his construction of postcoloniality as a form of writing. But, as collective expression, these signifiers entangle more complex and fundamental cultural formations such as the folktale, creolization, syncretism—indeed, the entire spectrum of Caribbean culture. From this particular point, Glissant moves strategically to recast the stories of national and cultural formation that have produced a sense of nonhistory in Martinique and the Carribbean into a rewriting of the area's errant "irruption into modernity."

These moments constitute the points of historical "entanglements" inscribed in the archive of diversion, to which one must return without essentializing its contents. Glissant carefully acknowledges that this awareness does not represent a return to identitarian forms of thinking, negritude, or even a nondiscursive understanding of creolization. What these entanglements ultimately invoke for him is "a prophetic view of the past," that is, the need to historicize errancy through artistic imagination and charge it with a constructionist role after the task of deconstruction is done. Two key examples would be a recognition of creolization as a global signifier that emphasizes cultural heterogeneity rather than race, and a radical valorization of orality in an age of performativity in which writing is no longer a narrowly defined practice.

Glissant's diversion thus provides an elaborate critique of both modern and postmodern notions of mimesis: neither the powerless subordination to colonial power often associated with the culture of underdevelopment nor an empowering deconstructive figure limited to theoretical work. Indeed, *Caribbean Discourse* could be read as a treatise on what Glissant calls *parallactics* (the displacement strategies of diversion). More specifically, Glissant explores through his study of Martinique the question of whether mimesis/mimicry—that intricate doubling that informs postcolonial culture—can find a historical grounding. In doing so, he presents a set of crucial theoretical problems whose value continued to increase for postcolonial criticism in the 1990s, as evident in the most recent works of Benita Parry, Henry Louis Gates Jr., Neil Lazarus, Cornel West, Stuart Hall, and others. As postmodern theorization moves beyond its initial stages of literary and epistemological avant-gardism, reelaborations of community, nationalism, and the social text, as well as other political applications of deconstructive insights, are coming to the fore.[53]

Postcolonial Horizons

In his influential essay on the topic of power and the aesthetics of vulgarity in the postcolony, Achille Mbembe accentuates the need to distinguish further between postmodern and postcolonial forms of discourse.[54] His study of Cameroon provides the backdrop for a series of observations on the postcolonial condition, inspired by Foucauldian notions of power and Bakhtinian categories of carnivalesque praxis. For Mbembe,

> the postcolonial mode of domination is as much a regime of constraints as a practice of conviviality and a stylistic of connivance—marked by innate caution, constant compromises, small tokens of fealty, and a precipitance to denunciate those who are labeled "subversive"—the analyst must be attentive to the myriad ways in which ordinary people bridle, trick, and actually toy with power instead of confronting it directly.[55]

This study obviously constitutes yet another attempt to articulate the doubling of mimicry/mimesis, though somewhat differently from those of Glissant and Bhabha outlined earlier.

What interests me here is that Mbembe's approach calls for neither resistance nor deconstruction, nor opposition, for it sees no commensurable
external sources of power implicit in the description of Foucauldian immanence. It fashions postcolonialism as the quintessence of postmodern simulacra. Mimicry/mimesis here turns into a micropolitics of power, which
produces a self-contained economy of subject positions in Cameroon. In
the absence of viable metanarratives, and in the presence of a global economic structure that he does not theorize, Mbembe seeks to isolate postcolonial power relations as an enclosed totality whose functional elements
respond only to an internal logic. Postcoloniality thus becomes a sight to
behold, like a film or an artistic object, or perhaps a Baudrillardian spec-
tacle: "the simulacral regime par excellence."[56] Glissant's call for relations
and entanglements—locally and globally—here seem nothing less than in-
congruous or anachronistic. Bhabha's search for subversive troping also
contrasts significantly with Mbembe's celebratory depiction of postcoloniality as a site where subjection to the law intersects with "the subject's deployment of a talent for play and a sense of fun which makes him *homo lu-
dens par excellence.*"[57]

It could be argued that Mbembe is only transferring deconstructive
emphasis from writing about writing to an emphasis on writing about the
bodies of the living—in other words, a shift from Derridean to Foucauldian
modes of troping. But, in either case, as in Benítez-Rojo's use of *choteo*, decolonization proper remains absent from postcolonial theorizing. It is not a
question of disclaiming the unquestionable value of the "art of improvisa-
tion" in the postcolony, or its "tendency to excess and disproportion," or
the "distinctive ways in which identities are multiplied, transformed, and
put into circulation."[58] Rather, the problem lies in the fact that these characteristics are present nearly everywhere today, and most certainly in the
metropoles of global capitalism. Furthermore, these features surface on
their own from nearly all modes of standard deconstructive analysis. Critical languages tend to produce their own object of study, and thus to ho-
mogenize it, even as they attempt to explicate differences. Deconstructive
work has masterfully applied this insight to nearly all forms of literary and
epistemological thought, except perhaps to itself.

Glissant writes about the meaning of this blind spot for Caribbean
writing:

> When I witness from a little distance the very interesting work done
> on a theoretical level in the West, it seems to me that two reactions are
> formed: I experience at the same time a feeling of the ridiculous and a
> feeling of the extreme importance of these ideas. The text must for us

(in our lived experience) be destabilized, because it must belong to a shared reality, and it is perhaps at this point that we actually relate to these ideas that have emerged elsewhere. Our critique of the act and the idea of literary creation is not derived from a "reaction" to theories which are proposed to us, but from a burning need for *modification*.[59]

One must wonder, nonetheless, if there is any basis for Glissant's optimism after his own detailed descriptions of dispossession, nonhistory, and lack of collective consciousness in *Caribbean Discourse*. It is important to note, however, that his faith in the future of the Caribbean, and even in the future of Martinique itself, is based on a different understanding of new theoretical insights, as well as their relation to contemporary history, most particularly his tendency to look on the contradictory forces of globalization in a promising light: "And so transversality, and not the universal transcendence of the sublime, has come to light. It took us a long time to learn this. We are the roots of a cross-cultural relationship. Submarine roots: that is, floating free, not fixed in position in some primordial spot, but extending in all directions in our world through its network of branches."[60]

Transversality, cross-cultural potential, creolization, and hybridity do not implode into a micropolitics of subjection in Glissant's discourse, as they do in Mbembe's. In *Caribbean Discourse,* theory assumes a relational dynamics that moves outward and sees the radical and contradictory changes that are taking place in the global community. His particular use of discursive theory spells out a level of critique that Gayatri Chakravorty Spivak has begun to address as well:

> Foucault is a brilliant thinker of the power-in-spacing, but the awareness of the topographical reinscription of imperialism does not inform his presuppositions. He is taken in by the restricted version of the West produced by that reinscription and thus helps to consolidate its effects. To buy a self-contained version of the West is to ignore its production by the imperialist project.[61]

Foucault should not, however, be singled out in this regard. Postmodernism as a whole tends to buy into the same self-contained version of the West as an enlarged global village. As such, the West becomes both a self-containment and an extension of its basic logic, as the globalist notion of neoliberalism becomes a new form of universalism.[62] Critiques of the West's modern legacy and its narratives depend primarily on an immanent gaze, an implicitly reformist orientation in an epoch weary of oppositional alternatives. Paget Henry and Paul Buhle's work on C. L. R. James is quite instructive in this regard. They see in James's work, as well as in Fanon's, a different mode of deconstructive practice, one that is severely limited when strictly confined to semiolinguistic doctrine: "The existence of multiple bases of deconstruction in James's discourse points to a linguistic foundationalism within poststructuralism that contradicts its explicit anti-essentialist stance. Embedded in the constituting claims that poststructuralism makes for language are contradictions that suggest that its thought rests on a resolution of the opposition of essentialism/anti-essentialism that is not consistent with its own deconstructive strictures."[63]

Postcolonialism is largely defined today not as a historical period, but rather by the postmodern constellation of questions brought to bear on the study of history, power relations, and subject formation. Less clearly prescribed is the degree to which postmodern and postcolonial approaches must include a specific and comprehensive analysis of the contemporary moment, whether it be the Caribbean, or of some other Third World area. Yet, even from an uncertain point of entry as far as Third World history is concerned, the critique of colonialism and imperialism implicit in postcolonial studies also seems to propel postmodernism in new and different directions. Postcolonial studies now often encompass certain aspects of the First World, and its study of so-called minority cultures, as well as the growing field of border cultures.[64] But there remains a need to probe more deeply into a loosely defined but all-encompasing notion of *writing* that deconstructs through foreclosure the continuity between colonial and postcolonial societies, a movement that, as we saw in Benítez-Rojo's work, tends to dismiss the modern period.[65]

The need to scrutinize more rigorously the very body of continental theory that informs it is now evident in the most acute postcolonial writers. Spivak's critique of "the benevolent Western intellectual" underscores this concern, for, as she explains, there are arenas into which "Derrida has not moved (or perhaps cannot move)."[66] Glissant's study of Martinique and the Caribbean also explicitly makes this point, even though he has not identified explicitly with postcolonialism as a rubric. In *Caribbean Discourse*, Glissant manages to engage the world of theory through the specificity of the local without recurring to historicist forms of narration. The complexity of his work lies precisely in the commitment to a theory that cultivates both edges of that performative impulse.

In this context, the substantial differences between Bhabha's and Glissant's modes of mapping what could be called postcolonial societies could not be of greater significance to contemporary critical thinking. Bhabha's entire critical project embodies a new type of writing as theory that aims to gather new force from the deconstruction of Third World narratives. It is both creative and incisive, though it understands these aims only from within the aesthetics of designification that has evolved in continental philosophy since Martin Heidegger. His postcoloniality emphasizes a writerly frontier in which otherness finds its place mainly as signifier, concrete historical entanglements implode into an invigorated but still universalizing theoretical troping, and political subversion becomes suggestive only as a rhetorical figure. Although he is aware of the value of writing as form of designification within the tradition of Western metanarratives, Glissant views writing from contradictory perspectives, most particularly by questioning its capacity to trope Third World historical entanglements.

It is in Glissant's grave doubts about the conception of writing as a new liberating frontier that we find his most striking critique of mainstream poststructural thinking. Indeed, he is eager to submit the privileged practice of writing, which he sees as an intricate part of the colonizing legacy, to a different deconstructive rigor, in which orality and performativity figure prominently:

> Today the oral can be preserved and be transmitted from one people to another. It appears that the written could increasingly perform the function of an archive and that writing would be reserved as an esoteric and magical art for a few. . . . The creative writer must not despair in the face of this phenomenon. For the only way, to my mind, of maintaining a place for writing (if this can be done)—that is, to remove it from being an esoteric practice or a banal reserve of information—would be to nourish it with the oral. If writing does not henceforth resist the temptation to transcendence, by, for instance, learning from oral practice and fashioning a theory from the latter if necessary, I think it will disappear as a cultural imperative from future societies. As Sameness will be exhausted by the surprising dynamism of Diversity, so writing will be confined to the closed and sacred world of literary activity.[67]

Glissant's critique of writing dramatizes the need to account for a new postmodern orality, as well as video culture and other performative arts that resist strict scriptural containment. His critique also extends to include the body in relation to orality in a manner that moves beyond Foucauldian notions of self-knowledge as sedimented technologies:

> The written requires nonmovement: the body does not move with the flow of what is said. The oral, on the other hand, is inseparable from

the movement of the body. There the spoken is inscribed not only in the posture of the body that makes it possible (squatting for a palaver, for instance, or the rhythmic tapping of feet in a circle when we keep time to music), but also in the almost semaphoric signals through which the body implies or emphasizes what is said. Utterance depends on posture, and perhaps is limited by it.[68]

Glissant intuits that postcolonial thinking must provide a different critical account of this global moment, its opportunities as well as its pitfalls. His search for a new understanding of collective agencies, and for the promise buried with ghosts of the past, retains a hope of renewal that has been mostly absent from postmodern insights. It is interesting to note, however, that Derrida's recent work echoes a struggle with similar concerns: "the alliance of a rejoining without conjoined mate, without organization, without party, without nation, without State, without property (The 'communism' that we will later nickname the new International)."[69] Unlike Derrida's work, however, Glissant's does include a stable First World state endowed by centuries of institutionalized nationhood, property systems, and democratic traditions. Glissant's call for theoretical difference thus has a different concern for historical evolvement:

> the methodological and fundamental distinction between diachrony and synchrony could also be seen as a *trick*; that, no longer capable of dominating the History of the world, the West chose this method of refining the idea that histories would no longer weigh so heavily on consciousness and self-expression. It is, however, simpler to consider this transformation, not as a trick, but as a kind of logical eventuality. In the face of a now shattered notion of History, the whole of which no one can claim to master nor even conceive, it was normal that the Western mind should advance a diversified Literature, which is scattered in all directions but whose meaning no one could claim to have mastered. Now, to follow the logic of these ideas to its conclusion, we should let the weight of lived experience "slip in." Literature is not only fragmented, it is henceforth shared. In it lie histories and the voice of peoples. We must reflect on a new relationship between history and literature. We need to live it differently.[70]

Dash's translation of *passer* in *Le discours antillais* as "slip in" may bring to mind Derrida's "slippage," but the reader needs to treat such associations with care. Glissant's call to allow the weight of experience to "slip in" to literature is a very poignant moment in his essay on history and literature. It signals a state of literary affairs that goes beyond designification toward a state in which narratives, performances, and oralities in the Third World construct a daily life aiming to a better future. *Caribbean Discourse* can therefore be seen as a liberationist text, and indeed, some may find this aspect somewhat naive. It does not call, however, for a nostalgic return to aesthetic values stemming from humanistic precepts. Furthermore, its optimistic moments are not reserved for the academic theorist, or even for the Caribbean. It speaks to the global village itself:

> One could imagine—this is, moreover, a movement that is emerging almost everywhere—a kind of revenge by oral languages over written ones, in the context of a global civilization of the nonwritten. Writing seems linked to the transcendental notion of the individual, which today is threatened by and giving way to a cross-cultural process. In such a context will perhaps appear global systems using imaginative strategies, not conceptual structures, languages that dazzle or shimmer instead of simply "reflecting." Whatever we think of such an eventuality, we must examine from this point on what conditions Creole must satisfy in order to have a place in this new order.[71]

"Slipping in," then, is perhaps Glissant's most artful appropriation of postmodern perspectives on language and the body. It could be read as a devious exercise of his brand of mimicry, or a Caribbean gaze at poststructuralist discursivity from within. It is thus a figure that comes full circle, back to the world, from postcolonial experiences to the First World as a shared legacy of experiences as well as rhetorical devices. Freeing the body through new oral discourses, mobilizing diversity, and imagining a future where our understanding of culture is not exclusively ruled by the boundaries of writing—these are some of its constitutive moves. "Whatever we think of such an eventuality," as Glissant himself seems to wonder, it is a construct that delves into the contradictory links between globalization and postmodernity. It is also Glissant's daring conjuration of a postdeconstructivist horizon, a different technology of the self, where art, theory, and history seek to defamiliarize postmodern cartographies that continue to pursue tantalizing but mainstreamed modes of implosion. For Glissant, Caribbean opaqueness provides a way out of this fashionable cul-de-sac.

5
The Lettered City
Power and Writing in Latin America

A lasting work is always responsible for an infinitely plastic ambiguity; it is every-thing for everyone, like the Apostle; it is a mirror that traces the features of the reader; it is also a map of the world.

Jorge Luis Borges, Other Inquisitions

Never have violence, inequality, exclusion, famine, and thus economic oppression affected as many human beings in the history of the Earth and humanity.

Jacques Derrida, Spectres of Marx

Although Ángel Rama was introduced in chapter 3 for his contribution to Latin American transculturation theory, most Latin Americanists would agree that he does not require an introduction. His earlier work on Latin American modernism charted the field for Latin America's literary specialists in the sixties and seventies, and his entire oeuvre, which includes two books published posthumously (he died in an airplane crash in Spain in 1984), continues to accrue value today as point of reference in debates over cultural studies and postcolonialism. Yet, even as his stature continues to grow in Latin America, Rama's work remains for the most part unavailable in English and beyond the reach of the English-speaking world of contemporary criticism. There are many reasons for this neglect. The renowned Peruvian novelist Mario Vargas Llosa has written that Rama "belonged to a lineage of critics who were truly influential, those who turned criticism into an artistic form comparable to other genres: a Sainte-Beuve, an Ortega y Gasset, an Arnold Bennett, an Edmund Wilson."[1] It is important to note, however, that Vargas Llosa's praise is intended to date Rama: it is a burial of sorts, an attempt to place the Uruguayan critic among the ranks of figures whose time has passed. Rama's critical acumen always ran counter to Vargas Llosa's theories of creative passion and daemonic inspiration. For Rama, literature spoke from and to a broad spectrum of cultural and social articulations.

More important, however, one should note that Vargas Llosa's critical obituary is based largely on Rama's early work on Latin American modernism and the novelistic boom of the sixties. It does not take into account Rama's posthumous texts, a key body of work published after 1983 and consisting of two books and many essays that bear considerably on contemporary poststructural theoretical debates and their application to Latin American cultural studies.[2] Thus, Rama entered many contemporary theoretical debates posthumously. If his work still speaks to us, it is not as a newly crowned figure in Latin America's literary pantheon, but as a challenging, contradictory, and far-reaching critical corpus. This chapter attempts to read him precisely in that light.

Of Rama's posthumous texts, none is more important in its complexity and reach than *La ciudad letrada* (*The Lettered City*, published in Spanish in 1984). A look at its reception among academic critics reveals a notable paradox: a decade and a half after its first Spanish edition, one hardly finds more than a half dozen published studies of this thick, risky essay.[3] Yet, at the same time, *The Lettered City* may well be the most frequently mentioned text in contemporary Latin American cultural studies. Always present in journalistic notes and bibliographies, it has become a benchmark of sorts, a legitimizing stopping point that is always mentioned, often glossed, but hardly ever scrutinized, on the way to other topics. As with Vargas Llosa's casual observation, one finds many citations of *The Lettered City* that simply aim to mark its presence as a key point in one's critical compass, often to leave it behind in passing praise of Rama's extensive oeuvre. It is also often cited for its intriguing title, largely taken as a self-referential signifier, or as a metaphor for a writerly horizon that does not require explanation in today's theoretical scene, and even less so in the world of Latin American contemporary fiction, which is often cited as the quintessential site of postmodern writing.

It may well be that *The Lettered City* has become a title that lives fully outside the body of the work it attempts to articulate. Needless to say, such forms of reading through citation and brief quotation often fail to ask if the notion of a "lettered city" could not indicate the sense of a constraining grid as much as a liberating space. Indeed, as we will see, Rama's text encompasses both meanings, thereby allowing us to understand the relationship between power and writing as always prone to constriction as much as deconstruction. Yet, an even more striking set of contradictions is found if one takes into consideration published criticism of this book. Those few instances that provide a detailed analysis of *The Lettered City* reveal that it has been simultaneously understood as a prototype of colonial, modern, postmodern, and postcolonial Latin American textuality—all at once. It could be argued that such a heterogeneous reception from academic critics derives from the complex singularity of Rama's text, as well as testifying to the importance it still holds for contemporary Latin American cultural studies. On the other hand, one could also ask if the mixed, if not contradictory, nature of critical assessments surrounding *The Lettered City* does not invite a more general discussion regarding the state of contemporary theory. Is the convergence of such different discourses on this text a testimony to its theoretical value, or is it a symptom of theoretical self-generation, a state in which marketability of critical discourses is directly proportional to imprecision? It is my aim in this chapter to attempt an exploration of *The Lettered City* that takes both sides of this question into consideration, that is, the proliferation of theoretical discourses as well as the growing number of discursive communities within Latin Americanism. One hastens to add that the 1997 publication of the first English edition of *The Lettered City* will undoubtedly evoke many more new readings of this book, particularly from within postcolonial and cultural studies frameworks that are now revising the postmodern schools of criticism that flourished in the United States and Britain during the 1970s and 1980s. Needless to say, this new, transnational context will more than likely contribute its own set of ambiguities. On one hand, it will provide an occasion to place Rama's text alongside others that now form a provisional critical canon in the study of postcolonialism and postnationalism. I have in mind particularly Edward Said's *Orientalism* (1978) and Benedict Anderson's *Imagined Communities* (1983), whose proximity to *La ciudad letrada* (1984), in topical range, formal aspirations, date of composition, and Foucauldian lineage, deserves some attention. On the other hand, such an empowerment, available largely, if not only, through the English-speaking world, deserves particular attention for its capacity to codify new Latin American discursive markets far removed from the literary and cultural logic of Latin America itself.

Rama's text, like Anderson's and Said's, bespeaks a discursive universe somewhere between epistemology and aesthetics, an "episthetics" or middle ground that encompasses a broad range of new methods of humanistic writing and scholarship that have emerged since the early 1970s. Indeed, in this globalizing context, Rama's book is less well known, but not only because of its unavailability in English. As noted earlier, even in Spanish there has been a dearth of careful readings. This may be explained, in part, by the difficulty of his texts, which are challenging hybrid constructs of humanistic and social-science theory, a dense combination of cultural criticism and historical research, and an extensive bibliographical reach that challenges a readership perhaps too accustomed to the new transnational codification of Latin Americanism. Moreover, *The Lettered City* is also constituted by a performative ambition. Its pages attempt a writing aware of its own commitment to form, though not an entirely ludic expression willing to abandon conceptual territory, but rather, a project combining historical understanding with writerly pleasure in a constant double movement.

In many ways, *The Lettered City* returns to basic themes and methods found in Rama's earlier research on the two great Latin American literary periods: the poetry of modernism between 1870 and 1920 and the extraordinary corpus of contemporary novels. Such would be his mode of tracing literary history through a rich Latin American intertextuality often understood as transculturation. But Rama's posthumous work also provides evidence of important contrasts with his earlier work. Of these, the most striking would be his examination of Latin America's writerly history as a colonial residue largely informed by Michel Foucault's notion of epistemic breaks in *The Order of Things*. This is less a direct application of Foucault's early principles, than a simultaneous deploying and problematizing of his discursive epistemology. In so doing, Rama shows a willingness to alter, if not endanger, his own previous modes of reading Latin America's modern culture. His main interest now becomes the extraordinary—one should say determining—weight of the lettered class in Latin America's colonial and postcolonial history. Rama takes this history on board as a direct relation between writing and colonial power, and sets out to examine it not in its contents but through its written forms. He understands the Foucauldian concept of episteme as a structuring map for our understanding of colonial relations. More than just looking at history as a text, or underlining the importance that texts acquire in our understanding of epistemic organization, Rama becomes fascinated with the notion that a new understanding of history as discourse could also allow us to examine how writing and the explosion of signs ensuing from the onset of European modernity endow the imaginary of colonial power in Latin America. Rama's focus on discourse simultaneously suggests its potential for empowerment and its constitution of prison house. His new emphasis on the colonial residue as a persistent epistemic configuration entails a radical departure from his earlier work on Latin American modernity as a clearly demarcated, autonomous period.

One ventures to say that *The Lettered City* is a true essay—in the double sense of providing a test as well as a rehearsal—of many theoretical aspects that have fueled debates in the years since it was published, many of which are central to Foucault's own work. It is now well understood that *The History of Sexuality* or *Technologies of the Self*, for example, constitute profound revisions of the discursive epistemology that was central to *The Order of Things* or *The Archaeology of Knowledge*.[4] It is important therefore to look at Rama's book as a mode of theoretical experimentation. His most careful readers to date have tended to look at other key aspects and problems, or touched on the question of colonial discourse as a structuring episteme only tangentially. Mabel Moraña, for example, makes a careful critique of the need to make more and greater distinctions in Rama's new history of Latin American culture as the product of a "lettered" class. She also calls for a more nuanced approach to the "autonomous nature of cultural practice" and of the independent role that writers assume in Rama's book.[5] Rolena Adorno provides a different critique. She praises Rama's attempt to study colonialism as a set of relations between language and power, as well as his reach beyond "the frontiers that separate literary or intellectual histories of Latin America from political and social history."[6] Yet, Adorno also reminds us that colonial writing constitutes a more extensive space—indeed, a "labyrinth of ideological rivalries"— that transcends the concept of the "enclosed lettered city" she sees in Rama's essay.[7] In a very different register, Carlos J. Alonso provides the only reading that takes Rama's Foucauldian debt as the starting point. It is his contention, however, that Rama's bid to take up the autonomy and self-referentiality of writing as a central tenet in understanding history is both equivocal and insufficient, even though it constitutes the key contribution of his book. Alonso maintains that, though profoundly flawed and ultimately dispensable, Rama's approach constitutes a symptom of the need for a truly postmodern final sweep of Latin America's penchant for sociohistorical critical methods.[8]

The underlying common thread one gathers from these widely differing views is that Rama's text has a way of provoking a richer dialogue about how one deploys discursive paradigms, all the more so when approaching Latin America's colonial order as a lingering presence during modern and postmodern periods. This does not necessarily mean that we can now assert, uncritically, Rama's place as a precursor of postcolonial studies. That would be an important trace that has so far been explored only by Josaphat Kubayanda, who has argued that Rama, as well as other Latin American writers such as Augusto Roa Bastos, should be read alongside Frantz Fanon.[9] My specific interest at this point, however, lies in the conditions of possibility for such a postcolonial appropriation; hence, it has more to do with the links between globalizing postmodernism and the production of critical discourses around Latin American literature.

I will argue that *The Lettered City* contains an early, but distinct and important, reading of the difficulties inherent in poststructural theorizing.

Obviously, in so doing, this text also reveals its own contradictions, which one would expect of any attempt to transcribe, critically and creatively, a major strand of European theory in the context of Latin American studies. Rama's posthumously published research comes directly at the main questions that inform poststructural theory armed with perhaps the most extensive understanding of Latin American literary and cultural modern traditions of any published critic at the time. This encounter, I believe, is centered on two central sets of questions: (1) If we understand discourse as the new core of historical knowledge that is largely constituted by textuality, how will we determine whether, when, and for whom writing may constitute a liberating transgression? and (2) If we understand the discursive, or "lettered," Latin American colonial order as a special moment of textual gestation that marks all of Latin American literature since the colonial period, how does one account for the widely divergent, if not opposed, ways of understanding such a transhistorical mode of periodization?

Theory as Legacy

All through Rama's text there is a constant presence of what was earlier defined as *episthetic* play, that is, a theoretical performance simultaneously imbued by aesthetics and epistemology. *The Lettered City* not only traces how words and signs gain autonomy in colonial Latin America; it is also an attempt to enact, if not dramatize, that very process as a contemporary strategy. The book's pulse is marked by the constant iteration of the term *lettered city*, a term that moves from the initial title to signify a more general description of an epochal epistemic construct that Rama continuously articulates, defines, and exemplifies, almost as if to meet the immensity of a reified colonial order with an utterance never satisfied with its own capacity to refer. This also explains the morphological strategy of deriving chapter subtitles from his key term—lettered city, ordered city, writerly city, modernized city, politicized city, revolutionized city—as if to show how nimbly a shifting signifier can operate even while under the hold of a given epistemic order. All of these mutations of the Latin American city-as-history respond to one logic: the intensification of the world of signs that Rama traces from the moment of the conquest through the formation of the Baroque period, or city, culminating in the modernized city, but signaling all the way through to even postmodern times.

> It is already evident in *El Bernardo* that design occupies the entire life of Bernardo de Balbuena. This is even more explicit in the 1624 prologue, in which he cites the Italian source (Boyardo, Ariosto). The

same occurs two centuries later, in Justo Sierra's proposal to obviate the "Spanish aqueduct" and continue designing from French literary sources.

Both [Bernardo de Balbuena and Justo Sierra] were urban planners by vocation, as were the overwhelming majority of Latin American intellectuals. Both worked as city planners who followed closely prodigious models laid out in literary texts, in the impeccable universe of signs that allowed them to think and dream the city, in order to claim that an ideal order would be embodied in its citizens.[10]

The question of the materiality of words, of their capacity to constitute their own reality, a reality that went beyond the representation of a previous given order, is obviously a central concern for Rama. This was not a new theme for him, even though it now intensifies considerably. He had already worked on and through this key topic in previous texts, notably in his *Transculturación narrativa en América Latina,* where Ferdinand de Saussure, Claude Lévi-Strauss, Theodor Adorno, and Max Horkheimer are discussed in the context of a contemporary understanding of the relation between signification and mythology.[11] What strikes Rama at this point is the intensity of this problem in Foucault's notion of epochal discourse as epistemic ordering. Thus, he begins to understand the Hispanic Baroque or the French classical period of the sixteenth and seventeenth centuries as a moment in which "words began to separate from things," giving way to "the independence of the signs."[12] From this moment on, through this new conduit of knowledge,

the immense Latin American extension of ideal cities will flow from here. They will be governed by an ordering reason that reveals itself in a hierarchical social order transposed to a geometric distributive order. . . . Thus, society and city do not connect, but their respective forms do; indeed, they are perceived as equivalent, allowing us to read society when we are reading a city map. To make this conversion possible, it was first necessary to work through a previous rational project, which was what magnified and made the order of signs indispensable, allowing it to claim the greatest operational freedom it could marshal.[13]

Here we can clearly observe a shift in Rama's previous understanding of history, which up to then had been primarily concerned with links between Latin American literary modernism and the specific features of modernity in societies that remained somewhat peripheral to its First World definitions. The theoretical groundwork of *The Lettered City* was laid at the end of the 1970s and the beginning of the 1980s, a period that in Latin American literary criticism still belongs to an in-between moment of late structuralism and its later strands, which include, particularly in U.S. Latin Americanism, early forms of deconstruction. This transitional moment is roughly present, in different ways, in the work of Foucault himself, as well as in Said's *Orientalism,* which, like Rama's text, is itself informed by early readings of Foucauldian epistemics. Like Rama, Said takes on board this newly formed way of theorizing the arbitrariness of the sign, the so-called abyss between language and world, but never quite accepting unconditionally, nor failing to see it as an opportunity to continue to theorize colonialism, imperialism, and agency, as would be perhaps the case with much of the literary deconstructionism of this moment.

Said would eventually write books that continued to problematize this theoretical legacy, as is evident from *The World, the Text, and the Critic,* and even more from *Culture and Imperialism.* It would be hazardous to guess what Rama would have written had he continued to live, but the early parallels with Said's work are not fortuitous. There are many ways of historicizing the Saussurean theoretical legacy and its subsequent evolution in literary studies, all the way into what I have called its contemporary episthetic moment. I would, however, hazard to sketch three general moments or tendencies that are often found in overviews: (1) the construction of epistemes, aggregates, and totalities prone to structuralist configuration and analysis; (2) the ensuing modes of deconstruction of such constructs, some strictly from the singularity of key or canonical texts, others with a more extensive model of how textuality and dispersal challenge history as well as literary studies; (3) the post-1989 moment in which humanistic studies are confronted like never before with globalization, the privatization of all academic and social spheres, and the advent of cultural studies as a full-blown academic specialization in the United States. These are obviously not fixed categories, nor do they denote firm temporal boundaries.[14] My fundamental interest here is to complicate any attempt that fails to account for the points of contact and contrast that contaminate these moments in rather unsettled ways.

To some readers, *The Lettered City* might correspond strictly to the set of concerns associated with a late-structuralist moment, but it is a bit more complicated than that. As stated earlier, its central preoccupation is the advent of a more arbitrary order of signification, or at least a more transparent way of understanding the pretenses of a representational order that was taken to constitute "the real" in Latin American intellectual history. This allows disciplinary knowledge to come under scrutiny as a series of heuristic structures or totalizations configured by archives, grammars, literary genres, city plans, and other forms of organizing the production and reception of the social imaginary. Textuality, here understood as not just literature but all forms of writing and sign production, thus assumes a privileged role for un-packing, and at the same time constituting a new totality out of the colonial order. Again, Rama's concern clearly parallels Foucault's "archaeological" moment regarding the classificatory power of disciplines, or Said's demarca-tion of how orientalism forms a particular kind of knowledge that brings a certain lettered order to its practitioners by producing the very object it purports to describe.[15]

The second, or deconstructionist, moment began to manifest itself in Latin American criticism toward the end of the 1970s in some American universities. It came precisely at a time when the Latin American novelistic boom was becoming a world-class corpus in the United States. It was also much more skilled than previous paradigms at working with the experi-mental nature of writers such as Jorge Luis Borges, Gabriel García Már-quez, Carlos Fuentes, Mario Vargas Llosa, and others who would eventually constitute a considerable part of the postmodern canon. Today, this is still a predominant paradigm, even as it becomes absorbed by more recent articu-lations of literary postmodernism, postcolonialism, or high-end cultural studies. It has achieved a significant degree of sophistication and institu-tional recognition, particularly through work published primarily in En-glish. Texts such as *Myth and Archive* by Roberto González Echevarría and *Inventing America* by José Rabasa continue to shape an already impressive bibliography. Interestingly, this mode of criticism also stems from a privi-leged sense of discursivity, now termed "writing," but it moves in a some-what different direction from the work produced in the first moment. Rather than formulating objects of study as totalized aggregates that en-compass history as discursive epistemes, it posits historical understanding and literary appreciation, often without distinguishing between the two, as an ongoing process of designification, particularly available when applied to major literary and philosophical texts. Its attention moves toward intensify-ing the practice of close reading as the ideal method for disinterring contra-dictions always present in discourse. The familiar regime of words or the epistemic grid of high structuralism now moves toward a liberating model implicit in the transgressive potential of deconstruction, particularly when drawn from the elaborate discursive patterns of literature and philosophy, an always-already polysemic presence that is said to exceed or subvert any representational bond between words and things.

What is generally assumed by this critical approach, particularly through literary deconstruction and metanarrative critique, is that the internal dynamics of specialized texts are equally inherent in all texts, or that model texts can be made to encompass the entire social realm.[16] This is the epistemological leap more prevalent among critical paradigms in the 1980s and early 1990s that Rama was already unwilling to take in *The Lettered City.* Today, that leap may be considerably more difficult, or open to debate. But what is important to note is how Rama already straddles the line between the two moments of the discursive legacy presented thus far, challenging each in different ways. At one level, based on his reading of Foucault, he undoubtedly assimilates an understanding of Latin American culture as a great archive of textuality, but he also confronts that totality with collective forms of popular and class culture that threaten to break the epistemic monolith. At another level, he fully apprehends the notion of semiotic excess internal to literary writing, but he also moves in an opposite direction by positing a way of looking at Latin American culture as a lettered order more than capable of absorbing individual acts of transgression, without failing to account for their artistic excellence.

Globalization, a term that lacks genuine specificity, can nonetheless serve provisionally to define a third moment in theoretical work. It is intended here to refer to the launching of a neoliberal market logic upon the blithe and ludic energies that dominated postmodern imaginaries up to 1989. With the end of the Cold War and the disappearance of the weaker side of an East/West, First World/Second World set of binaries, Western triumphalism began to manifest itself as globalization in the name of the end, whether of history, modernity, or ideology. It is now evident, however, that this vacuum is beginning to call forth more concrete approaches to questions of ethics and politics in theoretical work, as is evident in the angst expressed in Derrida's *Spectres of Marx*. Needless to say, it remains to be seen how far the liberatory or transgressive understanding of postmodern academic practice will be tested from within by this latest capitalist expansion. We can now observe much more clearly, for example, that earlier moments of poststructuralist understanding also had their own utopian, if not identitarian, longings. This is what Christopher Norris calls a tendency to give language and writing "nearly anthropomorphic attributes."[17] Indeed, the need to clarify or sort out what I have called our contemporary legacy has also been felt by Latin American critics and theorists, particularly those who work outside the U.S. academy. Carlos Rincón, one of the most prolific theorists of Latin America's postmodern literary scene, stipulates that it is high time for an "indispensable differentiation" regarding the "multiple interconnections among postmodernism, postcolonialism, and Latin Americanism, not only in terms of analytic-descriptive terminology, but also in terms of what constitutes contemporaneity."[18]

My argument here is not that the rich theoretical legacy of the past three decades has suddenly been rendered redundant, nor that its value has receded to what it was in a blissful epoch when theory was much less significant. I do want to suggest, however, that theory is now a rather muddled terrain in constant need of reassessment and clarification. Moreover, I would like to argue that certain early theoretical texts such as *The Lettered City*, which straddle the line between colonial and postcolonial subject matters, already contain many ambiguities that have of late become more evident in theoretical work. In short, it is my contention that Rama's attempt to engage Foucault's conceptual archaeology in the context of a nonsynchronous Latin American colonial legacy turns into a telling, albeit aporetic, confrontation between that very theory and its object.

Other attempts to theorize Latin American literature as an intricate part of the Western discursive legacy could serve as a pertinent background. One important example would be "neobaroque" theory, particularly as seen in the work of Severo Sarduy, which incorporates both structural and poststructural semiological precepts that first circulated in Latin American literary circles in unison with the advent of the novelistic boom period in the sixties and early seventies.[19] Rama's work, though chronologically close to that period, already affords significant contrasts: he studies literature as part of a cultural period composed of an array of texts that defies strict literary enclosure; he understands the links between literature and markets of reception, and he sees the great novels of the Latin American boom period as metatextual attempts to encompass an inexhaustible difference available only through multiple discourses and asynchronic constellations. It should not surprise us, therefore, that Rama becomes the first Latin American critic to engage Foucault—rather than Roland Barthes or Paul de Man—systematically, in a full-length study that afforded Rama a broader, more historical approach to the new discursive horizon. During the mid-1980s to early 1990s, other critics would attempt to incorporate Foucauldian categories into methods of deconstructionist close readings that had otherwise failed to render any workable sense of literary or cultural history. A key example mentioned earlier would be Roberto González Echevarría's *Myth and Archive*. Today, this emphasis has assumed an even greater importance in the growing awareness that postmodern methods of reading, particularly those canonized by literary criticism, are at once necessary and insufficient. Texts such as Walter Mignolo's *The Darker Side of the Renaissance* and Rincón's already cited *La no simultaneidad de lo simultáneo*

constitute new attempts to map the territory of Latin American literary/
cultural studies. But it is important to probe further how this contemporary problematic is already present in Rama's text, as an embryonic set of
symptoms and contradictions.

One problem that nearly all of Rama's readers observe is his unwilling-
ness to take stock of the ways in which a given text can subvert hegemonic
logic or the order sustained by Latin America's lettered class through various
centuries. Actually, as one can see in the following quotation, Rama does on
occasion distinguish the exceptional quality of certain texts and writers,
even if he appears unwilling to render them individually capable of counter-
vailing official history:

> Sor Juana's original (brilliant) move consists in having turned the dis-
> location between literary discourse and the world of affect into the
> central theme of her poetics. She managed to render suspect (hence
> the oneiric irruption of the *First Dream*) the belief that truth could
> only stem from the hemisphere of the occult, thus disrupting, if not
> destroying, rational discourse, which, while claiming autonomy and
> self-sufficiency, only managed to gather obscure impulses.[20]

Rama's critics will rightfully observe that his intellectual history does
not quite allow for the promise of textual irruption to come through in
seminal texts because he is much less concerned with exceptions than with a
structured totality. Indeed, Rama looks for a representational field of force
that functions almost as a pact between colonial power and organic intellectuals armed with the power to signify in ever more imaginative ways. He
fails to see—or, more accurately, resists—the notion that specific texts or
authors can be said to alter this relationship between power and signification, or that we can reconstruct the epistemic period solely based on the
transgressive qualities of a given text. Put in different ways, he seems to
challenge us to show how our newfound appreciation of rhetorical liminality is able to dent in any significant way the larger historical totality he creates out of this extraordinary lettered order of the colonial imaginary. One
hastens to add, however, that Rama's approach also discards, radically, many
other forms of Latin American criticism that were prevalent at the time and
that continue to populate the critical landscape in the United States as well
as in Latin America. I am referring not only to various forms of sociological
content analysis often found in dependency theory, but also to literary histories bound by generational theory, author-bound models of literary hagiography, impressionism, and various other forms of unbridled aesthetic
humanism. These methods, constituting modes of totalizing in their own

right that are often absorbed by postmodern eclecticism, could not be more at loggerheads with Rama's work.

In *The Lettered City*, but even more so in *Las máscaras democráticas del modernismo* (a series of essays collected for book publication by friends and colleagues after Rama's death), he incorporates all of his earlier research in a new matrix that not only includes experimentation with notions of history as discourse, but also attempts to study how the language of desire and the erotic affect our understanding of history. At this stage, for the first time in his prolific career, Rama sees the crucial role of women and women's writing in any attempt to configure the Latin American modernist imaginary. There are some differences between these two books, because the latter begins to move away from the concept of a "lettered culture" toward the possibility of a more "democratized culture" that stems from a more nuanced understanding of eroticism, desire, and women's writing. But both books are still bound by a theory of orality that constitutes the only really transgressive space conceived by Rama, and both reiterate a central skepticism regarding the role of lettered intellectuals: "the doctrinal discourse they imposed on poetry"; "the intellectual heroism of a few superior spirits, and the failure that awaited the majority of them."[21] Moreover, both texts respond to the new elaboration in Rama's work prior to his death: bringing literary intertextuality to a transcultural understanding of Latin American cultural forms and epistemic configuration, from colonial times to the advent of postmodernity.

A key moment in this new casting would be Rama's approach to political discourse, particularly the model he offers to study Latin American revolutions during the twentieth century. He writes that these recurrent historical events should be evaluated by placing a greater value on "deep social change," rather than on "violent rupture."[22] This distinction disrupts many mythical moments of a revolutionary narrative. It also brings Rama to sense the advent of a new historical era, by concluding that the 1970s mark the end of modern Latin American revolutions, "an epoch that has continued since 1911 in which the debates and protagonists look pretty much alike and their fight with universal circumstances varies only to the degree that it worsens."[23] Rama's critics have thus far failed to notice this new periodization of the almost sacred popular terrain of Latin American revolutions from a new historical schema that takes on board colonial and neocolonial intellectual residues. Notice how he approaches the difference between social change and lettered representation in what is incontestably the most marked chapter of Latin America's contemporary revolutionary legacy:

The direct consequence of the politicization of the city will be a new functional conception of the political party, with the development of a new democratic base and other side effects that were never known to nineteenth-century political parties. This trend will continue during the twentieth century until the latter decades when the old regime of freemason lodges will reappear as new militarized nuclei (focos) that will require a new legitimizing theory to adjust well-entrenched customs: this is the well-known pamphlet by Regis Debray, *Revolution in the Revolution* (1962), which transcribes the Cuban revolutionary conception at the time, a conception that no longer does justice to the revolutionary movement that was indeed able to involve ample sectors of society, a conception that already began to become mystified with that little book by Franqui, *The Twelve.*[24]

One can also observe here how Rama leans on the distinction between a revolution and its discursive representation in order to exonerate deep social change from verbal mystifications of violent rupture. This is obviously a complex and controversial reading of revolution, undoubtedly an alternative to contemporary critiques of modern master narratives that tend simply to dismiss Latin American revolutionary movements without further ado, as if they were just a forgettable or misguided episode in history. It is also important to place Rama's complex critique in light of his personal story at the time of his death, the short period he spent living and working in the United States. During the early 1980s, Rama's work profited tremendously from the time afforded him by a Woodrow Wilson fellowship and University of Maryland visiting appointments, but it should also be noted that he suffered intense political harassment and personal denigration during those years from those who sought to deny him a work visa to continue working in the United States.[25] At the heart of Ramas's exploration of the intertextual relations between literature and cultural studies lies a very Gramscian set of concerns and categories: most prominently, the function of intellectuals and the production of social-symbolic capital. This approach yields a different understanding of subversion that is not strictly bound to major texts and literary moments but involves what Rama calls the "real city." By this term, he does not mean a return to realism; rather, he intends an apprehension of the social text as a transcultural pivot of conflicting forces. This is why Rama attempts to configure a countercanon that expands our sense of colonial and premodern Latin American textuality. The main elements of such a canon would include: orality as a social formation, graffiti as collective writing, unorthodox grammars such as Simón Rodríguez's writing experiments, rereadings of texts such as the picaresque novel *El Periquillo Sarniento,* and, above all, the idea of popular speech. Hence, Rama's notion of transgression and resistance looks toward a multiplicity of conflictive voices and cultural forms that goes beyond the reach of narrative heteroglossia and the privileging of writing as the only site of difference and otherness.

The Other City

It is difficult to find critical texts informed by deconstruction that are willing to encompass the social realm without neutralizing it or turning it into a literary trope that immediately reduces the social to an undifferentiated coefficient of writerly polysemy. This could well constitute one of the specific challenges for literary Latin Americanism and its postmodern metafictions, particularly as they turn into a paradigm for otherness as rhetorical space in figures such as Menard, Bustrófedon, and Melquíades. One needs to ask what is gained, and lost, as Latin American literature turns into a prototype of postmodern writing, or is seen as the exotic source of a magic realism marketable on a worldwide scale. Nonetheless, signs of a more complex and heterogeneous criticism are already present in the work of Beatriz Sarlo, Néstor García Canclini, Roberto Schwarz, and Nelly Richard, among others.[26] That they generally write, work, and produce theory in Latin America itself is a telling, though not a singularly determining, factor in their more nuanced approach. What differentiates their writing is not simply that they operate from a different locus of enunciation, a concept that is quite capable of reintroducing a weak but celebrated sense of inchoate pluralism in which all loci claim truth and beauty at once. The problem has more to do with how sites of legitimation constitute markets that govern the production and reception of influential critical discourses. Like Rama, these Latin American critics approach contemporary developments in literary theory as an ongoing instability that also encompasses the social realm. They work in settings in which the institutional structure of their disciplines is not a stable, autonomous constellation of research universities. Hence, their work tends to take episthetic work beyond its customary hermeneutical interplay to another terrain that can extend to the deconstruction of dominant postmodern aesthetics. In the last few paragraphs of Néstor García Canclini's *Consumidores y ciudadanos* (Consumers and citizens), for example, one finds the call for new forms of urban subject formation and the public sphere in Latin American cities:

> Any realistic look at our contemporary societies will not find it difficult to conclude there are few reasons to be in favor of the excluded and the exploited. Walter Benjamin used to say that only because of

our love for the downtrodden do we manage to conserve hope. I will add that it is still possible to justify solidarity, as artists, writers, and scientists, to the extent that we enjoy a certain degree of emancipation, or at least that we have an interest in keeping emancipation and renovation of the real—indeed, a certain utopian sense—as part of the social realm. During the seventies and eighties, postmodern thought taught us to liberate ourselves from the illusions implicit in metanarratives that promised totalizing and totalitarian emancipations. Perhaps it is time to emancipate ourselves from our disenchantment.[27]

But perhaps the most elaborate attempt to articulate a detailed deconstruction of society as a discursive category is found in Ernesto Laclau's *New Reflections on the Revolution of Our Time.*[28] Indeed, Laclau's text may well constitute a test case of the interesting contradictions that ensue when one transposes Derridean epistemology from the literary to the social. In the chapter titled "The Impossibility of Society," for instance, one finds a set of distinctions that may be usefully juxtaposed to Rama's notion of the "real city." For example, though Laclau underlines the centrality of the term *discourse,* he warns that such a term must be "liberated from its restrictive meaning as writing or speech."[29] He also assigns a special role to the "infinite play of differences," but he insists that it does not derive so much from the internal dynamism of specific texts as from the social space:

> The great advance carried out by structuralism was the recognition of the relational character of any social identity; its limit was its transformation of those relations into a system, into an identifiable and intelligible object (i.e., into an essence). But if we maintain the relational character of any identity and if, at the same time, we renounce the fixation of those identities in a system, then the social must be identified with the infinite play of differences, that is, with what in the strictest sense of the term we can call *discourse*—on the condition, of course, that we liberate the concept of discourse from its restrictive meaning as speech and writing. . . . The social always exceeds the limits of the attempts to constitute society. At the same time, however, that "totality" does not disappear: if the suture it attempts is ultimately impossible, it is nevertheless possible to proceed to a relative fixation of the social through the institution of nodal points.[30]

Laclau assigns the key notion of "excess in meaning" to the sphere of the social, or what he terms "the infinitude of the social," whose contours always exceed the limits of representational order or any unitary concept of society. An understanding of "excess" as an interplay pertaining to the social sphere constitutes an interesting contrast with literary deconstructionism that tends to locate this phenomenon only in writing or relies heavily on a standard binary between language and the social, whereby the former is inherently excessive and the latter enclosing. Laclau disturbs that handy binary by introducing a different set of oppositions: the distinction between the social and society, as well as the distinction between the social and both speech and writing. Laclau's conceptualization of discourse allow us to redraw those boundaries, not only in a closer reading of his own book, but also as a propaedeutic for understanding *The Lettered City*. Moreover, a social grounding of excess enables us to open a space of discursive negotiation and contestation that goes beyond literary heteroglossia. This in turn augments the notion of textuality in significant ways: (1) the realm of the social includes ongoing political and economic conflicts that destabilize a critical practice whose radical claims seldom dare go beyond the shelter of distant texts and the inner sanctum of academic institutions; (2) it disrupts the conceptual slide that neutralizes pertinent differences between signifiers such as literature, writing, epistemology, and finally the social. As Laclau maneuvers around these theoretical turns, he arrives at a paradoxical juncture also present in Rama's text: the constant dissemination within the social makes it impossible to articulate society as a totality, yet that totality does not disappear, because the social is never reducible to "the constant interplay of differences" but instead can also respond to attempts to limit that interplay, that is, the forces that seek to "contain it within the confines of a given order." Inasmuch as it is a totality, society is unattainable; but it is possible to proceed toward a relative construction of the social through nodal points that are "subject to different determinations and overdeterminations."[31]

Laclau's articulation typifies how inherently flexible Saussurean metalanguage can be, and how immanently transferable its central conduits have become. It could be said that the historic *langue/parole* split that informs Derrida's center/margin opposition, or Homi Bhabha's pedagogy/performance divide, is here transferred to a different terrain, as Laclau attempts to examine the society/the social interplay. This reorientation of the Saussurean binary is also evident in Rama's earlier attempt to demarcate the lettered city from the real city. Needless to say, it remains to be seen whether any poststructural articulation that leans on a binary opposition or split is finally able to escape its structural limitations. Flirting with binaries leaves it unclear if they are ever really abandoned, rather than just momentarily submerged to be reinstated once again. What Laclau and Rama introduce in to this persistent problematic is a specific attempt to extend the play of differences and semiotic excess to the broadly social and cultural domains. More important, for Rama, society is represented by the complicity between social order and writing in the lettered cities during the colonial period. Both are breached only by the social as represented by the excesses of meaning found in Amerindian orality, in the marginal spaces of colonial everyday life, and in the hybrid chaos of urban centers attempting to modernize: "with their leagues of unknown people, their constant waves of construction and demolition, their accelerated rhythms, and the mutations introduced by their new customs."[32] Rama's real city is therefore not stably demarcated, innocent, unitary. It is instead a relational matrix stemming from a representational crisis that composes the interplay of excesses inherent in a far-reaching set of social nodes that organize Latin America's epistemic horizon: city/countryside, elite/popular, resistance/complicity, Americanism/Eurocentrism, writing/orality, among others. Rama's real/lettered city dyad could thus be understood as an attempt to grasp social forms and contents that tend to escape more stable demarcations of the binary model:

> Seen from the ardent infiltration of our everyday experiences, and from a past that we transport secretly within us, and inside the texture of our dreams, it is possible to suspect that the ideal city did not copy a precise European model over the Western shore of the Atlantic, as it has been often said of our always mimetic upper classes. But those cities were also an invention made with an appreciable margin of originality; they were daughters of a desire that is freer than all the real models, and even more frenzied. Moreover, given their aspiration to become *real-izable*, they would enter into a murky amalgam with the surrounding reality.[33]

Such a reading of colonial desire entails a double movement: it discards the simple idea of representational mimesis, or governing conventional accounts of the relations between writing and the social, while claiming a space somewhere between the real and the real-izable. The latter aspect can only be understood through Rama's concept of orality as transculturation, that is, as the aggregate of multiple languages that converge on Latin America's popular culture: alternative modes of writing, undecidable gestures, and marginal, resistant modes of signifying that include a historical understanding of graffiti and musical forms such as *corridos* and tangos. He observes, for example, that the popular novel *El Periquillo Sarniento*, published in 1816 by the Mexican writer José Joaquín Fernández de Lizardi, "is much more of a threat to the lettered city than to the Spanish monarchy, or even the Catholic church."[34]

It should be emphasized that Rama is concerned with a form of orality that deviates substantially from Derrida's notion of speech as "presence." In his critique of the Western philosophical tradition, Derrida carefully deconstructs presence as the presumed authority of oral speech, behind which there always lies an arche-writing of sorts. For Rama, however, orality does not constitute a cult of originary presence; rather, it names an internal gaze directed at the colonial and neocolonial forms of epistemic excess, an attempt to delve into the discursive resources of the Creole verbal order from the colonial epoch to our times. A key moment in this order appears in the problem of linguistic transmission of American words to the narrative structures of Spanish language, a topic that Rama traces through various important writers over a period of three centuries. It is found in the reconversion of legal codes of Carlos de Sigüenza y Góngora, as well as the *costumbrista* novel filled with glossaries, and is later turned into theories of the Latin American Baroque by the contemporary Cuban novelist Alejo Carpentier. Here we see another instance of a colonial residue, for, according to Rama, Carpentier remains caught in this lingering problem of American linguistic reconversion inasmuch as he only manages to substitute for previous glossaries a new code of metalinguistic explication.[35]

Reconversion, the process of translating Latin American languages and cultures into Spanish narrative forms, becomes a preoccupation among Latin American writers whom Rama also attempts to deconstruct, in his profoundly alternative ways, through his own understanding of radical transculturation. Perhaps the most elaborate example he gives is the social thought of Simón Rodríguez, which "is situated in a pre-Saussurean, anti-Derridean line, and which recognizes in language an oral tradition independent of writing that is formed in a rather different way."[36] It should be noted here that Rama's work exhibits frequent traces of engagement with continental critics and philosophers such as Adorno, Lévi-Strauss, Gilles Deleuze, Félix Guattari, and Foucault, particularly in his last books. It is not evident how much of an opportunity he had to study Derrida before he died, but it is clear he is aware of how the latter structures his critique of orality and Western logocentrism in *De la grammatologie* (1967).[37] Rama even makes an allusion to Jean-Jacques Rousseau's *Essay on the Origin of Languages* by way of a quotation from Simón Rodríguez that is both subtle and complex in its possible reading of Derrida's critique. The mystical force often ascribed to Rousseau's sense of oral speech, a self-sufficient medium that organizes society as an organic totality, is not Rama's interest. He understands orality as a site where the difficult crisscrossing of chronologies and discourses becomes history. This is best illustrated in his bid to locate historical change in oral traditions that are otherwise unavailable to the notion of myth proposed by Lévi-Strauss:

> Orality modulates itself within a cultural flow that is in permanent composition and transformation. Lévi-Strauss's observation that all variants compose the same myth is still pertinent to this matter. But orality allows us to recognize how the adaptation of different concrete circumstances takes place. It also allows us to introduce what amounts to a historical factor that is often difficult to measure from within the myths of aboriginal cultures, but which is more attainable through the verbal inventiveness of rural cultures. Through that historical factor we can ascertain new variants within traditional flows that generally seem atemporal, thereby illustrating how historical circumstances are adapted.[38]

Rama's critiques of structuralism and poststructuralism make clear how his work is situated in a significant chapter of Latin America's own encounter with the theoretical legacy that runs through Foucault and Derrida. It is also clear that even if Rama does not offer a close reading of these key European sources, he brings them to a pivotal give-and-take with his previous essays and research projects, themselves in constant theoretical and thematic movement. It could further be said that, like Derrida, Rama understands orality as a sort of arche-writing that constitutes a historical order sustained by norms, hierarchies, and verbal oppositions, even if he differs with Derrida over whether writing can be opposed to orality on a universal plane. The reason for that quibble emerges when Rama's own casting of orality diverges from the Saussurean legacy of structuralist and poststructuralist signification. As the passage cited earlier illustrates, Rama finds a central example of subaltern orality in some Latin American rural cultures. Another instance would be found in the multiple transcultural relationships he sees between writing and orality, a nonsynchronous text that springs from Latin America as a multilingual, multiethnic, and multinational construct. Rama's linguistic model—also underscored in the work of linguists and anthropologists such as Eugenio Coseriu and Martin Lienhard—is more hybrid in its appropriation of different alphabetic forms and colonial models of writing than those available to Western metaphysics and its more contemporary revisions.

There is ample room to disagree over how Rama's work may be understood today, but it seems clear that the main set of concerns guiding it is increasingly evident. *The Lettered City* endeavors to bring the social text and colonial residues within the range of poststructural theory. The former is obviously the central concern of cultural studies, the latter of postcolonialism. Furthermore, it could be argued that both aspects constitute an index of the shortcomings implicit in the poststructural methods that Rama somehow managed to detect fifteen years earlier. Perhaps I can illustrate this point by appealing to a text mentioned earlier—Walter Mignolo's *The Darker Side of the Renaissance*—which sets forth a political history of orality and the different writerly systems that were prevalent during Latin America's colonial period. The pivotal moment in this book, notwithstanding the author's unsuccessful attempts to downplay its implications, is an extensive examination of Derridean presuppositions in the contexts of colonial philology and semiotics. Mignolo, an Argentine critic originally trained as a philologist and semiotician, attempts to provide a comparative linguistic history of orality, which he sees as the basis for a potential school of Latin American postcolonial studies. What follows is an enumeration of the most important propositions that Mignolo finds wanting in Derrida's work. Together they provide not only a different accent on orality, but also an attempt to underscore the role of orality in the history of imperialism that reveals striking parallels with Rama's main postulates.

- Derrida's crucial insights do not transcend a certain evolutionary prejudice. They presuppose that with the invention of the alphabet, the history of writing takes a road that overcomes all alternative forms.
- There are nonalphabetical forms of writing as well as alternative forms to the Greco-Roman alphabet.
- One could begin with the grammars of Antonio de Nebrija instead of Rousseau: for Nebrija, the letter did not represent the voice, but the domestication of voice, a crucial step in the constitution of contemporary imperial states, as well as in the colonization of non-Western languages.
- During the colonial expansion, certain systems of writing sustained a different relationship between writing and the sounds of language that complicates the evolutionary history of letters in the Western tradition.
- Western logocentrism shows its limits when it confronts forms of knowledge and meaning that are based on alternative forms of speech and writing.

- The deconstruction of Western metaphysics is not preoccupied with the structure of power that allowed alphabetic writing to establish a hierarchy of cultures that in turn allowed the extension of its image of superiority.[39]

Horst Ruthrof argues in his *Semantics and the Body* that linguistically dominated literary theories have failed to include the "re-emergence of the corporeal in the linguistic structures which they emphasize,"[40] thereby echoing Édouard Glissant's *Caribbean Discourse* in the call for a new post-colonial understanding of the ways in which orality and the body unhinge the reification of writing. By "corporeal," Ruthrof means a realm of language that defies the predominantly syntactical enclosure inherent in theories derived from Saussurean epistemology. Although he finds Derrida's work slightly less driven to that enclosure (in comparison to, say, Jean Baudrillard, Paul de Man, or Jean-François Lyotard), he insists that "the discrepancy of reference and speech modalities" must be dealt with through an intersemiotic and heterosemiotic engagement that the theories based on the linguistic turn are unlikely to offer, particularly for multicultural societies, which "can only be enriched by the inevitable modification of standard meaning events by alternative representations."[41]

Dissemination and Reordering

The Lettered City has a wayward quality about it, perhaps the only appropriate manner for an essay that takes so many risks and dares so much. As I have argued, this text constitutes a pronounced shift from Rama's previous essays on Latin American modernism and contemporary narrative that is best viewed in the continuum of contemporary theoretical work, itself filled with trials and errors during the past three decades. Only in that sense of accumulated dispersal could one see Rama's text peeping from his Latin American outpost into the contemporary postmodern sense of chaos. We may ask, however, if the 1990s did not shift that sense of dispersal toward a reordering of sorts, to a logic of privatization and the market often misread as just academic wars over the fate of print culture. This has no doubt led to a certain urgency in the work of theory, evident, for example, in such otherwise different texts as Derrida's *Spectres of Marx* and Aijaz Ahmad's *In Theory*. Each struggles, in distinct but analogous ways, to register the drama of this particular moment, to see how our present is a legacy filled with attainment as well as contradictions, revisions, and misplaced bets. Rama's work should not be exempt from that urgency. His work affords the possibility of grasping margins, supplements, and residues from Latin American cultural history to question that privilege generally reserved for literary masters as the only story worth retelling, or deconstructing. That wayward articulation takes us to an alternative reading of Latin America's discursive dispersal, that is, to Rama's categories of colonial residue discussed earlier: subaltern social thought, subversive orthography, the social realm as epistemic excess, peripheral modernity as real-izable cities, unlettered revolutions, and the languages of graffiti, tangos, and *corridos*.

The questions raised by Rama have an undeniably contemporary tenor. They can be correlated within the contradictory sense in which today's cultural studies and postcolonial thought simultaneously attempt to challenge and invoke the same theoretical legacy of the past three decades. I would add that Rama's work leads to an appraisal of the conflictive impact of global capitalism and market forces on cultural formation that currently confounds theoretical work. I am referring to the voices that now seek to contain and reorder discursive dispersal from within the bosom of Western art and philosophy. An emblematic instance is Harold Bloom's *The Western Canon*. Bloom warns that we have lost a sense of values in literary study, and that the primacy of great Western literature has come under siege from a new gendered, multicultural context. It is important to ask here, I believe, how one of the most influential figures in U.S. literary criticism comes to terms not so much with contemporary theory, but with the social text surrounding it. It could be said, following Rama's critical categories, that Bloom has identified the postmodern "real city" as consigned by an indifferentiated catalog of alternative cultural studies textuality threatening to claim too big a space in U.S. universities. Bloom labors to expose the contemporary academy, but his main philippic is aimed at the absence of aesthetic sensibility in today's social realm.

How might we take Bloom's charge seriously, and to what extent is Rama's work relevant here? Bloom seems to be asking us if we have not witnessed, or perhaps even abetted, the process of debasing academic disciplines and their object of study. But who is to blame for this degradation? New generations of assistant professors insufficiently refined? Universities restructured by privatizing globalization? The enlarged domain of mass media? Greater access to education on the part of women and racial minorities? Interdisciplinary cultural studies? New genres of autobiographical narcissism? These have admittedly produced extraordinary tensions, but the question of contemporary aesthetics and sensibility requires a more nuanced reading of the social text than is given by Bloom. Consider Néstor García Canclini's description of a new Latin American urban citizenry:

> Forty years after the electronic media took over the public sphere and became the principal formative agent of the collective imaginary, the

ministries of culture continue to be fully committed to the fine arts. In the best of cases, they also concern themselves a bit with traditional popular cultures, but they almost never have anything to say or do about modern urban cultures such as rock, tabloid narratives, photo-narratives, videos, in short, the media that move the thought and sensibilities of the masses. They are therefore disengaged from the scenarios of consumption that constitute what we could perhaps call the aesthetic basis of citizenship.[42]

Is it possible to reconcile the theoretical work of the past three decades, a process that originally included an enthusiastic younger Bloom, with the dynamic marketing of contemporary cultural forms and imaginaries? Are spaces for critique and contestation still available? Three responses are typically given: (1) make the university a pillar of resistance for the lettered values in force prior to postmodern dispersion and cultural studies; (2) redraw the boundaries of critical and artistic values originally promulgated by post-structural theory to accommodate the neoliberal reordering of the academy through market logic and cultural studies; (3) configure a new set of critical and aesthetic relations out of diverse cultural forms, critical theories, and market strategies. Rama, in my view, speaks to the third alternative, even though his frame of reference remains largely literary. Bloom, on the other hand, appears to long for the autonomous space afforded to good taste implicit in the first response. But Bloom's agenda is arguably more complex and could be said to approximate the second position in certain ways. His aim is not quite to reestablish the exclusivity of traditional humanistic order, but rather to reorder literary studies on the basis of a new canon of world literature capable of including a few non-European authors that could be organically translated into English. This program implies the possibility of a global hermeneutic based on a somewhat expanded corpus, a community of readers guarded by well-trained professionals, and enough well-funded, or at least sustainable, libraries and university presses. Global, though still largely Western, literature would then reach a higher level of universality than was known to the modernist paradigm, while at the same time it would depend less on the exigencies of localized cultural distinctions still spawned by global marketing. The constitution of a world literary canon, produced through English translations, would then be able to return value to literary studies, reaffirming at the same time the institutional space of tradition in the face of the mass-mediatic dispersion of academic disciplines. Such would be a deeper account of Bloom's alternative reordering: a post-postmodern realignment of theoretical dispersal inspired by a previous order, a move to transcend the most transgressive elements of the poststructuralist legacy. It is not clear, however, if Bloom's literary sensibility could absorb the pressures of a modified canon sufficiently expanded to cover the world in any meaningful way. It is also not clear that one language can bear the weight of literary hierarchy and simultaneously serve as the currency of exchange through translation. A monolingual concept of comparative literature could well sustain a "world literature," but even though English provides the prism through which transnational literary valuation is refracted, it is quite likely that this more catholic form of literariness will be transformed by cultural forces and new readings it cannot really dissipate. Indeed, as the lingua franca of globalization, English may already be compromised as a true conduit of Western canon formation, for the House of English is now filled with permanent guests for whom the distinction between a native and a second language has been permanently transformed.

These same disjunctions are even clearer in the work of Richard Rorty, a prominent figure in contemporary American philosophy. His latest books and essays seek to define more concretely the confrontation between postmodern theory, the old lettered order, and global cultural dispersion.[43] He argues that Derridean deconstruction and Foucauldian critique of metanarratives should be understood more as a continuation of, rather than a rupture within, Western hermeneutics. Furthermore, he claims that they are only meaningful in the space of literature, philosophy, and the fine arts. Hence, a profoundly equivocal dispersion of values takes place when these theories are taken to the space of popular culture, politics, or the social. In such transferrals, they become displacements prone to take too seriously the liberationist projections implicit in those discourses, as if one could really create a utopian moment from them, or the social radicalism of modern metanarratives could be preserved through them. Somewhat analogously to the end of history theories proposed by Francis Fukuyama, Rorty insists that postmodernity has no need to aspire to new horizons; it needs only to consolidate the values and institutions of what he calls the "North Atlantic Postmodern Bourgeois Democracies," taking into consideration that these constitute the truly postmodern model, because they have been able to "take privacy to the highest degree known to history, encompassing an unequaled margin of individual gratification, opinions, lifestyles, and means of self-promotion."[44] The new subject of these communities, like its philosophers, participates in a self-sufficient internal dialogue that has no need for a new theoretical universality. Thus, the attendant critiques of its metanarratives by this hermeneutical tradition only respond to its own immanent adjustments, and the problematics of difference derived therefrom do not imply a reduction of the space between public and private morality, but rather the knowledge that there is nothing beyond of any consequence. Only a reflexive writerly exploration of these traditions is valuable or necessary.[45]

Many readers of Foucault, Derrida, or de Man, including an entire generation of Latin American critics trained in U.S. universities formed by their work, may be somewhat surprised by Bloom's and Rorty's alternative reordering. Up to now, there was always the thought that attendant upon the deconstruction of modernity there remained a breath of liberationist spirit, an impulse or a flutter conjured by a new epistemology that would reinvent or rewrite history, even if it meant a more localized sense of justice and a less ambitious recipe for collective well-being. But the self-sufficiency of that promise has lost some of its force, as is evident in Derrida's own attempt to recast it by reverting to the emancipatory specters of Marx's different sense of promise.[46] More than a surprise, Bloom's and Rorty's proposals suggest an index, or a symptom, of how theoretical work scrambles to respond to a threatening dislocation it had not suspected. García Canclini's call for a new concept of citizenry is undoubtedly informed by a different response to the same challenge. In this context, one can see that Rama's essay provides an early sign of these very symptoms. He sets out to split the high/low cultural binary that is typically preserved in even the most radical theoretical work. More important, the radical force of capitalism's ceaseless revolutionizing, which is deeply inscribed in Latin America's cultural history, assumes a central role in his theoretical categories.

How will humanist and posthumanist theory draw lessons from its invaluable past while producing at the same time a more dynamic critique of a social text in which the private ambitions of all subjects, including those with few resources, are constantly stimulated through fandom, consumerism, and other attempts to market imaginaries? If that inventory is a significant part of aesthetic experience in contemporary societies, it is not clear how a monolingual world literary canon will respond to it. It is also doubtful that the aggregate of North Atlantic Postmodern Bourgeois Democracies provides even a pragmatic register of that inventory of excess, and much less a critical one. Rama's work commands our attention in this context. Notwithstanding the totalizing impulse of *The Lettered City*'s archaeological reach, some of its premises remain powerful and provocative. Rama recognized that cultural forms, like words, are profoundly transformative but can hardly constitute autonomous forms of resistance. What is required, according to Rama, would be a more complex understanding of how human desires and the excesses of meaning are continuously drafted by both the discourses of culture and market forces. Without this engagement, which Rama approached with the conviction of a theoretical heretic, the work of theory remains trapped inside the "lettered cities"; at best, it can only return to them in calculated gestures of lamentation and nostalgia, a strategy that will prove inadequate to revitalize the dynamic elements of the Western tradition at this particular moment of global capitalism. In any contest between market forces and cultural nostalgia, the latter must perforce become the tool, however unwittingly, of the former.

6
Globalization, Neoliberalism, and Cultural Studies

Adults try to cope with the challenge of change by "using their heads," trusting in logic, and drawing on experience. But as kids we followed our hearts as much as our heads. We trusted our creative instincts, our intuition, because our logical thinking skills had not yet developed. And since we had not been around long enough to learn much from the past, we did not get trapped by our old solutions. We did not get hung up on tradition.

"Act like a Child," in Culture Shift:
The Employee Handbook for Changing Corporate Culture

There is something attractive in the idea of learning to unlearn, in the invitation to contemporaneity, in the vitality of forgetfulness. But, is this levity what we want to claim as an aesthetic for our everyday lives?

Martin Hopenhayn, Ni apocalípticos ni integrados

"Globalization" strives to name our current epoch, to signify it with a grandiosity and imprecision available to no other term. New investment and communications frontiers, more opportunities and markets for everyone, mass culture across national borders—globalization conjures utopian images as if guided by remote control and inexhaustible benevolence. Beyond that propitious surface, globalization also signals an intensified fusion of cultural, political, and financial interests that closely correlates with postmodern constructs in the cultural terrain and neoliberalism in the political sphere. Each term accentuates a different angle, yet all three—globalization, postmodernism, and neoliberalism—have come to occupy the same horizon. They respond to a logic that fuses marketing, culture, and politics into a performative doctrine not far from a new metanarrative. As signifiers go, particularly those that float between the academy and new cultural production, globalization by now may have overshadowed postmodernism inasmuch as market forces entail their own radical critique of modern traditions. Neoliberalism, on the other hand, is not commonly used by cultural critics in the United

States to describe the reigning political philosophy of globalization.[1] Given the once great tradition of American liberalism, it would seem natural to resist naming something so contrary with a term so morphologically close. In Latin America, on the other hand, the postmodern cultural logic is almost unavailable without a neoliberal political sense, and both are increasingly absorbed by the engulfing rhetoric of globalization.

In any case, regardless of terminological inclinations, any attempt to depict today's cultural logic is bound to meet lexical equivocation. The postmodern scene is riddled with many alarming shifts, not all of them confined to the sphere of academic disciplines. In the United States, for instance, public distress over labor markets, media content, migration control, and the preservation of English as the national language is on the rise. Indeed, the idea of a blissful bond between cultural and commercial interests so inherent to globalization met its limits during the 1990s, leading to deeper questions of national and regional identity in many parts of the world: France contested GATT (General Agreement on Tariffs and Trade) over the right to subsidize its film industry; conservative Midwestern groups in the United States formed armed militias that view the federal government as an agent of foreign financial interests; labor unions in Mexico and the United States are becoming transnational as a strategy against globalization; Mayan Indians in Mexico's Chiapas state continue to struggle against NAFTA (North American Free Trade Agreement) for the right to cultivate corn on a scale commensurate with indigenous traditions and modernizing needs. This chapter will move from Latin Americanism to pursue its conditions of possibility in the question of the role performed by the language of humanistic theory in the new global order.

The Chilean theorist Martin Hopenhayn has made a point of studying the "synchrony between the market offensive and a cofunctional postmodernist cultural sensitizing."[2] By market offensive, Hopenhayn means, of course, neoliberalism, a term that is quite prevalent in Latin America and other parts of the developing world where the 1970s and 1980s failed to usher in a new age of unwavering optimism and expanding economies. Neoliberal political doctrine, according to Hopenhayn, spells out certain features that are obviously cofunctional with globalization as well as postmodernism: the market is understood as the only social institution that provides order without coercion, politics and the state lose their transformational capacity except when they seek privatization, consumerism becomes inherently emancipatory in the absence of liberationist discourses, critique of utopias is largely reserved for egalitarian utopias, and the blanket deconstruction of modernizing schemes transforms structural underdevelopment into healthy examples of diversity and localized heterogeneity.[3]

Neoliberal precepts evidently translate today's cultural logic of ambiguity in a more blatant fashion, accentuating a political wisdom whose contentious repercussions are now becoming more evident than the celebrated sense of liminality of postmodernism and the free-floating expansionism of globalization. The Argentine cultural theorist Néstor García Canclini argues for the need to acknowledge this shift in the following terms:

> I believe that an anthropological relativism that rests on a simple acknowledgment of floating differences has shown sufficient limitations for us not to stay there. The need to construct a way of knowing that is interculturally valid becomes all the more imperative in an epoch in which cultures and societies are constantly confronted in various spheres and markets: economic, communicational, migration, and tourism. We have a dire need for political and everyday practices that are based in a transcultural ethics, sustained by ways of knowing that combine the acknowledgment of different social styles with rational norms of multiethnic and supranational modes of coexistence.[4]

Such a broadening scope may well prove vital, not only for academic research on globalization, but for inquiry into the changing roles of education and universities. Market values have become an unspecified sort of wisdom in a post–Cold War period that brings all areas of knowledge and research under review. In the United States, this scrutiny finds its most dramatic instance in the ongoing national focus on humanistic scholarship and teaching, in which privatizing strategies occupy an increasingly central role. Thus far, this has only yielded perplexing questions that kindle academic and political debates regarding the ways in which culturally oriented disciplines— once core elements of a liberal education—have responded to new historical pressures during the past few decades. Most important among these questions are perhaps those pertaining to the changing role of theory, writing, and marketing in new humanistic research.

In his book on contemporary American writers (Norman Mailer, Thomas Pynchon, Joseph McElroy, and Don DeLillo), Joseph Tabbi observes that "literary ambition and the cult of originality has reached hitherto unheard-of intensities in a technological age where performance, the conversion of mind and raw talent into a visible and negotiable product, is the only recognized value."[5] Similar performative pressures abound in the world of critical and theoretical production. Many scholars now see themselves primarily as writers who look on discourse production as an end in itself. Such work draws much of its force from an inward look at literary, cultural, and philosophical traditions, as well as from the search for specialized metadiscourses. It could be argued that poststructuralist paradigms gave initial form and content to much of this production, but many of its central features are now predominant in a generalized way. From the more epistemic postmodern forms and styles of writing, to literary deconstructionism and new historicism, to the more socially bound cultural, gender, and ethnic studies, avenues and expectations for publication have continued to escalate in the recent past. Two seemingly disparate elements are featured in this research economy: rhetorical self-consciousness and an accelerated production of texts. Both have also successfully, and at times imaginatively, responded to an ever-growing demand from print and electronic sources. Needless to say, humanistic research is not immune to the hypereconomy. Much less obvious, however, may be the notion that within such a culture, writing and market forces mirror each other with particular intensity.

Attention to the complicity of language and narration in the formation of conceptual thought is arguably the most salient feature of contemporary literary research. Roland Barthes's notion of writing as an intransitive transaction, Paul de Man's emphasis on rhetoric and troping as master codes of polysemia, Jacques Derrida's call for incessant designification and hypercriticism as a form of agency, Judith Butler's gender performativity as feminist praxis, and Homi Bhabha's theoretical lyricism as postcolonial politics are but a few examples of a burgeoning sense of novelty spanning various generations of writerly critics. Inventiveness, imagination, formal exploration—indeed, many of the powerful aspects of creative writing—are no longer foreign to the production of critical discourses, imbued as they are by a new sensitivity to knowledge production as verbal process. Both patrons and critics of postmodernism acknowledge its commanding presence in today's critical horizons—an experience of the sublime for Jean-François Lyotard, an apotheosis for Slavoj Žižek. In that sense, "writing" has acquired a meaning all its own, signifying a new ontological frontier that overpowers whatever differences remain at play within various new theoretical methods. As the following critique by Terry Eagleton attests, even Marxist critics who champion the need to "always historicize" speak through the lineaments of such paradigms:

> Style in Jameson is the excess or self-delight which escapes even his own most strenuously analytical habits, that which slips through the very dialectical forms it so persuasively delineates. This, rather than the discussions of Bloch or Marcuse, is the truly utopian dimension of

his work, a shadowy presence coupled at every point to his analyses, a lateral gesture so all-pervasive that, like utopia or desire itself, it refuses definitive figuration and echoes in the mind simply as the rhetorical *verso* or buzz of inexhaustible implications of his grand narrative themes.[6]

Eagleton's spotlight on Fredric Jameson's rhetorical fervor is a valiant attempt to straddle a fine line. He would like to insist that Jameson is far from confusing or conflating the demands of criticism with those of creative writing, but he must also concede that he sees in Jameson's style how the growing awareness of the workings of language has greatly enhanced our understanding of performativity in all forms of discourse, most particularly in those disciplines that shape our sense of historical, political, and aesthetic values. Indeed, that line remains quite difficult to straddle, not only for Marxists, but for other historically oriented modes of analysis as well. Although the new focus on rhetoric and troping informs the contention that writing constitutes a new way of examining the status quo, it remains to be seen how such a claim performs as a critical instrument beyond the realm of academic discourses. Weaving literary and philosophical motifs without further rigors can give way to a politics of writing willing to cash in the conceptual presuppositions of research for writerly practices whose relationship to knowledge production and dissemination deserves much greater scrutiny.

It is not that easy, however, to find a space where the links between rhetorical prowess and theoretical discourse can be submitted to a broader social debate without succumbing to ideological harangues. One hesitates to even approach the Alan Sokal incident in 1996, but some of its symptoms remain heuristically valuable for an exploration of those very links. The *New York Times* gave front-page coverage to an article by Sokal titled "Postmodern Gravity Deconstructed, Slyly." With a clearly chosen tone of mockery, the opening paragraph proclaimed: "A New York University physicist, fed up with what he sees as the excesses of the academic left, hoodwinked a well-known journal into publishing a parody thick with gibberish as though it were serious scholarly work."[7] Professor Sokal's prank fueled many ongoing academic debates, even though it only glossed their most critical aspects in the most superficial manner. Sokal's essay had been submitted to *Social Text,* a journal dedicated to theoretical and cultural studies in humanities and some social sciences. The piece was accepted and published in a special issue on the relationship between scientific research, documented facts, and the cultural construction of scholarly disciplines and discourses. Sokal's admitted aim was to ridicule such research—its methods of proof, style of argumentation, and peer-review process—by replicating it in the most convincing fashion, that is, with semiobscure clichés linking physics, epistemic relativism, and an overall absence of foundational truths. Sokal added that his antic was executed not only on behalf of factual scientific knowledge, but also as a man of the left who spent various summers teaching math in Nicaragua, and as a self-described feminist.

In response, the *Times* published a Op-Ed piece by Stanley Fish a few days later. In a lengthy, hermetically argued essay, Fish explained the difference between the physical properties of the real world and accounts of that world that are produced by observers and "are therefore relative to their capacities, education, training, etc."[8] In his defense of discourse analysis and the intrinsically linguistic nature of knowledge and disciplines, Fish added that "it is not the world or its properties but the vocabularies in whose terms we know them that are socially constructed—fashioned by human beings—which is why our understanding of those properties is continually changing."[9] Fish's response, though free of jargon and meticulously argued, nonetheless failed to address the most ardent question at the bottom of Sokal's hoax: Has the focus on the socially constructed nature of disciplines lent itself to a predictable and easily obtained pedagogy of rhetorical devices as performance? Is such a pedagogy more conducive to a trendy style of writing than to Fish's own methods of arguing the workings of intellectual history? Are there journals all too willing to publish theoretical work of that sort? Is there a significant market for it? Even more important, he failed to explain the rhetorical appeal of Sokal's original text, regardless of his avowed intention. At the very center of the *Times's* title page, in a box framed with large scare quotes, a double-spaced citation of Sokal's well-versed mimicry reads: "the μ of Euclid and the *G* of Newton, formerly thought to be constant and universal, are now perceived in their ineluctable historicity; and the putative observer becomes fatally decentered, disconnected from any epistemic link to a space-time point."[10]

Poststructural and postmodern modes of critique are old enough to have created their own myths. One such myth could be that were it not for the work of key figures such as Paul de Man, Michel Foucault, and Jacques Derrida, humanistic discourse would have remained properly focused on traditional aesthetic values and proven historical grounds. Such thinking not only fails to account for the profound differences between these theorists but, more important, it fails to account for the revolutionary energy of contemporary capitalism, particularly its impact on cultural forms and academic boundaries. This is an aspect that neither Sokal, nor Fish, nor the

New York Times seemed willing to consider in their eagerness to attack or defend an entire array of different disciplines—cultural studies, speech acts, deconstruction, feminism, and postmodernism—as an undifferentiated constellation of symptoms detached from the rest of society. Very few critical projects attempt to contextualize these theoretical paradigms or their key figures, either locally in their diversity and contradictions or in a truly transnational framework that brings specificity to cultural dispersal, neoliberalism, and globalization. Interestingly enough, the most notable examples of such scrutiny correspond to the work of diasporic and Third World women theorists for whom in-betweenness incurs more than epistemological liminality. One thinks of Gayatri Chakravorty Spivak's attempt to advance a postcolonial critique of Foucauldian and mainstream deconstruction, or Beatriz Sarlo's readings of Argentinean neoliberalism, or Nelly Richard's work on postmodern cultural debates in Chile during the late 1980s and early 1990s.[11]

Indeed, what is often left unexamined is that the academy is hardly a place that fosters radical paradigms, and that disciplinary shifts and theoretical discourse owe much more to the marketing strategies that call on graduate programs, academic journals, publishing presses, and professional conferences to produce and disseminate innovative academic texts with a higher degree of commercial self-awareness than ever before. Novelty as immanence and self-referentiality turns into agency in the commodification of knowledge that ultimately codifies writerly products in the academic marketplace. "The mechanisms of corporate capitalism," writes Tabbi, "have by now evolved to the point where they are themselves a kind of avant-garde, fomenting a state of constant revolution in international markets that is not to be 'resisted' by the subtlest postmodern irony or the most inventive of aesthetic intelligentsias."[12] What these strategies have mainstreamed, in the context of postmodernity, globalization, or neoliberalism, is a basic set of new critical positions that are no less relevant to contemporary economic realities than to new theoretical knowledge: skepticism toward the living social text, a shifting conception of difference as privatized theoretical agency, and a new frontier of criticism as performative art.

More than cultural debates, or relativism, theoretical work continued to energize new strands of humanistic research during the 1990s, albeit in the midst of a more complex understanding of theory, as the contradictory constellation of cultural, political, and economic affairs intensifies. Nelly Richard writes of "a diffuse feeling" that accompanies contemporary epochal changes, an enveloping confusion "marked by the *dissemination* and *contamination* of meaning: a crisis of totality and pluralization of the fragment, a crisis of singularity and a multiplication of differences."[13] Recent scholarship on postcolonial and cultural studies draws energy from this diffusion, even though these approaches are increasingly aware of the need to bridge new aesthetic and philosophical practices with other intellectual communities, and, more important, with the public sphere.[14] For others, such as Harold Bloom and Richard Rorty, the most pressing need would be the opposite: to find ways of negotiating a return of the deconstructive legacy back to established aesthetic principles of Western traditions, in the hope of detaining the most deleterious effects of globalization and neoliberalism on the academy. But the efficacy of theory-laden discourse must be examined not only within the world of humanistic scholarship, but also in the marketing of avant-garde products and practices. Whether as self-referential agency, intransitive self-reflection, or designifying performance, "writing as research" resonates with "the real" in ways that are often unexpected.

In a brilliant book titled *Semantics and the Body*, which I will quote at some length, Horst Ruthrof provides the most systematic explanation of how postmodern writing resonates with globalization. "The postmodern," he explains,

> can be observed in the flattening of the semantics by way of hyperbole. If everything is hyperbolic, nothing is. The postmodern is a style of superterms not only in art but also in the culture of technology. We speak of supercolliders, superconductivity, superstrings, superfluidity, supervacancy, supercomputers, SuperCALC, supercommunication, the "hyperreal," the "hypertelic," and let us not forget the information superhighway and the infobahn. Yet there seems little doubt that the flatline effect of the superterm style conceals its oppositional shadow: the intensification of hierarchization and the possibilities of control.[15]

From this perspective, I would argue that Sokal's piece could perhaps be seen as a form of discursive mimicry that draws from technoscientific as much as cultural hyperbole, which explains the ease with which he managed to bridge two cultures of research into one stylistic gloss. According to Ruthrof, the conditions of possibility for a postmodern politics depend on our awareness that "there are features in both the postmodern nontechnical and technoscientific discourses which display affinities of a kind and degree absent in previous social structures. I propose to look at this at least partly repressed Other of the postmodern in terms of the digital as a radically reduced syntax."[16] Indeed, could we not see in these affinities how academic paradigms and their attendant markets work through language and rhetoric to unhinge subjects from their ontological bearings, as Sokal's mimicry admirably registers with much greater acuity than the excesses of cultural studies? "Looking at discursivity," adds Ruthrof, "as a gradation from culturally saturated discourses—such as jokes, the literary, myth, or everyday speech—to technical and formal language, we can observe a fundamental reduction of reference and a deixis towards zero."[17] Hence, I would argue, what seems to have been lost in the legacy of the "linguistic turn" and its scientific critics is that such writing does not simply impose itself from the ivory tower, but rather is the preferred idiom for capturing the very diffuse essence of contemporary capitalism. Again, I turn to Ruthrof for a comprehensive attempt to explain this apparent paradox:

> At the metaphenomenal level of postmodern theorization the digital syntax shines through in an emphasis on discontinuities (Foucault), dissemination, antitelos, and différance (Derrida), and a war against totalization (Lyotard). Yet here we again turn into the paradoxical semantics of the postmodern and the asymmetry of the digital syntax of the postmodern surface serving two kinds of semantics in opposing ways. Superficially, the postmodern displays itself as a world of seemingly free play with the attractions of an aesthetic and, for some, even an emancipatory promise. If, on the other hand, we see the political will of an economic master reading, the same syntax concentrates bureaucratic power and economic control of global populations. How are these two possible at the same time?
>
> Indifferent differentiation, of which the digital is the most recent technical form, equally supports a semantics of phenomenal free play of dissemination and a semantics of control. The freedom of meaning which we celebrate in the former finds its semantic Doppelgänger in the latter. The irony is that the emancipatory potential of semantic freedom dissolves unless it is realized in a political culture with a will to projection. Without the will to engage in social projection the semantic free play of the postmodern is no match for the well-organized meaning structures of economic production and its military back-up. Here the syntax of indifferent information can be optimized by strict hierarchization. Nothing is lost, and everything can be viewed from the most promising parameters, reorganized at digital speeds, multiplexed, and put to productive use on a global scale.[18]

Indifferent differentiation thus allows globalization to evolve as a cultural sphere of production that encroaches upon the more open-ended and celebratory notions of postmodernism that critics such as Jean Baudrillard and Jean-François Lyotard continue to hold unabatedly.[19] Again, what is forgotten is how, in a climate claiming to be beyond metanarratives and guiding principles, critical or theoretical writing is still likely to mirror rather than contest the surrounding logic of hyperproduction: the specific application of its claims as critical discourse need not be self-evident beyond the capacity to produce and reproduce itself. In "Aesthetics and Post-Politics: From Fujimori to the Gulf War," Beatriz Sarlo writes:

> Intellectual discursive forms are despised by a communicative populism that copies the strategies of the media, hoping to put itself in touch with a popular culture found in the traces that the media leave in the collective imaginary. For the aesthetics of advertising, the truth is indifferent, not because it recognizes truth as a construction but rather because truth is simply superfluous in the face of the hyperrealism of broadcast news or the audiovisual simulation of discourses.[20]

These forces are obviously reshaping universities and academic markets. New concepts such as "student-centered research universities," "scholarship of application," and "scholarship of dissemination" are now central to planning and reconfiguring the future of many U.S. universities. This is, to a considerable degree, a language meant to probe how humanities and the less empirically oriented social sciences can come closer to the educational needs of today's undergraduates, while simultaneously responding to regional cultural and economic needs.[21] An even more telling index of the same pressures may be found in the national dialogue on American culture proposed by Sheldon Hackney, former head of the National Endowment for the Humanities (NEH), a gesture whose primary purpose was to bridge the deep lines of division in America's growing multicultural society and restore public support for federally funded research in the humanities.[22] One could argue whether these measures really speak to the voids resulting from dominant paradigms in the humanities, or whether they emerge from a much deeper set of contradictions, among which lies an educational system blamed for its own obsolescence and a neoliberal culture disinclined to acknowledge the cost of meaningful schooling at all levels. Yet, nothing could seem more politically exigent than a careful observation of the absences left behind by three decades of humanistic theoretical proliferation, its gains, its losses, as well as its embarrassing quirks, such as its general disdain for social and pedagogical relevance, and its profound resistance to exploring how poststructuralist theories resonate with, or perhaps even accommodate, economic globalization and neoliberalism.

Marketing humanistic endeavors today revolves around packaging of images—careers, knowledge, curriculum, and programs—indeed, all the nitty-gritty features of the business world that were inimical to the training and spirit of traditional humanists, and perhaps may still be to some posthumanists. The academy, increasingly dependent on the scientific model that equates grants with research value, now asks humanists to openly embrace the rigors of marketability: a constant stress on funding, grants, workload measured by students-per-class averages, links to regional economies, community outreach, curricular innovation, publications that bring notoriety if not visibility, and trend-setting if not cutting-edge research projects. Indeed, an increasing commercialization of professional roles has profoundly transformed the recipe for success at most research universities since the 1970s. This is taking place at a time when universities come under highly contradictory pressures. No longer the primary agents of cultural transmission, universities are nonetheless being called on to stand as bastions of resistance to the very economic pressures that promote globalization. Undergraduates now arrive at the university with an internalized anthology filled with cultural references and interests largely derived from video culture and the service industry, the two main agents of global acculturation. Any debate over the ways to transform, or simply accommodate, that anthology into a useful and critical academic experience is likely to challenge avant-garde research as much as traditional paradigms in the humanities.

The prevailing problems in American—and, for that matter, global—education are many, and they are obviously subject to contradictory views. As the Sokal incident indicates, one of the most narrowly defined (but frequently asked) questions is whether humanistic culture will survive American-style postmodernism, not economic globalization, or political neoliberalism. The irony could be that, despite all claims to the contrary, humanistic research remains institutionally bound to academic boundaries that privilege high culture through literature and philosophy. What remains insufficiently explored is whether the deepest challenges now felt be that tradition come from its own theoretical precepts or from the pressures of globalization. Needless to say, academic institutions and disciplines will attempt to adjust. Accordingly, ongoing critiques of modernity's metanarratives will require new strategies that seem less threatening to an expanded, differently organized, conception of Western models and posthumanist practices. The work of deconstruction may have already begun to yield to a more congenial inscription of postmodern literature, art, and criticism as transnational literacy.

This process of readjustment will obviously continue to arouse considerable tension, because the reconfirmation of the Western tradition now faces an internal split between transnational economic interests and national cultural constraints. The encounter is not new but much more pronounced:

how to preserve the established institutional support for the study of high culture while accommodating the growth of mass cultural forms. It is quite symptomatic that American literary studies—perhaps unsuspecting of the eventual spread toward postmodern cultural studies and other complications—embraced certain deconstructive precepts in the late seventies that were, in many ways, a natural extension of New Criticism. Other possible paradigms that were perhaps less hermetic but more capable of exploring interdisciplinary links between literature and mass cultural production were shunned.[23] I have in mind German critical theory, various strands of reception critique, and several schools of cultural semiotics exemplified in the work of Jurij Lotman, Feruccio Rossi Landi, Umberto Eco, and Algirdas Julien Greimas.[24] It is pertinent to note that eclectic theorists such as Donna Haraway continue to turn to these paradigms, if anything to disturb the taboo.[25] One could also point to the ways in which Mikhail Bakhtin's notion of carnival was domesticated into a universal and transhistorical literary trope, or the turning away from Charles Sanders Peirce, whose own notion of signs was profoundly more semantic. These choices chart moments of containing the intellectual grounds for theorizing culture within a strictly literary hermeneutic. Indeed, it is only with the advent of the postcolonial accent on postmodernism that questions of ethnicity, multiculturalism, and other residues from Third Worldism resurfaced once again, as cultural studies, and attempted to introduce the body, orality, musicality, and other intersemiotic exigencies from a discursive legacy that had purged itself from semantics, semiotics, and other cultural entanglements.

The institutional structure of literary studies, particularly in the American university system, has shown the capacity to renew itself even from within posthumanist paradigms. This is not to deny that many scholars, whether traditionalists or transgressors, are beginning to doubt these regenerative powers or feel that the process of literary and theoretical recanonization has been profoundly radicalized in recent times. Yet, one should note, once again, that the sense of instability, as well as the need for constant readjustments, transcends academic disciplines; it is a symptom of a much broader uncertainty that is deeply embedded in contemporary social fabric. Joseph Tabbi reminds us that "Discrepancies between the collectivist market and an advertising cult of individuality produce aggravations in the capitalist system that, far from disrupting it and ultimately causing its collapse, have proven necessary to its continuation."[26] For research universities, the adjustment will be fraught with contradictions, particularly in the area of the humanities, for the latter continue to depend more than ever on philanthropists (native as well as foreign) who look on culture as a repository of foundational texts; thus, the strains on institutions wanting to uphold humanistic traditions in which literature occupies a special place, while global capitalism promotes a new image of a middle-class citizen-consumer whose training and imaginary derive from an anthology of mass cultural forms, hi-tech vocational training, and financial service industries. Increasingly, donors and foundations react to these trends by attempting to influence the actual appointment of faculty in the best U.S. research universities. The *Chronicle of Higher Education* reports on this trend in a feature article: George Washington University was offered $100,000 a year by the Olin Foundation for a post in American history on condition that it hire a pre-selected candidate; Princeton University has come under scrutiny over faculty appointments resulting from a Turkish government donation of $750,000; and Yale University was forced to return a $20-million gift from Lee M. Bass because of pressure to hire a certain type of scholars for courses on Western culture.[27]

What is not often asked, and much less studied, is how these strains challenge a contemporary theoretical paradigm whose very identity is based on its potential for transgression. Indeed, one can already observe attempts to reinvigorate literary studies by subscribing it to a postmodern model of textual virtuosity that somehow preserves the primacy of the literary tradition.[28] The clearest example could well be Harold Bloom's book *The Western Canon*. The return to disciplinary boundaries is only to be expected, particularly from those who see the need to rescue literary studies from recent epistemological excesses. But that revision also leaves behind a significant void that cultural studies—as well as programs that emphasize women's studies, ethnic studies, or other new fields—must attempt to fill. Although there are important questions regarding cultural studies as a new academic market, these programs try to engage the world of culture and political experiences in ways that are not quite legitimized by the institutional structure of literary studies in the American academy, be it the older New Criticism, structuralism, or the most recent strand of high postmodernism.

Whether or not "cultural studies" will Balkanize literary studies, politicize humanities at large, or stand as an undergraduate version of inchoate postmodern theory remains an open question. To critics like Harold Bloom and Richard Rorty, these programs constitute a denial of literary and cultural values driven by trends such as multiculturalism, or the celebration of media in contemporary culture. To Stuart Hall and R. Radhakrishnan, on the other hand, cultural studies calls for serious but novel links with literature, history, and philosophy, as well as mass culture, thereby broadening the critical spectrum through which we intervene in contemporary society as active intellectual entities. In any case, the study of culture and literature requires new and perhaps reciprocal approaches that are nearly always overlooked by many of today's popular debates over culture wars and curricular changes in American universities. Silviano Santiago, one of Brazil's leading writers and critics, speaks of the need to discover "new ways of 'reading' cultural productions that are not embodied in writing, understanding that there exists in the mass dissemination of simulacra a universe that needs to be explored in order to develop an aesthetic sensitivity and strategies that are relevant to the present."[29]

The new market-media influence on academic research and disciplinary shifts must also face ethical questions that postmodern critiques tend to ignore. One of them, perhaps the central one, is the dwindling career opportunities for graduate students in many humanities disciplines. Trade publications such as *Profession* (MLA reports), the *Chronicle of Higher Education,* and *Lingua Franca,* among others, have surveyed this question, though not always to a point where serious scrutiny is brought to bear on the types of scholarly training obtained in the disciplines in question. Graduate career training as an ethical question goes beyond paring down established elite programs to an optimal size self-regulated by the market. This corrective measure will not suffice for large programs in state universities where graduate students have become, by the force of numbers, the most significant body of educators without a potential career opportunity in the foreseeable future. The question asked is if highly specialized doctoral work in literary or cultural studies provides expertise transferable to other professions. Highly placed critics whose recruiting class always yields a star or two may shun the utilitarian resonance of this question, but new unions of graduate students take it more seriously. The highly influential National Research Council (NRC) has thus far also avoided this question. Its ten-year study of graduate education in the United States published in 1995 ranked programs on various key parameters but failed to include any evaluation of "output" measures, such as placement of graduate students.[30]

These challenges—be they ethical or intellectual—are not quite driven by overall economic hardship. Indeed, current financial constraints on university education come at a time of extraordinary economic expansion in the private sector, at least in United States and most of Europe. It is likely that downsizing and privatizing university research will be driven by market forces whose allegiance to humanistic cultural values—traditional or not— will remain doubtful. The ranks of adjuncts will likely continue to swell. Yet, this is also the climate in which cultural, gender, ethnicity, media studies—a list that should also include the growing sphere of English writing programs—have proliferated, partially in response to demographic changes in the student population. A simple look at the increasing numbers of women, Latinos, African Americans, and Asian Americans attending college should suffice. Their interest in becoming subjects of study is not so much a desire for "nation building," or a disdain for Western culture, as an instance of self-awareness in a marketing environment all too willing to respond to, and reward, new performative impulses. It seems odd to celebrate a national economy fully invested in the wisdom of multinationalism while insisting on a national culture that mourns all the corresponding multicultural consequences. Equally odd, however, would be to ignore the strain such contradictions present to established academic traditions and their corresponding claim on what American values should be. Needless to say, the pretense that a vague notion of multiculturalism will offer the most proper response deserves scrutiny.

Staunch opposition to cultural studies is obviously driven by nostalgia for the magic 1950s, or some other unspecified notion of the past whose academic wholeness is taken for granted. But resistance to such trends goes further. As the Sokal exposé reveals, mainstream journalism also feels duty-bound to look on cultural studies with dismissive glances, linking them with Marxism, deconstruction, and any sort of feminism in a grand sweeping gesture of blame somehow linked with the 1960s, which are together responsible for the current problems in American education. It should be noted, moreover, that with some exceptions, literary deconstruction itself has not quite welcomed the new focus on culture spurred by demographic changes and globalization. Serious deconstructionism—as Richard Rorty reminds us in his essay "Tales of Two Disciplines"—is a sound, well-established academic practice within the Western humanistic tradition that ought not to be confused with cultural studies, feminism, gay studies, or other new ancillary fields. As long as it remained exclusively linked to the study of literature and philosophy, Rorty explains, deconstruction was not only legitimate, but a welcome force of renovation for both English and philosophy departments. But if English departments are now besieged by culturalists, feminists, and ethnicists, he argues, then they are likely to suffer as philosophy did with the advent of the analytic paradigm. Let there be new structures, he adds—such as a discrete but safe department of poetics, for example—for the sake of youth in love with books and scholarly learning as we used to know it.

Interestingly, Rorty's mourning for a high form of literary and philosophical deconstruction goes hand in hand with his mourning for Western poetics, its metaphysics and its history, as if the two were indelibly embedded in a self-reflexive aesthetic whole. His way of saving canonical deconstruction at this moment of cultural and economic dispersal—a deep concern for Rorty—would thus require a reverse reconfiguration of knowledge, a small place at the margins, so to speak, rather than a closer look at Western deconstruction's main contradictions: its role in a postmodern celebration of difference that turns to mourning for fear of contamination with women and ethnic studies and an inability to apply its ambitiously radical critique of modernity in a critical look at the contradictory challenges of neoliberal doctrines. Separating deconstruction from multiculturalism also fails to probe into the ways in which they might actually complement each other, as Nancy Fraser explains:

> It is no accident that both deconstructive antiessentialism and pluralist multiculturalism fail in the same way, for the weaknesses of both share a common root: both fail to connect a cultural politics of identity and difference to a social politics of justice and equality. Both fail, that is, to link struggles for recognition to struggles for redistribution. Neither appreciates the crux of the connection: cultural differences can be freely elaborated and democratically mediated only on the basis of social equality.[31]

NAFTA and GATT provide clear examples of the radical impulses that disturb humanist as well as posthumanist theoretical work. They unearth unforeseen cultural anxieties that are rehearsed in the political realm with a corresponding demand for higher education to provide both meaning and resistance to those very pressures for the sake of traditional cultural values. Neoliberal politics feeds on this endemic cycle, fraught as it is with coarse arguments over the canon and multiculturalism. Whether or not new studies of this or that type are legitimate academic pursuits that provide use-value to these pressures, ascertaining the value of new research will require a debate for which there is a scarcity of imaginative models, as Nancy Fraser seems to suggest. In a similar vein, Spivak reminds us that

> there is a mad scramble on among highly placed intellectuals to establish their "colonial origins" these days. Such efforts belong with the impatience of world-systems literary theory, with portmanteau theories of postcoloniality, with the isolationism of both multiculturalism and antiracism; they cannot keep the fracture or wound open. This is the infinite responsibility of the emergent dominant engaged in graduate education in the humanities. Otherwise, we side with the sanctimonious pronouncement of a Lynn Cheney: of course I support multicultural education; I want each child to know that he can succeed.[32]

Global market forces forge paradigm shifts and new academic structures, universities adapt to their changing roles, and ethical questions regarding career opportunities in many disciplines will be raised, but taking new humanistic research beyond political correctness and neoliberal multiculturalism may well require reenergizing and problematizing the postmodern/ deconstructive legacy. Its designifying force is as necessary as insufficient, when it comes to providing a move toward a critical role in a context of academic marketing and global systems. That move may not necessarily be led by our most entrenched graduate disciplines, perhaps not even those at the cutting edge of theoretical paradigms. In an essay on the importance of Rigoberta Menchú's testimonial narrative for the American academy, John Beverley offers the following moment of self-reflection:

> I am beginning to think that my sense of testimonio as a kind of anti-literature may well neglect the fact that the Althusserian idea of "theoretical antihumanism" on which it is based is passing, for all practical purposes, from leftist professors like myself to pragmatic administrators concerned with downsizing and adapting the traditional humanities curriculum to suit the emerging requirements of economic globalization, with its new emphasis on media, communications, and cybernetics.[33]

Responses to Harold Bloom's *The Western Canon* provide an interesting case in point, particularly if one goes beyond the immediacy of Manichaean journalistic glosses. Bloom's book has received much greater play for daring to display the term *canon* in its title than for the theoretical basis that informs his choices. One wonders if an impressionable undergraduate audience, or the print media that has celebrated the book for taking a prescriptive stand on the side of literary history, will find many of Bloom's categories of inclusion representative of canonical values in a classic humanistic sense. Bloom's heavy reliance on various synchronic and panhistoric theoretical presuppositions, for example, is not quite equal to the unburdened defense of traditional Western aesthetics and American values that many commentators have inferred from his book, even if he has all-too-willingly enjoyed the publicity provided by such misreadings. Indeed, Bloom's Freudian extrapolations of generational angst among writers and his use of formalist notions to define strangeness and innovation in literature are but one step removed from certain strands of a literary deconstructionism that has flourished in the best American graduate schools since the 1970s, which Bloom now blames for the Balkanization of literary studies. What is of concern to Bloom is not a continuation of aesthetically bound close readings—a congenial and perhaps generational refinement of approaches to the Western tradition that links formalism, New Criticism, and deconstruction proper—but the advent of new modes of organizing knowledge and various studies programs, particularly women and ethnic configurations.

This is what brings Bloom to the almost desperate conclusion—just a few steps beyond Rorty—that there is no future in the university for brilliant and sensitive students; it also brings him to blame deconstruction at large for diluting itself, for lending itself to illegitimate applications such as multicultural studies. In any case, having rejected the market-driven reorganization of academic programs (though not its corresponding salary structure for star professors), it remains to be seen whether Bloom would be willing to participate in a hypothetical department of poetics, such as Rorty's, or if he would rather close down humanities departments altogether in one apocalyptic swoop, to be replaced, perhaps, by churches and synagogues to carry on legitimate forms of exegesis. Needless to say, humanistic research, market forces, and writing itself are caught in a web of intricate but paradoxical relations that require more than just mourning, or, for that matter, celebration. At stake is whether a new concept of transnational literacy will likely emerge from attempts to refashion the Western canon as world literature, and whether such a construct will in any way accommodate the most critical edges of deconstructive work. "If we were transnationally literate," Spivak reminds us, "we might read sectors that are stylistically non-competitive with the spectacular experimental fiction of certain sections of hybridity, or postcoloniality with a disarticulating rather than a comparative point of view."[34]

Various recent scholarly contributions warrant special attention for their capacity to move beyond media debates to confront the inherent ambiguities of the problem at hand. Two substantive examples are Jacques Derrida's "Spectres of Marx," an abridged version of his book *Spectres of Marx: The State of the Debt, the Work of Mourning, and the New International,* and Arif Dirlik's "The Postcolonial Aura: Third World Criticism in the Age of Global Capitalism," closely following the lines of research in his *After the Revolution: Waking to Global Capitalism.* Ordinarily, Derrida and Dirlik are not read together. Their respective cultures of research have been, generally speaking, mutually exclusive: the former, a French philosopher championing poststructural epistemology; the latter, a Turkish historian calling for an account of ongoing Third World structural differences under the policies of globalization. The two intricately complex and polemical pieces come together, perhaps unexpectedly, in the prevailing context of neoliberal academic production.

"Never in history," writes Derrida, "has the horizon of the thing whose survival is being celebrated (namely, all the old models of the capitalist and liberal world) been as dark, threatening, and threatened."[35] Readers of Derrida will be immediately struck by this rare entry into the murky text of lived experience, a position somewhat removed from his more customary critique of modernity's archive of canonical philosophy.[36] That sudden need to focus on political experiences carries an unusual sense of alarm for Derrida, a moment he defines as a "new dogmatic power" of a "techno-mediatic nature" that "conditions and threatens any democracy," a power of immensely complex apparatuses—including that of scholarly or academic culture—but one in which all elements "cooperate at every moment to assure the hegemony or the imperialism in question through the mediation of the media."[37] Even more surprising, if not uncharacteristic, is Derrida's implicit doubt as to the theoretical tools necessary to meet this challenge, for he poses the need to amend deconstruction—to reinvest in it, so to speak—with a certain spirit of Marxism, a spirit not to be confused with programmatic totalizations or grand utopias, but rather with traces of what Walter Benjamin called "weak messianic force."

It seems that with a closer look at the neoliberal reorganization of world orders Derrida has drawn a more negative conclusion than those who look at global capitalism mainly as a disjunctive moment of postmodernist decentralization; or that Derrida is attempting to disassociate deconstruction proper from celebratory postmodernism by focusing on the need to deconstruct the culture of contemporary capitalism itself, a task for which he ultimately needs to call on the horizon of a new, but yet old, promise: "Not only must one not renounce the emancipatory desire, it is necessary to insist on it more than ever. . . . This is the condition of a repoliticization, perhaps of another concept of the political."[38]

I emphasize these aspects of Derrida's puzzling essay because they embody historical entanglements that will undoubtedly prove challenging to the critical paradigm modeled on his own work, moments such as his call for a new Enlightenment for the twenty-first century and for a rearticulation of democracy and emancipation that he sees clearly threatened by the increasingly neoliberal quality of postmodern dissemination. I hasten to add, however, that the political in Derrida is always an immanently guarded moment hardly willing to give ground without reclaiming it. Thus, his wish "to open up access to an affirmative thinking of the messianic and emancipatory promise" is to be understood as the promise of promise, "not as ontolo-theological or teleo-escatological programme or design."[39] Similarly, his call for a new International is also a deconstructive one, a gesture of fidelity to a certain spirit of Marxism that "barely deserves the name community, [for] it belongs only to anonymity."[40]

It is crucial to observe how far Derrida's analysis of the tones of mourning in the would-be Western celebration of hegemony provides a critical look at our contradictory moment in history, its market-driven cultural forces, its absorption of academic scholarship in all its facets, and the kinds of nostalgic grieving it can induce. Yet, he offers this with a certain degree of mourning of his own, perhaps from the immediate impact of GATT on the politics of contemporary French culture, or his perception of a growing culture of Islamic fundamentalism in neighboring territories, or perhaps from having had to reorient his deconstructive paradigm by reformulating some aspects of hypercriticism and constant dissemination in order to focus on the need for a discourse of promise and counterconjuration. Like Bloom and Rorty, Derrida is alarming and alarmed, though arguably moving in a somewhat different direction, perhaps closer to the concerns outlined by Nancy Fraser.

The future of deconstruction is obviously very much on Derrida's mind, hence his surprising call to imbue it with the spirit of postsocialist Marxism, perhaps a discrete attempt on his part to engage deconstruction's shortcomings at a time when the cultural logic of late capitalism shifts from postmodernist dispersion toward neoliberal enclosure. His essay signals the advent of an all-absorbing cultural economy whose global reach constitutes a definable force of opposition to his project. Yet, it is not quite clear how Derrida distinguishes the present moment from the historical forces of the preceding twenty-five years. The final demise of the Soviet bloc is certainly new, but all the principal forces that now constitute neoliberal politics and transnational globalization have been present for quite some time—a time frame that roughly coincides with the celebration of postmodern decentralization that has been largely theorized through deconstruction; hence, perhaps, Derrida's concern for turning the practice of deconstruction away from this, its own, immediate history, moving it a bit more toward the edge of political critique, and even recharging it with a slight utopian angst.

What Derrida's reluctant but clearly self-questioning text does not provide, however, is a window to or from the Third World, a view that would have perhaps allowed him to arrive at his current position somewhat sooner. After all, his sudden interest in the neoliberal impact on academic culture reveals a trace of Eurocentric detachment that remains largely undeconstructed. Scholars in the so-called Third World—Latin America, Africa, Asia, or diasporic populations within Euro-American metropolitan centers—have been cogently addressing this void for decades. Their work, however, is never present in Derrida's new insights and discoveries, in spite of the fact that it has by now accrued considerable theoretical value, particularly in the critique of postmodern precepts.[41] Martin Hopenhayn, for example, has eloquently stressed the growing need to open the study of culture to include the discourses of social communication, everyday life, production and consumption, work and leisure, and the constitution of collective identities. He argues that a theory largely bound to epistemological immanence is "trapped between two alternatives, neither of which is very satisfactory: either to declare its competence exclusively in the epistemological realm, or to project, metonymically, that realm onto society, in which case the social turns into an epiphenomenon, a transposition, or a concomitance of the production of knowledge."[42]

This "other" look at theory and the global "technomediatic" moment also finds a considerable source in Arif Dirlik's own understanding of postcolonialism—one that I find quite suggestive, even if I do not share in its totality:

> What is truly remarkable is that a consideration of the relationship between postcolonialism and global capitalism should be absent from the writings of postcolonial intellectuals, an absence all the more remarkable because this relationship, which pertains not only to cultural and epistemological but also social and political formations, is arguably less abstract and more direct than any relationship between global capitalism and postmodernism.[43]

He finds a key example in work on contemporary China, particularly in ways in which "Confucianism has been rendered into a prime mover of capitalist development and has also found quite a sympathetic ear among First World ideologues who now look to a Confucian ethic to relieve the crisis of capitalism."[44]

Although his aim is postcolonialism, by isolating its debt to postmodern principles Dirlik provides a most pointed critique of the latter: the need to deconstruct its own universalizing premises such as its persistent Euro-American cultural centeredness and its stability within the very space and time of global capitalism. This is the very relationship that I believe Derrida has finally attempted to explore in his book as a way to save deconstruction from neoliberal absorption and indiscriminate celebratory dispersal. Dirlik's primary aim, however, is to call attention to the absence of such a critique among a few prominent postcolonialists without hardly a word about the First World theorists on whom such work depends. He expounds that it is in the theoretical space formerly occupied by the Third World where global capitalism becomes more dramatic, and where any attempt to theorize its effects with the arsenal of postmodernism will only produce intransitive forms of deconstruction whose transgressive force is always enclosed within writing and other avant-garde performative practices. According to Dirlik, Homi Bhabha's approach to theoretical production provides a dramatic example of such intransitivity.[45]

The full range of issues raised in Dirlik's work would require a more expansive critique, but I will approach those that are most crucial to my arguments in these concluding pages. Dirlik's rather stern criticism of diasporic intellectuals such as Bhabha, for instance, highlights two main facets: their failure to include a structural account of global capitalism in its current neoliberal moment, and their construction of an in-betweenness that mirrors their own Western predicament more than that of the Third World.[46] Indeed, postcolonialism generates a discourse about the Third World that is largely produced, marketed, and consumed in the First World, a sentiment clearly echoed in Stuart Hall's growing doubts about the industry of cultural studies in the United States:

> There is no moment now, in American cultural studies, where we are not able, extensively and without end, to theorize power—politics, race, class, and gender, subjugation, domination, exclusion, marginality, Otherness, etc. There are ways of constituting power as an easy-floating signifier which just leaves the crude exercise and connections of power and culture altogether emptied of any signification.[47]

What Dirlik is not inclined to observe, however, is how postcolonialism provides a key register for an increasing number of different voices within the West, not only diasporic, but also for a new and growing sense of ethnic otherness. Many new and significant literary voices in the United States, for example, correspond to Latinos and Asian Americans, who must now be read differently, perhaps as native speakers of English as a second language, a growing category whose cultural and ethnic bearings remain different or plural. Obviously, these voices are not immune from the logic of appropriation that concerns Hall. Indeed, Latino and Latin Americanist criticism within the United States often produces and promotes use-value criteria that are then transferred to Latin America as universally valid. A most telling example is found in Rigoberta Menchú's testimonial narrative, a catalyst for multicultural and feminist causes in the United States that work differently in Latin America.[48] The question is not only whether the subaltern can speak, but whether there will be an open and meaningful dialogue between diasporic, resident, and traveling intellectuals as to who and what constitutes subalternity in time and space. Spivak has initiated this dialogue in "Teaching for the Times," in which she explores the relationship between globalization and transnational literacy, as well as curricular implications for both graduate and undergraduate levels. Spivak also proposes that the African American is the postcolonial subject in the United States, whereas the Latino/Chicano corresponds to the diasporic discourse studies.[49] It is a debatable attempt to demarcate postcoloniality in the United States, but it contributes nonetheless to clarifying the grounds in which multicultural and subaltern theories are marketed in the American academy.[50]

Dirlik does not quite say it, but he invites the reader to think of post-colonialism as a graduate-school version of anodyne undergraduate multi-culturalism. Yet, it could be argued that postcolonial and diasporic voices are expanding in the growing Third Worldness of the First World, un-doubtedly a different referentiality than that of exiled or visiting intellectu-als who see themselves as more direct, and perhaps faithful, interlocutors of the Third World. To this, Dirlik would likely counter that Western Third Worldness is at best an equivocal terrain. He would also see shifts within postmodern paradigms as more likely to have an impact on how the First World sees itself than on the Third World itself, particularly if, as Stuart Hall argues, such shifts remain bound to a concept of political agency ex-clusively defined by the aesthetics of troping. In short, Dirlik's main argu-ment attempts to challenge the very theoretical problem that Derrida hesi-tantly intimates—that the utopia implicit in the postmodern aesthetic impulse may no longer pass without further historical entanglements such as those posed by globalization.

One could extend Dirlik's critique to explore the way in which post-colonial thinking introduces political strains that postmodernism would not ordinarily engage, such as rereadings of the Western canon more closely informed by Third World cultural flows and influences likely to be present as well—though differently organized—in the work of diasporic intermedi-aries. But Dirlik remains unconvinced of the notion that intellectuals in the diaspora hold theoretically strategic positions, or that they are more readily inclined to bridge different modes of intellectual production and consump-tion. This debate could obviously benefit from the work of other postcolo-nial critics such as Radhakrishnan, who, while sharing many of Dirlik's critiques, still find benefit in exploring the theoretical implications of dias-poric positionality.[51] Édouard Glissant's *Caribbean Discourse* would be an-other important source in this regard, for his work stems from a Caribbean experience in which diasporic theory is by definition closer to that of the Third World than, for instance, to the United States or Britain. Unlike Bhabha's postmodern inscription of Fanon's writing, which transposes the latter's colonial experiences onto a strictly rhetorical and individual symbolic postcolonial plane, Glissant argues that figures such as mimicry, liminality, and in-betweenness must draw from the ongoing historical entanglements of areas such as the Caribbean if they are to contribute anything specific to metropolitan theory.[52] Spivak's most recent work, though still closer to linguistic immanence than Glissant's, reveals a growing concern with retaining the notion of praxis as a mode of deconstruction to our global moment: "Since we are imprisoned in and habituated to capitalism, we might try to look at the allegory of capitalism not in terms of capitalism as the source of authoritative reference but in terms of the constant small failures in and interruptions to its logic, which help to recode it and produce our unity."[53]

Dirlik's prose calls for a new sense of historical exigency, a scrutiny whose denotative impulse guides his accounts of ongoing political and economic hierarchies, as well as their impact on cultural developments and knowledge formation. This urgency draws from the same spirit that Derrida's newfound need intimates, even though the latter's own stylistic rigors allow him only an oblique approximation to the immediacy of such needs. Derrida speaks to the specters of Marx, but only through the rhetorical impetus of Shakespeare's ghosts, whose distant tones and exquisite elocutionary force escort his theoretical performance. Dirlik, on the other hand, concedes at times that a structural understanding of cultural economies will also require greater awareness of how discursive sedimentation and rhetorical maneuvers shape "the real." Through their distinct styles and disciplinary paradigms, both are intricately captivated by their attempts to discern the pressures of globalization on disciplinary boundaries and modes of writing. It may not be equally evident in Derrida's and Dirlik's rhetorical devices, but they unquestionably respond to the same array of conflicts and predicaments in ways that, contrary to neoliberal wisdom and postmodern precepts, are not mutually exclusive. Their writing, if closely observed, will challenge and disturb exclusive circles of readership, be they Third World Marxism, Euro-American postmodernism, or other vintages in between. It is a writing clearly aware of the culs-de-sac of postmodern theorizing that Ruthrof outlines as undifferentiated difference, abandonment of the ties between syntax and semantics, and an "uneasy alliance between the philosophical fathers of the linguistic turn and the posthermeneutic tradition

[that] has robbed many disciplines of interpretive will."[54] Radicalness and transgression, to the extent that such overused terms still retain meaning in academic work, may well require further calls to calibrate contemporary scholarship beyond correctness and nostalgia, to reclaim a critical edge for our times from the self-reflecting mirrors of mourning and celebration.

Notes

Preface

1. All translations are by the author, unless indicated otherwise.

2. Lisa Lowe and David Lloyd, "Introduction," in *The Politics of Culture in the Shadow of Capital,* ed. Lisa Lowe and David Lloyd (Durham, N.C.: Duke University Press, 1997), pp. 1–32.

3. Ibid., p. 1.

4. Horst Ruthrof, *Semantics and the Body: Meaning from Frege to the Postmodern,* p. 253.

1. Latin Americanism and the Turns beyond Modernity

1. The influential work of scholars such as Jean Franco, Gerald Martin, John Beverley, Djelal Kadir, and Roberto González Echevarría, among other Latin Americanists working in the United States, is mainly written in English. British Hispanists who have turned their attention to Latin American literature, in English, now include Paul Julian Smith and Malcolm Read. The work of Sylvia Molloy and Beatriz Sarlo, generally written in Spanish, has been increasingly translated to English.

2. Ángel Rama has argued convincingly that the Latin American literary boom ought to be studied, at least in part, as an international publishing event largely affected by U.S. academic readers and publishing presses ("El boom en perspectiva," pp. 1–85).

3. The bibliography here is extensive, but a very useful sample is provided by the critical anthology *The Real Thing,* ed. Georg M. Gugelberger (Durham: Duke University Press, 1996).

4. John Barth, *The Friday Book: Essays and Other Nonfiction*; Hans Robert Jauss, "The Theory of Reception: A Retrospective of Its Unrecognized Prehistory"; Fredric Jameson, "Third World Literature in an Era of Multinational Capitalism."

5. Benedict Anderson, *Imagined Communities*; Edward Said, *Orientalism*.

6. Neil Larson, *Reading North by South*, p. 1.

7. Nelly Richard, *La estratificación de los márgenes*, p. 74.

8. A startling contrast is found in Santiago Colás's celebratory monograph on Argentine literary postmodernism, *Postmodernity in Latin America: The Argentine Paradigm*.

9. Martin Hopenhayn, *Ni apocalípticos ni integrados: Aventuras de la modernidad en América*, p. 63.

10. Norbert Lechner, ed., *Cultura política y democratización*.

11. See, for example, an attempt to constitute Borges's fiction as the only ontological project viable for contemporary critics in Alberto Moreiras, "Pastiche Identity and Allegory of Allegory." Another example would be the attempt to place Severo Sarduy's work as the main source of postmodern horizons, in Roberto González Echevarría, *La ruta de Severo Sarduy*.

12. See Klor de Alva, "Colonialism and Postcolonialism as (Latin) American Mirages"; Rolena Adorno, "Reconsidering Colonial Discourse for Sixteenth- and Seventeenth-Century Spanish America"; and Fernando Coronil, "Can Postcoloniality Be Decolonized? Imperial Banality and Postcolonial Power."

13. Hernán Vidal, "A Perspective from Literary Criticism."

14. The most elaborate recent examples are found in Djelal Kadir, *The Other Writing*, and Santiago Colás, "Of Creole Symptoms, Cuban Fantasies, and Other Latin American Postcolonial Ideologies."

15. John Beverley's *testimonio* paradigm and its most important critics are discussed later in this chapter.

16. Patricia Seed, "Colonial and Postcolonial Discourse"; Walter Mignolo, "Colonial and Postcolonial Discourse: Cultural Critique or Academic Colonialism?"

17. Henry A. Giroux, *Border Crossings*; Neil Lazarus, "National Consciousness and the Specificity of (Post)colonial Intellectualism"; R. Radhakrishan, "Postcoloniality and the Boundaries of Identity"; Arif Dirlik, "The Postcolonial Aura: Third World Criticism in the Age of Global Capitalism"; Aijaz Ahmad, *In Theory*.

18. See, for example, Gustavo Pérez Firmat, ed. *Do the Americas Have a Common Literature?*, and Paul Julian Smith, *The Body Hispanic*.

19. In 1996 and 1997, new critical anthologies on Latin American literature in the context of current theoretical debates began to appear with more frequency. Among them, perhaps the most comprehensive is *Revista Iberoamericana*, no. 75 (1997), edited by Mabel Moraña.

20. Walter Mignolo's work on Latin American postcolonialism pro-

vides an interesting example of how a pluralist multicultural dispersion can easily set in on loci of enunciation criteria. His semiotic and philological expertise brings to bear many interesting questions to the history of orality in colonial times, as evidenced in *The Darker Side of the Renaissance*. On the other hand, the notion of multiple loci of enunciations, while laudatory as an extension of a liberal academy that manages to include as postcolonial, say, Roberto Fernández Retamar alongside Spivak and Gloria Anzaldúa without further ado, ultimately enacts little theoretical specificity for postcolonialism.

21. George Yúdice, Jean Franco, and Juan Flores, eds., *On Edge: The Crisis of Contemporary Latin American Culture*; John Beverley and José Oviedo, eds., *The Postmodernism Debate in Latin America*; Amaryll Chanady, ed., *Latin American Identity and Constructions of Difference*. For the debate in the *Latin American Research Review,* see Adorno, "Reconsidering Colonial Discourse"; Mignolo, "Colonial and Postcolonial Discourse"; Seed, "Colonial and Postcolonial Discourse"; and Vidal, "A Perspective from Literary Criticism." See also Walter Mignolo, "Editor's Introduction."

22. *Nueva Revista de Crítica Literaria,* nos. 45–47 (1992–1993); *Nuevo Texto Crítico,* nos. 28–29 (1993); *Papeles de Montevideo* (Montevideo, Uruguay) 1.1 (1997); *Teoría y política de la construcción de identidades y diferencias en América Latina y el Caribe,* ed. Daniel Matos; *Posmodernidad en la periferia,* ed. Hermann Herlinghaous and Monika Walter; *Las culturas de fin de siglo en América Latina,* Josefina Ludmer, ed. (Buenos Aires: Beatriz Viterbo, 1994); *Cultura y Tercer Mundo,* ed. Beatriz González Stephan (Caracas: Nueva Sociedad, 1996); *Culturas en globalización,* ed. Néstor García Canclini (Caracas: Nueva Sociedad, 1996).

23. This journal, guided by a transnational board of cultural and literary critics, is edited in England.

24. *Critical Inquiry* 15 (1989): 224.

25. Ibid.

26. Gates seems particularly concerned here with the kind of postcolonial reading that overturns any attempt to value colonial discourse in and of itself (*Critical Inquiry* 17 [1991]: 458).

27. Gayatri Chakravorty Spivak, "Poststructuralism, Marginality, Postcoloniality, and Value," p. 297.

28. See Stephen Slemon's excellent article on this point, "Magic Realism and Post-Colonial Discourse."

29. Fredric Jameson, "On Magic Realism in Film."

30. Spivak, "Poststructuralism, Marginality, Postcoloniality, and Value," p. 222.

31. Ibid.

32. Homi K. Bhabha, "Remembering Fanon: Self, Psyche, and the Colonial Condition," pp. 120–23.

33. Of the recent critical anthologies, *Latin American Identity and Constructions of Difference* (edited by Amaryll Chanady) provides a telling example of this view. An introduction and an epilogue serve as metropolitan (United States and Canada) bookends to nine essay chapters of Latin American Third Worldness. The latter are mostly attempts to theorize Latin American identity and difference from within the area's cultural/literary experience; their authors are grounded in the rich array of Latin American heterogeneous discourses, and yet also informed by new theoretical insights. On the other hand, the bookend supplements, written by the editor and Alberto Moreiras, respectively, assume the tone of corrective counterpoints of Euro-American theoretical use-value for a U.S. university audience, for which this important volume is obviously intended. Accordingly, these bookend supplements offer Derridean and Borgesian lessons as bold new horizons for Latin America's future understanding of itself.

34. Jean Franco, "The Nation as Imagined Community," p. 210.

35. Spivak, "Poststructuralism, Marginality, Postcoloniality, and Value," p. 222.

36. Dirlik, "The Postcolonial Aura," p. 337.

37. Ibid., p. 350.

38. On the question of modernizations in the age of postmodernism, Arturo Escobar provides a suggestive, though perhaps utopian, preview of alternative models in "Imagining a Post-Development Era?"

39. "Notes on the 'Post-Colonial,'" p. 103.

40. Ibid., p. 102.

41. Beverley and Oviedo, *The Postmodernism Debate in Latin America,* p. 15.

42. John Beverley and Marc Zimmerman, *Literature and Politics in the Central American Revolutions.* Throughout this book, Beverley makes a convincing argument that Latin America's postmodernity is not just a subject of theorization but a social and political reality that can be observed in recent revolutionary movements such as the one in Central America. His work does not include a study of how postmodern deconstructionism has deployed itself in U.S. Latin American literary criticism and how such authoritative readings have kept postmodern political culture as such beyond the bounds of mainstream studies. That, in part, is the focus of this chapter.

43. Franco, "The Nation as Imagined Community," p. 210.

44. These questions are explored with greater detail in chapter 2.

45. Roberto González Echevarría, *The Voice of the Masters: Writing and Authority in Modern Latin American Literature*, p. 4.

46. Djelal Kadir, *Questing Fictions*, p. 35.

47. Ibid., p. 40.

48. Ibid., p. 91.

49. Spivak, "Poststructuralism, Marginality, Postcoloniality, and Value," p. 228.

50. Roberto González Echevarría, *Myth and Archive*, p. 144.

51. Ibid., pp. 180–84.

52. Carlos Alonso, *The Spanish American Regional Novel: Modernity and Autochthony*, pp. 35–36.

53. Colás, *Postmodernity in Latin America*.

54. Santiago Colás, "What's Wrong with Representation?: Testimonio and Democratic Culture," p. 164. Colás includes the work of González Echevarría in the first mode but gives no other example.

55. Ibid. p. 171. Colás appears to advance this position and then produce a semiretrieval in the same paragraph through a quote of Nancy Fraser. One is left to conclude that his postmodern critique is somewhere in between these views. A fuller discussion of the globalizing turn in postmodern theory will be found in chapter 6.

56. José Rabasa, "Of Zapatismo: Reflections on the Folkloric and the Impossible in a Subaltern Insurrection," p. 408.

57. Alberto Moreiras, "The Aura of Testimonio," p. 198.

58. The invocation of Borges for a postsymbolic praxis is found in Alberto Moreira's "Pastiche Identity and Allegory of Allegory," in Chanady, *Latin American Identity and Constructions of Difference*, p. 231.

59. Ibid., p. 233.

60. Peter Dews, *The Logic of Disintegration*, p. 78.

61. Richard, *La estratificación de los márgenes*, p. 101.

62. This critique will be taken up in detail in chapters 4 and 6.

63. For a critique of containment of potential semiotic dispersal by aesthetic poststructuralism, see Román de la Campa, "Mainstreaming Poststructuralist and Feminist Thought: Jonathan Culler's Poetics."

64. Rabasa, "Of Zapatismo," p. 404.

65. See chapter 3 for a more detailed discussion of transculturation. See also Fernando Coronil, "Challenging Colonial Histories: *Cuban Counterpoint*/Ortiz's Counterfetishism." It is also important to note the recent Latin American Subaltern Studies Group, whose collective "Founding Statement" is included in Beverley and Oviedo, *The Postmodernism Debate in Latin America*.

66. Deconstructions of transculturation have provided considerable insights, even though they often rehearse a new aesthetic triumphalism meant to deny the historical realism any relevance except as rhetorical mastery. See, for example, Antonio Benítez-Rojo, *La isla que se repite;* Gustavo Pérez Firmat, *The Cuban Condition*; and Alberto Moreiras, "Transculturación narrativa y pérdida de sentido."

67. Juan Carlos Mariátegui, *Siete ensayos de interpretación de la realidad peruana*; José María Arguedas, *El zorro de arriba y el zorro de abajo*; Fernando Ortiz, *Contrapunteo cubano del tabaco y el azúcar;* Ángel Rama, *Transculturación narrativa en América Latina* (Rama's work is discussed in more detail in chapters 3 and 4); Néstor García Canclini, *Hybrid Cultures: Strategies for Entering and Leaving Modernity.*

68. Rabasa, "Of Zapatismo," p. 420.

69. Ibid.

70. Enrique Dussel, "Eurocentrism and Modernity," p. 67.

71. Lucía Guerra Cunningham, "Las sombras de la escritura: hacia una teoría de la producción literaria de la mujer latinoamericana," p. 143.

72. Debra Castillo, *Talking Back: Toward a Latin American Feminist Literary Criticism,* p. 36.

73. Jean Franco, "Apuntes sobre la crítica feminista y la literatura hispanoamericana," p. 42.

74. Stephen Slemon provides an interesting discussion of a dual strategy, a "reach for a positive (post-colonial) referentiality . . . alongside a counter-discursive parodic energy—one which a post-modernist methodology would at least notice if not always specify" ("Modernism's Last Post," p. 7).

75. Beatriz Sarlo, "Aesthetics and Post-Politics: From Fujimori to the Gulf War."

76. Martin Hopenhayn, "Postmodernism and Neoliberalism in Latin America," p. 98.

77. See Ken Silverstein and Alexander Cockburn, "The Killers and the Killing."

78. See Paco Ignacio Taibo II, "Zapatista! The Phoenix Rises."

79. Rossana Reguillo, "Chiapas: la otra cara de la modernidad mexicana," p. 8.

2. Postmodernism and Revolution

1. Murray Kempton, "U.S. Sanctions for Salvadoran Atrocities."

2. Ibid.

3. The work of CISPES (Committee in Solidarity with the People of El Salvador) is an important example. In the art world, *Cineaste* published a

number of very informative surveys of new documentaries on Central America during the 1980s.

4. Sheldon Hackney, "Organizing a National Conversation."

5. Jacques Derrida, "Spectres of Marx," p. 37; emphasis in the original.

6. Ibid.

7. Carlos Rincón provides an original critique of Borges's influence on current European theorists in "The Peripheral Center of Postmodernism: On Borges, García Márquez, and Alterity."

8. This story is found in Néstor García Canclini, *Hybrid Cultures: Strategies for Entering and Leaving Modernity,* p. 75.

9. Jorge Luis Borges, *Labyrinths,* p. 8.

10. This particular reading very much informs two paradigmatic examples of Latin American literary deconstructionism: Alberto Moreiras, "Pastiche Identity and Allegory of Allegory," pp. 204–38; and Roberto González Echevarría, "The Novel as Myth and Archive: Ruins and Relics of Tlön," in *Myth and Archive,* pp. 142–86. For a more balanced reading of Borges and an assessment of the main lines of reception his work has inspired in Euro-American institutions, see Beatriz Sarlo, *Jorge Luis Borges: A Writer on the Edge*; and Jean Franco, "The Utopia of a Tired Man: Jorge Luis Borges."

11. Santiago Colás, "What's Wrong with Representation?: Testimonio and Democratic Culture." Colás attempts to explain this postmodern aesthetic liberation with the following observation: "But postmodernism's recognition that the aesthetic is grounded on a violence done to the marginal does not translate into a real concern for violence done to the marginal person. The marginal cannot be the locus of counterhegemonic subjectivity precisely because it is the oppression of the marginal that 'excites'—that motivates—the written representations of postmodernism" (p. 169). One is left to ponder how counterhegemonic aesthetics translates into politics, how freeing the text from any real concern for violence done to people will ultimately elucidate what postmodern excitement means.

12. Carlos Castañeda, *Compañero: The Life and Death of Che Guevara* (New York: Knopf, 1997); David Deutschmann, ed., *Che Guevara Reader: Writings on Guerrilla Strategy, Politics and Revolution* (Melbourne and New York: Ocean Press, 1997); Henry Butterfield Rian, *The Fall of Che Guevara* (New York: Oxford University Press, 1997); Michael Ratner and Michael Steven Smith, eds., *Che Guevara and the FBI* (Melbourne and New York: Ocean Press, 1997).

13. Hugh Thomas, *The Spanish Civil War,* and *Cuba: The Pursuit of Freedom.*

14. Donald C. Hodges, *Intellectual Foundations of the Nicaraguan Revolution*, pp. 167–72.

15. The original Spanish title of Che's *Guerrilla Warfare* is *La guerra de guerrillas*.

16. Borges, *Labyrinths*, p. 13.

17. González Echevarría's reading of this story as a Borgesian deconstruction of the ideological and literary projects behind the realist fiction of the time is thorough and imaginative, but, in typical de Manian dogma, it leaves nothing but literary unwriting of social projects to be celebrated from afar. By this account, Latin America becomes a triumphant repository of literary monuments that unmask the inherent impossibility of all social projects or any discourse that does not acknowledge itself primarily as fiction, the ultimate and unavoidable character of all historical reflection. This narrow application of deconstructive insights is even more dramatic in Djelal Kadir's *Questing Fictions*, and with greater fervor, in his more recent *The Other Writing*.

18. Derrida, "Spectres of Marx," p. 56. Needless to say, Derrida does not propose here a dialectical understanding of how such a debt persists, but in this essay he does problematize the relation between deconstruction and the social realm, perhaps in a fashion never seen in his earlier work. He looks here at neoliberal hegemony as a contemporary ideological problem embodied in specific political forces, a risk that many literary deconstructionists prefer to eschew.

19. Paul de Man, *Blindness and Insight: Essays in the Rhetoric of Contemporary Criticism*, p. 165.

20. Arif Dirlik provides a very well argued critique in "The Postcolonial Aura: Third World Criticism in the Age of Global Capitalism," pp. 312–49.

21. Quoted in John Beverley and Marc Zimmerman, *Literature and Politics in the Central American Revolutions*, p. 53.

22. José Rabasa, "Of Zapatismo: Reflections on the Folkloric and the Impossible in a Subaltern Insurrection," p. 420.

23. See Beverley and Zimmerman, *Literature and Politics in the Central American Revolutions*, chapters 3 and 5 in particular. My literary reading of revolution in this chapter brings me to think that the work of García Márquez, or Borges for that matter, remains open to appropriation and misappropriation, just like Darío's poetry.

24. My quotes from Eduardo Galeano's book derive from the earlier Spanish text, *Guatemala: país ocupado* (my translations). Julio Cortázar's "Apocalypse at Solentiname" is in his *Nicaragua, tan violentamente dulce*.

25. Galeano, *Guatemala: país ocupado,* p. 11.

26. Ibid., p. 56.

27. Barbara Harlow, *Resistance Literature,* p. 79.

28. Ibid., p. 77.

29. Ibid.

30. Cortázar, *Nicaragua, tan violentamente dulce,* p. 19.

31. Ibid.

32. Borges, *Labyrinths,* p. 17.

33. Quoted in George Yúdice, "Marginality and the Ethics of Survival," p. 234. It should be observed that Yúdice is quoting from a different edition than mine: *Salvador* (New York: Washington Square Press, 1983).

34. Ibid.

35. Ibid.

36. Ibid. See also Mary Louise Pratt's incisive reading in her *Imperial Eyes,* pp. 225–27.

37. Didion, *Salvador,* p. 13.

38. Borges, *Labyrinth,* p. 10.

39. Didion, *Salvador,* p. 15.

40. Ibid., p. 36.

41. Ibid., p. 53.

42. Ibid., p. 54.

43. Ibid., p. 59.

44. Ibid., p. 64; emphasis in the original. After many years, Didion has concluded that a "systematic obfuscation" of massacres in El Salvador has followed in the U.S. media ("Something Horrible in El Salvador," *New York Review of Books* 41.13[1997], pp. 8–13.

45. Enrique Dussel, "Eurocentrism and Modernity," p. 69.

46. Ibid., p. 55.

47. I am indebted to Robert W. Benson for his analysis of the Zapatista revolution's reliance on the Mexican constitution. See his "Mexican Reform Can't Be Trickle-Down Kind."

3. Of Border Artists and Transculturation

1. This is a concern that Butler appears to have taken quite seriously in subsequent work. See, for example, Judith Butler, *Bodies That Matter* (New York: Routledge, 1993).

2. Nancy Fraser, *Justice Interruptus,* p. 218.

3. Homi K. Bhabha, "DissemiNation: Time Narrative and the Margins of the Modern Nation."

4. Aijaz Ahmad offers a different view in his "Postcolonialism: What's in a Name?"

5. See *Poetics Today* 15.4 (winter 1994) and 16.1 (spring 1995).

6. Homi K. Bhabha, "Postcolonial Authority and Postmodern Guilt," p. 66.

7. These postcolonial positions become immediately transferable to postmodern forms of standard deconstructive practice so long as they privilege rhetoric and literature as a master code through which other cultural forms and history must be read. See, for example, Carlos J. Alonso's reading of Bhabha in "The Burden of Modernity."

8. See Peter Dews, particularly the Introduction to *The Logic of Disintegration*.

9. Jacques Derrida "Spectres of Marx."

10. Nelly Richard, *La estratificación de los márgenes*.

11. On the question of Latin Americanisms, see Román de la Campa, "On Latin Americanism and the Postcolonial Turn."

12. For a much broader treatment of Latin American postmodernism in English, three anthologies are worthy of note: *On Edge: The Crisis of Contemporary Latin American Culture,* ed. George Yúdice, Jean Franco, and Juan Flores; *The Postmodernism Debate in Latin America,* ed. John Beverley and José Oviedo; and *Latin American Identity and Constructions of Difference,* ed. Amaryll Chanady.

13. The most elaborate example of this paradigm within Latin American criticism is found in the work of Djelal Kadir. See his *Questing Fictions* and *The Other Writing*.

14. Mary Beth Sheridan, "Latin American Soaps Get Gritty," *Newsday,* December 28, 1997, p. 83.

15. Walter Mignolo, "Afterword." Mignolo looks into the importance of Rodolfo Kusch's work for contemporary Latin Americanism. The latter's key works include *Geocultura del hombre americano*.

16. Juan Villegas looks at this tendency in "La estrategia llamada transculturación." His critique of the totalizing impulse of transculturation seems useful, even though his counterproposals remain obscure and contradictory.

17. Alberto Moreiras's understanding of transculturation is perhaps the clearest example of this view. See his "Transculturación y pérdida del sentido."

18. See Antonio Benítez-Rojo, *The Repeating Island*; and Gustavo Pérez Firmat, *The Cuban Condition*.

19. A recent anthology will likely have considerable impact in the rereading of transculturation: Mabel Moraña, ed., *Ángel Rama y los estudios latinoamericanos* (1997). My specific citations here refer to two of its essays:

Abel Trigo, "De la transculturación (a/en) lo transnacional," and Juan Poblete, "Rama/Foucault/González Echevarría: el problema de la construcción del espacio discursivo del siglo diecinueve latinoamericano."

20. Lisa Lowe and David Lloyd, "Introduction," in *The Politics of Culture in the Shadow of Capital*, p. 16.

21. Ibid.

22. For a panoramic view of Ortiz's work, see *Bio-Bibliografía de Don Fernando Ortiz*, Havana: Biblioteca Nacional José Martí, 1970); see also Julio LeRiverend Ortiz, ed. *Orbita de Fernando Ortiz.*

23. Néstor García Canclini, *Hybrid Cultures: Strategies for Entering and Leaving Modernity*, p. 172.

24. Ibid., pp. 153–70.

25. John Barth, *The Friday Book: Essays and Other Nonfiction.*

26. Carlos Rincón's *La no simultaneidad de lo simultáneo* provides a fresh look at these problems.

27. Ernesto Laclau makes an important distinction between society and the social in his *New Reflections on the Revolution of Our Time*, pp. 89–93.

28. Derrida, "Spectres of Marx," p. 38.

29. *Poetics Today* 15.4 (winter 1994) and 16.1 (spring 1995).

30. This is clearly evidenced, though more as a dismissive gloss than as a clearly argued position, in Carlos J. Alonso, "Rama y sus retoños: Figuring the Nineteenth Century in Spanish America."

31. Jean Franco, "Ángel Rama y la transculturación narrativa en América Latina"; Saúl Sosnowski, "Ángel Rama: un sendero en el bosque de palabras"; Jorge Ruffinelli, "Ángel Rama: la carrera del crítico de fondo"; Jesús Díaz Caballero, "La transculturación en la novela regionalista: El caso sur andino peruano en la obra de Arguedas"; Neil Larsen, *Modernism and Hegemony: A Materialist Critique of Aesthetic Agency.*

32. Rama, *Transculturación narrativa en América Latina*, p. 33 n. 22.

33. See Richard Rorty's own struggle with this crisis point in his "Tales of Two Disciplines."

34. Rama, *Transculturación narrativa*, p. 71.

35. Ibid., p. 74; emphasis added.

36. Ibid., p. 51.

37. Ibid., p.52

38. This is a full-length development of Derrida's essay "Spectres of Marx."

39. Two of these rereadings are particularly relevant: Fernando Coronil, "Challenging Colonial Histories: *Cuban Counterpoint*/Ortiz's Counterfetishism"; Maribel Ortiz, "Modernidad conflictiva: Ángel Rama y el estudio de la literatura latinoamericana."

40. Fernando Ortiz, *Contrapunteo cubano del tabaco y el azúcar,* p. 5.

41. My discussion of Ortiz follows in part some of the arguments included in my earlier essay "Relectura y redescubrimiento del *Contrapunteo cubano.*"

42. For a full-scale discussion of *testimonio* and postmodernism, see John Beverley and Marc Zimmerman, *Literature and Politics in the Central American Revolutions.*

43. This is, in essence, Nelly Richard's argument against what she sees as a new canon formation of Latin Americanism as *testimonio* guided by U.S. critics, and John Beverley in particular. It is an important argument worthy of a detailed analysis. Suffice it to say, for now, that a more thorough study of Latin Americanisms in the United States will reveal other more established strands of literary Latin Americanisms, such as boom and postboom writing, for which *testimonio* is just not literature. The question, then, is, How is *testimonio* read in Latin America versus the United States, and more particularly, how is Rigoberta Menchú deconstructed in Latin America, and in certain Latin American countries, versus the United States? Each of these questions goes beyond the simple assignation of *testimonio* as a new postmodern canon that suddenly replaces boom and postboom discourses. See Nelly Richard, "Bordes, diseminación, postmodernismo: una metáfora latinoamericana de fin de siglo."

44. Ortiz, *Contrapunteo,* p. 38.

45. James Clifford, *The Predicament of Culture,* p. 113.

46. Homi K. Bhabha's theory of otherness exemplifies the turn toward rhetorical space. See his "Remembering Fanon: Self, Psyche, and the Colonial Condition." For a different view, see Henry Louis Gates Jr.'s critique of Bhabha in "Critical Fanonism."

47. Edward Said, "Representing the Colonized: Anthropology's Interlocutors."

48. Enrique Dussel, "The Reason of the Other."

49. Gayatri Chakravorty Spivak's well-known essay "Can the Subaltern Speak?" is crucial in this regard. See also a subsequent discussion: Gayatri Chakravorty Spivak, "Subaltern Talk."

50. Richard, *La estratificación de los márgenes,* p. 35.

51. Clifford, *The Predicament of Culture,* p. 17.

4. Mimicry and the Uncanny in Caribbean Discourse

1. Édouard Glissant, *Caribbean Discourse,* p. 2.

2. Ibid.

3. Jacques Derrida, *Spectres of Marx,* p. 54.

4. Fredric Jameson, "Third World Literature in an Era of Multinational Capitalism."

5. Glissant, *Caribbean Discourse*, 4.

6. Arif Dirlik, *After the Revolution: Waking to Global Capitalism.*

7. Homi K. Bhabha, "Remembering Fanon: Self, Psyche, and the Colonial Condition."

8. Henry Louis Gates Jr., "Critical Fanonism."

9. Stuart Hall, "Cultural Identity and Diaspora."

10. Carlos Rincón, "The Peripheral Center of Postmodernism: On Borges, García Márquez, and Alterity."

11. Jorge Luis Borges, "Pierre Menard, Author of the *Quixote*," in *Labyrinths*. See also chapter 2 for a fuller discussion of Borges and postmodern writing.

12. Glissant, *Caribbean Discourse*, p. 77.

13. Ibid., p. 3.

14. An elaborate discussion of these pressures on Caribbean discursivity and feminism is found in Sylvia Wynter, "Beyond the World of Man: Glissant and the New Discourse of the Antilles."

15. Antonio Benítez-Rojo, *La isla que se repite: El Caribe y la perspectiva posmoderna*, p. vii.

16. See Paul de Man, *Blindness and Insight: Essays in the Rhetoric of Contemporary Criticism*; *Allegories of Reading*; and *The Resistance to Theory.*

17. Roberto González Echevarría, *Alejo Carpentier: The Pilgrim at Home* and *La ruta de Severo Sarduy*; Enrico Mario Santí, *Escritura y tradición: texto, crítica y poética en la literatura latinoamericana*; Gustavo Pérez Firmat, *The Cuban Condition* and *Life on the Hyphen: The Cuban American Way.*

18. Benítez-Rojo, *The Repeating Island*, p. 84.

19. Jean-François Lyotard, *The Postmodern Condition: A Report on Knowledge* and *The Differend: Phrases in Dispute.*

20. Román de la Campa, "Relectura y redescubrimiento del Contrapunteo cubano"; Pérez Firmat, *The Cuban Condition.*

21. Fernando Coronil, "Challenging Colonial Histories: *Cuban Counterpoint/*Ortiz's Counterfetishism," p. 104.

22. Benítez-Rojo, *The Repeating Island*, p. 10.

23. See, in particular, de Man's chapter "Literary History and Literary Modernity," in *Blindness and Insight.*

24. Benítez-Rojo, *The Repeating Island*, p. 108.

25. Judith Butler writes about this doubt in "Contingent Foundations: Feminism and the Question of Postmodernism."

26. Benítez-Rojo, *The Repeating Island,* pp. 23, 29.

27. Ibid., p. 23.

28. Wynter, "Beyond the World of Man," p. 639.

29. Lucien Taylor, "The Same Difference."

30. J. Michael Dash, "Introduction" to *Caribbean Discourse,* p. xii.

31. Ibid., p. xi.

32. Taylor, "The Same Difference," p. 99.

33. Dash, *Édouard Glissant,* pp. 24–25.

34. See Bernadette Callier, "Édouard Glissant: A Creative Critic."

35. Glissant, *Caribbean Discourse,* p. 19.

36. Ibid., p. 64.

37. Debra L. Anderson, *Decolonizing the Text: Glissantian Readings in Caribbean and African-American Literatures,* p. 118.

38. Glissant, *Caribbean Discrouse,* p. 4.

39. Ibid., p. 2.

40. Ibid., p. 195.

41. Ibid., p. 220.

42. Ibid., p. 201.

43. Ibid., p. 220.

44. On *testimonio* and postmodernism, see John Beverley and Marc Zimmerman, *Literature and Politics in the Central American Revolutions.*

45. See the questions raised in this regard by Amaryll Chanady in the "Introduction" to *Latin American Identity and Constructions of Difference.*

46. Glissant, *Caribbean Discourse,* pp. 19–20.

47. Taylor, "The Same Difference," 108–9.

48. Dash, *Édouard Glissant,* p. 148.

49. Dash, "Introduction," p. ix.

50. Homi K. Bhabha, "Of Mimicry and Man: The Ambivalence of Colonial Discourse," p. 128.

51. Ibid., p. 129.

52. Homi K. Bhabha, "Remembering Fanon: Self, Psyche, and the Colonial Condition," p. 298.

53. Two different but insightful new formulations are Neil Lazarus, "National Consciousness and the Specificity of (Post)colonial Intellectualism," and Ernesto Laclau, *New Reflections on the Revolution of Our Time.* See also Ernesto Laclau, ed., *The Making of Political Identities.*

54. Achille Mbembe, "The Banality of Power and the Aesthetics of Vulgarity in the Postcolony."

55. Ibid., p. 22.

56. Ibid., p. 11.

57. Ibid., p. 5.

58. Ibid., p. 6. These are some of Mbembe's categories that I underscore to indicate their importance as well as their insufficiency.

59. Glissant, *Caribbean Discourse,* p. 148.

60. Ibid., p. 67.

61. Gayatri Chakravorty Spivak, "Can the Subaltern Speak?"

62. Martin Hopenhayn, "Postmodernism and Neoliberalism in Latin America."

63. Paget Henry and Paul Buhle, eds., *C. L. R. James's Caribbean,* p. 147.

64. This is clearly outlined by Henry Giroux, *Border Crossings.*

65. See also Santiago Colás, "Of Creole Symptoms, Cuban Fantasies, and Other Latin American Postcolonial Ideologies."

66. Spivak, "Can the Subaltern Speak?" pp. 88–89.

67. Glissant, *Caribbean Discourse,* p. 101.

68. Ibid., p. 122.

69. Derrida, *Spectres of Marx,* p. 29.

70. Glissant, *Caribbean Discourse,* pp. 76–77.

71. Ibid., pp. 126–27.

5. The Lettered City

1. Mario Vargas Llosa, "Prologue" to Ángel Rama, *La ciudad letrada,* viii. It is indeed striking that this prologue makes no mention of Rama's text. It is more of a tribute to Rama after his death.

2. Rama's other posthumous book, *Las máscaras democráticas del modernismo,* was published in 1985. Unlike *The Lettered City,* its composition was not completely designed by Rama but by colleagues and editors. It is, nonetheless, a collection of Rama's late essays, which are discussed in this chapter.

3. Among the published studies of this book are the following: Rolena Adorno, "La ciudad letrada y los discursos coloniales"; Mabel Moraña, "De la ciudad letrada al imaginario nacionalista: contribuciones de Ángel Rama a la invención de América"; Josaphat Kubayanda, "Order and Conflict: Yo el Supremo in Light of Rama's *ciudad letrada* Theory"; and Carlos J. Alonso, "Rama y sus retoños: Figuring the Nineteenth Century Spanish America." See also Julio Ramos, *Desencuentros de la modernidad en América Latina: literatura y política en el siglo XIX* (Mexico City: Fondo de Cultura, 1989), a book that includes many valuable insights on Rama's work.

4. For a comprehensive and comparative critique of Foucault's work,

see Peter Boyne, *Foucault and Derrida: The Other Side of Reason,* and Christopher Norris, *Truth and the Ethics of Criticism.*

5. Moraña, "De la ciudad letrada al imaginario nacionalista," p. 47.

6. Adorno, "La ciudad letrada y los discursos coloniales," p. 4.

7. Ibid., p. 5.

8. Alonso, "Rama y sus retoños," pp. 286–87.

9. Kubayanda, "Order and Conflict," p. 130.

10. Rama, *La ciudad letrada,* p. 34.

11. A more detailed discussion of *Tranculturación narrativa en América Latina* is found in chapter 3.

12. Rama, *La ciudad letrada,* p. 4.

13. Ibid.

14. See Manfred Fran's *What Is Neostructuralism?* for a novel critique of the unsuspected links between structuralism and poststructuralism, as well as for an attempt to provide a dialogue between German and French theoretical approaches to these strands.

15. Boyne, *Foucault and Derrida,* provides an important critique of how Foucault moved beyond this stage and what aspects remained in his later work.

16. José Rabasa's *Inventing America* contains an elaborate illustration of this epistemology.

17. Norris, *Truth and the Ethics of Criticism,* p. 126.

18. Carlos Rincón, *La no simultaneidad de lo simultáneo,* p. 222.

19. Sarduy's *Escrito sobre un cuerpo* and Barroco are representative articulations.

20. Rama, *La ciudad letrada,* p. 34.

21. Rama, *Las máscaras democráticas del modernismo,* pp. 166, 167.

22. Rama, *La ciudad letrada,* p. 137.

23. Ibid., p. 140.

24. Ibid., p. 144. Rama's reference here is to Carlos Franqui's book *Cuba: el libro de los doce.*

25. See the author's comments in the book's acknowledgments, as well as Hugo Achugar's Prologue to *La ciudad letrada.*

26. Beatriz Sarlo, *Escenas de la vida posmoderna*; Néstor García Canclini, *Consumidores y ciudadanos*; Roberto Schwarz, "Brazilian Culture: Nationalism by Elimination"; Nelly Richard, *La estratificación de los márgenes.*

27. García Canclini, *Consumidores y ciudadanos,* pp. 197–98.

28. Ernesto Laclau, *New Reflections on the Revolution of Our Time,* p. 91.

29. Ibid., p. 90.

30. Ibid.

31. Ibid., p. 91.

32. Rama, *La ciudad letrada,* p. 123.

33. Ibid., p. 116.

34. Ibid., p. 59.

35. Ibid., pp. 53–54.

36. Ibid., p. 47.

37. See Christopher Norris's detailed analysis of this particular aspect in *Paul de Man, Deconstruction and the Critique of Aesthetic Ideology,* p. 153.

38. Rama, *La ciudad letrada,* p. 88.

39. Walter Mignolo, *The Darker Side of the Renaissance,* pp. 318–22.

40. Horst Ruthrof, *Semantics and the Body,* p. 261.

41. Ibid.

42. García Canclini, *Consumidores y ciudadanos,* p. 185.

43. Richard Rorty, "Tales of Two Disciplines."

44. Richard Rorty, *Objectivity, Relativism, and Truth,* p. 198.

45. For a broad discussion of these problems, see Cristopher Norris, *The Truth about Postmodernism.*

46. A more detailed discussion of Derrida's book on Marx, *Spectres of Marx,* and the current state of deconstruction is taken up in chapter 6.

6. Globalization, Neoliberalism, and Cultural Studies

An early version of this essay was read at the "Politics of Research" conference held at Rutgers University, Humanities Center, October 20–21, 1994.

1. I am in full agreement with Nelly Richard's appraisal that "When one gets beyond the facile equation of postmodernism and market neoliberalism, it becomes readily apparent that some postmodernist texts activate (new) energies of resistance and critical opposition, while others deactivate them" ("Reply to Vidal [from Chile]," p. 308). My contention in this chapter is, however, that, unlike Chile and other parts of the developing world, the links between postmodernism and neoliberal doctrines remain to be fully explored in the United States.

2. Martin Hopenhayn, "Postmodernism and Neoliberalism."

3. Ibid., pp. 98–99.

4. Néstor García Canclini, "Cultural Studies: Towards a U.S.–Latin American Intercultural Exchange," unpublished manuscript of a lecture given at the State University of New York at Stony Brook, April 15, 1997.

5. Joseph Tabbi, *Postmodern Sublime, Technology and American Writing from Mailer to Cyberpunk,* p. 12.

6. Terry Eagleton, *Against the Grain*, p. 66.

7. Andrew Steele, "Postmodern Gravity Deconstructed, Slyly," *New York Times*, May 18, 1996, p. A1.

8. Stanley Fish, "Professor Sokal's Bad Joke," *New York Times*, May 21, 1996, p. A23. For Alan Sokol's original essay, see "Transgressing the Boundaries: Toward a Transformative Hermeneutics of Quantum Gravity."

9. Ibid.

10. Ibid.

11. Spivak's work consistently attempts to draw a postcolonial feminist critique from poststructural sources, thereby challenging each of these paradigms in specific ways. Most relevant in this regard are her critique and reappraisal of Foucault in the essays "Can the Subaltern Speak?" and "More on Power/Knowledge." See also Nelly Richard, *La estratificación de los márgenes*. For Beatriz Sarlo, see *Escenas de la vida posmoderna* and *Jorge Luis Borges: A Writer on the Edge*.

12. Tabbi, *Postmodern Sublime, Technology and American Writing from Mailer to Cyberpunk*, p. 10. In this passage, Tabbi is paraphrasing Žižek.

13. Nelly Richard, "Cultural Peripheries: Latin America and Postmodernist De-centering," p. 217; emphasis in the original.

14. Henry A. Giroux's work attempts to make these connections between the world of theory and the field of pedagogy. See, for example, his *Living Dangerously*.

15. Horst Ruthrof, *Semantics and the Body*, p. 182.

16. Ibid.

17. Ibid.

18. Ibid., p. 250.

19. Fredric Jameson's well-known work on postmodernism details a more ambivalent understanding. The notion of a cultural domain that still remains somewhat autonomous suggests a modernist logic difficult to sustain in post–Cold War neoliberalism. Jameson's *Postmodernism, or the Cultural Logic of Late Capitalism* is essential on this topic.

20. Beatriz Sarlo, "Aesthetics and Post-Politics: From Fujimori to the Gulf War," In *The Postmodernism Debate in Latin America*, pp. 252–53.

21. Ernest Boyer's Carnegie Foundation studies have made calls for a more diverse understanding of scholarship along these lines. See *Chronicle of Higher Education*, February 16, 1994.

22. Current attempts by the U.S. Congress to eliminate the NEH and the National Endowment for the Arts (NEA), among other federal agencies promoting public funding for cultural and artistic projects, are a case in point. See Sheldon Hackney, "Organizing a National Conversation."

23. This process is evident in Jonathan Culler's work, particularly his quick transition from structuralism to deconstruction with a book on semiotics in between: *The Pursuit of Signs* (1981) is tightly squeezed between *Structuralist Poetics* (1981) and *On Deconstruction* (1982). See also Román de la Campa, "Mainstreaming Poststructuralist and Feminist Thought: Jonathan Culler's Poetics."

24. For an interesting, though restrictive, discussion of semiotics within deconstructive parameters, see Wlad Godzich, "The Semiotics of Semiotics," in *The Culture of Literacy* (Cambridge: Harvard University Press, 1994).

25. See Haraway's deployment of the Greimasian semiotic square in "The Promises of Monsters: A Regenerative Politics for Inappropriate/d Others."

26. Slavoj Žižek, *The Sublime Object of Ideology*, p. 52.

27. Courtney Leatherman, "New Facts about the Old Left," *Chronicle of Higher Education,* June 7, 1996, p. A16.

28. The work of Djelal Kadir provides a dramatic register of this tension. See *The Other Writing.*

29. Silviano Santiago, "Reading and Discursive Intensities," p. 246.

30. According to the NRC, it failed to do so because it could not obtain the funds to conduct a significant study. It is logical to assume, however, that this was not a priority for the NRC, given that its surveys are conducted in ten-year intervals (National Research Council, "Report on Graduate Programs," 1995).

31. Nancy Fraser, "Multiculturalism, Antiessentialism, and Radical Democracy," in *Justice Interruptus,* p. 186.

32. Gayatri Chakravorty Spivak, "Teaching for the Times," p. 484.

33. John Beverley, "The Real Thing," p. 116.

34. Spivak, "Teaching for the Times," p. 483.

35. Jacques Derrida, "Spectres of Marx," p. 38.

36. *Spectres of Marx* has elicited a number of critical essays. See, for example: Aijaz Ahmad, "Reconciling Derrida: *Spectres of Marx* and Deconstructive Politics"; Fredric Jameson, "Marx's Purloined Letter"; and Tom Lewis, "The Politics of 'Hauntology' in Derrida's *Spectres of Marx*" (unpublished manuscript).

37. Derrida, "Spectres of Marx," p. 39.

38. Ibid., p. 52.

39. Ibid.

40. Ibid., p. 53.

41. The "postcolonial turn" in postmodern theory is open to debate,

but it has managed to redirect attention to Third World and diasporic intellectuals, more than any other discourse before, and not only to those writing today, but to those belonging to colonial and neocolonial periods as well. Many new anthologies have entered this new market; among them, the reader *Colonial Discourse and Post-Colonial Theory*, ed. Patrick Williams and Laura Chrisman, is particularly valuable.

42. Martin Hopenhayn, *Ni apocalípticos ni integrados: Aventuras de la modernidad en América*, p. 125.

43. Arif Dirlik, *After the Revolution: Waking to Global Capitalism*, p. 354.

44. Ibid., p. 341.

45. Ibid., p. 333.

46. For a more nuanced reading of diasporic intellectuals, see R. Radhakrishnan's "Postcoloniality and the Boundaries of Identity"; and Román de la Campa, "On Latin Americanism and the Postcolonial Turn."

47. Stuart Hall, "Cultural Studies and Its Theoretical Legacies," p. 283.

48. See Nelly Richard's argument against this appropriation in "Bordes, diseminación, postmodernismo: una metáfora latinoamericana de fin de siglo."

49. Spivak, "Teaching for the Times," p. 479.

50. Spivak's argument is based on a reading that sees the links between Chicano and Latino discourses as global aspirations based on the "Our America" theme inspired by José Martí. She does not, however, examine its nineteenth-century origins or explain its current value. She also identifies "new immigrant intellectuals" with negotiable nationality and postcolonial theory without further ado. Nonetheless, her attempt to chart new territory on the question of transnational literacy in this essay is a laudable contribution.

51. R. Radhakrishnan, "Postcoloniality and the Boundaries of Identity." See also Radhakrishnan's "Ethnic Identity and Post-Structuralist Difference."

52. Homi K. Bhabha, "Remembering Fanon: Self, Psyche, and the Colonial Condition"; see Glissant's critique of the culture of writing in *Caribbean Discourse*.

53. Spivak, "Teaching for the Times," p. 483.

54. Ruthrof, *Semantics and the Body*, p. 259.

Bibliography

Adorno, Rolena. "La ciudad letrada y los discursos coloniales." *Hispamérica* 16.48 (December 1987): 3–24.

———. "Reconsidering Colonial Discourse for Sixteenth- and Seventeenth-Century Spanish America." *Latin American Research Review* 28.3 (1993): 120–34.

———. "Positioning the Text." In *Literature and Society: Centers and Margins,* ed. José García, Betina Kaplan, Carlos Lechner, Andrea Parra, and Mario Santana. New York: Department of Spanish and Portuguese, Columbia University, 1994.

Ahmad, Aijaz. *In Theory.* London: Verso, 1992.

———. "Postcolonialism: What's in a Name?" In *Late Imperial Cultures,* ed. Román de la Campa, E. Ann Kaplan, and Michael Sprinker. London: Verso, 1995. 11–32.

———. "Reconciling Derrida: *Spectres of Marx* and Deconstructive Politics." *New Left Review* 208 (November–December 1996): 88–106.

Alonso, Carlos J. *The Spanish American Regional Novel: Modernity and Authochtony.* Cambridge: Cambridge University Press, 1989.

———. "Rama y sus retoños: Figuring the Nineteenth Century in Spanish America." *Revista de Estudios Hispánicos* 28 (1994): 283–91.

———. "The Burden of Modernity." *Modern Language Quarterly* 57.2, special issue, ed. Doris Sommer. (1996): 227–37.

Anderson, Benedict. *Imagined Communities.* London: Verso, 1983.

Anderson, Debra L. *Decolonizing the Text: Glissantian Readings in Caribbean and African-American Literatures.* New York: Peter Lang, 1995.

Arguedas, José María. *El zorro de arriba y el zorro de abajo.* Havana: Casa de las Américas, 1965.

Barth, John. *The Friday Book: Essays and Other Nonfiction.* New York: Putnam's, 1984.

Bayo Giroud, Alberto. *150 Questions for a Guerrilla.* Boulder, Colo.: Panther Publications, 1962.

Benítez-Rojo, Antonio. *La isla que se repite: El Caribe y la perspectiva posmoderna.* Hanover, N.H.: Ediciones del Norte, 1989.

——. *The Repeating Island.* Trans. James Maraniss. Durham, N.C.: Duke University Press, 1992.

Benson, Robert W. "Mexican Reform Can't Be Trickle-Down Kind." *Newsday,* July 28, 1994, A40.

Beverley, John. *Against Literature.* Minneapolis: University of Minnesota Press, 1993.

——. "The Real Thing." In *The Real Thing,* ed. Georg M Gugelberger. Durham, N.C.: Duke University Press, 1996. 266–87.

Beverly, John, and José Oviedo, eds. *The Postmodernism Debate in Latin America.* Durham, N.C.: Duke University Press, 1994.

Beverley, John, and Marc Zimmerman. *Literature and Politics in the Central American Revolutions.* Austin: University of Texas Press, 1990.

Bhabha, Homi K. "Of Mimicry and Man: The Ambivalence of Colonial Discourse." *October* 28 (1984): 125–33.

——. "DissemiNation: Time Narrative and the Margins of the Modern Nation." In *Nation and Narration.* London: Routledge, 1990. 291–321.

——. "Postcolonial Authority and Postmodern Guilt." In *Cultural Studies,* ed. Lawrence Grossberg, Cary Nelson, and Paula A. Treichler. New York: Routledge, 1992. 56–68.

——. "Remembering Fanon: Self, Psyche, and the Colonial Condition." In *Colonial Discourse and Post-Colonial Theory,* eds. Patrick Williams and Laura Chrisman. New York: Columbia University Press, 1994. 112–23.

Bloom, Harold. *The Western Canon.* New York: Harcourt Brace and Company, 1994.

Borges, Jorge Luis. *Labyrinths.* Ed. Donald Yates and James E. Irby. New York: New Directions Books, 1964.

——. *Other Inquisitions, 1937–1952.* Trans. Ruth L. C. Simms. Austin: University of Texas Press, 1964.

Boyne, Peter. *Foucault and Derrida: The Other Side of Reason.* London: Unwin Hyman, 1990.

Butler, Judith. "Contingent Foundations: Feminism and the Question of

Postmodernism." In *Feminists Theorize the Political,* eds. Judith Butler and Joan Scott. New York: Routledge, 1990. 3–28.

————. *Gender Trouble: Feminism and the Subversion of Identity.* New York: Routledge, 1990.

Callier, Bernadette. "Édouard Glissant: A Creative Critic." *World Literature Today* 63.4 (1989): 589–92.

Castillo, Debra. *Talking Back: Toward a Latin American Feminist Literary Criticism.* Ithaca, N.Y.: Cornell University Press, 1992.

Chanady, Amaryll, ed. *Latin American Identity and Constructions of Difference.* Hispanic Issues, vol. 10. Minneapolis: University of Minnesota Press, 1994.

Clifford, James. *The Predicament of Culture.* Cambridge: Harvard University Press, 1988.

Colás, Santiago. *Postmodernity in Latin America: The Argentine Paradigm.* Durham, N.C.: Duke University Press, 1994.

————. "Of Creole Symptoms, Cuban Fantasies, and Other Latin American Postcolonial Ideologies." *PMLA* 110.3 (1995): 382–96.

————. "What's Wrong with Representation?: Testimonio and Democratic Culture." In *The Real Thing,* ed. Georg M. Gugelberger. Durham, N.C.: Duke University Press, 1996. 161–72.

Coronil, Fernando. "Can Postcoloniality Be Decolonized? Imperial Banality and Postcolonial Power." *Public Culture* 5 (1992): 90–115.

————. "Challenging Colonial Histories: *Cuban Counterpoint/*Ortiz's Counterfetishism." In *Critical Theory, Cultural Politics, and the Latin American Narrative,* eds. Steven M. Bell, Albert H. LeMay, and Leonard Orr. South Bend, Ind.: Notre Dame University Press, 1993. 61–80.

Cortázar, Julio. *Nicaragua, tan violentamente dulce.* Barcelona: Muchnik Editores, 1984.

Culler, Jonathan. *The Pursuit of Signs.* Ithaca, N.Y.: Cornell University Press, 1981.

————. *Structuralist Poetics.* Ithaca, N.Y.: Cornell University Press, 1981.

————. *On Deconstruction.* Ithaca, N.Y.: Cornell University Press, 1982.

Culture Shift: The Employee Handbook for Changing Corporate Culture. New York, 1996.

Dash, J. Michael. "Introduction." In *Caribbean Discourse.* Trans. J. Michael Dash. Charlottesville: University of Virginia Press, 1989.

————. *Édouard Glissant.* New York: Cambridge University Press, 1995.

de Alva, Klor. "Colonialism and Postcolonialism as (Latin) American Mirages." *Colonial Latin American Review* 1.1–2 (1992): 2–23.

de la Campa, Román. "Relectura y redescubrimiento del *Contrapunteo cubano.*" *Areito* 7.27 (1980): 46–48.

———. "Mainstreaming Poststructuralist and Feminist Thought: Jonathan Culler's Poetics." *M/MLA* 23 (1985): 29–37.

———. "Hibridez posmoderna y transculturación: políticas de montaje en torno a Latinoamérica." *Hispamérica* 20.69 (1994): 3–22.

———. "On Latin Americanism and the Postcolonial Turn." *Canadian Review of Comparative Literature* 22.3–4 (December 1995): 745–71.

———. "Postmodernism and Revolution: A Central American Case Study." In *Late Imperial Culture,* ed. Román de la Campa, E. Ann Kaplan, and Michael Sprinker. New York: Verso, 1995. 122–48.

———. "Latinoamérica y sus nuevos cartógrafos: discurso poscolonial, diásporas intelectuales y enunciación fronteriza." In *Crítica cultural y teoría literaria latinoamericana,* ed. Mabel Moraña. Pittsburgh: Instituto Internacional de Literatura Latinoamericana, 1996. 697–719.

de Man, Paul. *Blindness and Insight: Essays in the Rhetoric of Contemporary Criticism.* Oxford: Oxford University Press, 1971.

———. *Allegories of Reading.* New Haven: Yale University Press, 1979.

———. *The Resistance to Theory.* Minneapolis: University of Minnesota Press, 1986.

Derrida, Jacques. *Of Grammatology.* Baltimore: Johns Hopkins University Press, 1976.

———. "Spectres of Marx." *New Left Review* 205 (May–June 1994): 31–58.

———. *Spectres of Marx: The State of the Debt, the Work of Mourning, and the New International.* New York: Routledge, 1994.

Dews, Peter. *The Logic of Disintegration.* London: Verso, 1987.

Díaz Caballero, Jesús. "La transculturación en la novela regionalista: El caso sur andino peruano en la obra de Arguedas." *Revista de crítica literaria latinoamericana* 13.25 (1987): 155–72.

Didion, Joan. *Salvador.* New York: Simon and Schuster, 1983.

———. *Salvador.* New York: Washington Square Press, 1983.

———. "Something Horrible in El Salvador." *New York Review of Books* 41.13(1997), 8–13.

Dirlik, Arif. *After the Revolution: Waking to Global Capitalism.* Hanover, N.H.: New England University Press, 1994.

———. "The Postcolonial Aura: Third World Criticism in the Age of Global Capitalism." *Critical Inquiry* 20 (winter 1994): 331–50.

Dussel, Enrique. "Eurocentrism and Modernity." *boundary 2* 20.3 (1993): 65–76.

———. "The Reason of the Other." *boundary 2* 20.3 (1993): 65–76.

Eagleton, Terry. *Against the Grain.* London: Verso, 1986.

Escobar, Arturo. "Imagining a Post-Development Era?" *Social Text* 31.31 (1992): 20–56.

Fish, Stanley. "Professor Sokal's Bad Joke." *New York Times,* May 21, 1996, A23.

Foucault, Michel. *The Order of Things: An Archaeology of the Human Sciences.* New York: Vintage Books, 1973.

———. "Technologies of the Self." In *Technologies of the Self,* ed. Luther H. Martin, Huck Gutman, and Patrick H. Hutton. Amherst: University of Massachussets Press, 1988. 16–50.

Franco, Jean. "The Utopia of a Tired Man: Jorge Luis Borges." *Social Text* (fall 1981): 52–79.

———. "Ángel Rama y la transculturación narrativa en América Latina." *Sin Nombre* 14.3 (1984): 32–43.

———. "Apuntes sobre la crítica feminista y la literatura hispano-americana." *Hispamérica* 15.45 (1986): 38–45.

———. "The Nation as Imagined Community." In *The New Historicism,* ed. H. Aram Veeser. New York: Routledge, 1989.

Frank, Manfred. *What Is Neostructuralism?* Minneapolis: University of Minnesota Press, 1989.

Franqui, Carlos. *Cuba: el libro de los doce.* Mexico City: Ediciones Era, 1966.

Fraser, Nancy. *Justice Interruptus.* New York: Routledge, 1994.

Galeano, Eduardo. *Guatemala: país ocupado.* Mexico City: Editorial Nuestro Tiempo, 1967.

———. *Guatemala, Occupied Country.* New York: Monthly Review Press, 1969.

———. *Open Veins of Latin America.* Trans. Cedric Belfrage. New York: Monthly Review Press, 1973.

García Canclini, Néstor. *Consumidores y ciudadanos.* Mexico City: Grijaldo, 1995.

———. *Hybrid Cultures: Strategies for Entering and Leaving Modernity.* Trans. Christopher L. Chiappari and Silvia L. López. Minneapolis: University of Minnesota Press, 1995.

García Márquez, Gabriel. *One Hundred Years of Solitude.* Trans. Gregory Rabassa. New York: Harper and Row, 1970.

Gates, Henry Louis, Jr. "Critical Fanonism." *Critical Inquiry* 17 (1991): 457–70.

Giroux, Henry A. *Border Crossings.* New York: Routledge, 1992.

————. *Living Dangerously.* New York: Peter Lang, 1993.

Glissant, Édouard. *Le discours antillais.* Paris: Seuil, 1981.

————. *Caribbean Discourse.* Trans. J. Michael Dash. Charlottesville: University of Virginia Press, 1989.

————. *Poétique de la relation.* Paris: Gallimard, 1990.

González Echevarría, Roberto. *Alejo Carpentier: The Pilgrim at Home.* Ithaca, N.Y.: Cornell University Press, 1977.

————. *The Voice of the Masters: Writing and Authority in Modern Latin American Literature.* Austin: University of Texas Press, 1985.

————. *La ruta de Severo Sarduy.* Hanover, N.H.: Ediciones del Norte, 1987.

————. *Myth and Archive.* Cambridge: Cambridge University Press, 1990.

Guerra Cunningham, Lucía. "Las sombras de la escritura: hacia una teoría de la producción literaria de la mujer latinoamericana." In *Cultural and Historical Grounding for Hispanic and Luso-Brazilian Feminist Literary Criticism,* ed. Hernán Vidal. Minneapolis: University of Minnesota Press, 1989. 138–60.

Guevara, Che. *La guerra de guerrillas.* Havana: Editorial de Ciencias Sociales, 1978.

Hackney, Sheldon. "Organizing a National Conversation." *Chronicle of Higher Education,* April 20, 1994.

Hall, Stuart. "Cultural Studies and Its Theoretical Legacies." In *Cultural Studies,* ed. Lawrence Grossberg, Cary Nelson, and Paula A. Treichler. New York: Routledge, 1992. 277–94.

————."Cultural Identity and Diaspora." In *Colonial Discourse and Post-Colonial Theory,* eds. Patrick Williams and Laura Chrisman. New York: Columbia University Press, 1994. 392–403.

Haraway, Donna. "The Promises of Monsters: A Regenerative Politics for Inappropriate/d Others. In *Cultural Studies,* ed. Lawrence Grossberg, Cary Nelson, and Paula A. Treichler. New York: Routledge, 1992. 295–338.

Harlow, Barbara. *Resistance Literature.* New York: Methuen, 1987.

Henry, Paget, and Paul Buhle, eds. *C. L. R. James's Caribbean.* Durham, N.C.: Duke University Press, 1992.

Herlinghaous, Hermann, and Monika Walter, eds. *Posmodernidad en la periferia.* Berlin: Langer Verlag, 1994.

Hodges, Donald C. *Intellectual Foundations of the Nicaraguan Revolution.* Austin: University of Texas Press, 1986.

————. *Sandino's Communism.* Austin: University of Texas Press, 1992.

Hopenhayn, Martin. "Postmodernism and Neoliberalism in Latin America." *boundary 2* 20.3 (1993): 93–109.

———. *Ni apocalípticos ni integrados: Aventuras de la modernidad en América.* Mexico City: Fondo de Cultura Económica, 1994.

———. "Postmodernism and Neoliberalism." In *The Postmodernism Debate in Latin America,* eds. John Beverley, Michael Aronna, and José Oviedo. Durham, N.C.: Duke University Press, 1995.

Hutcheon, Linda. "Introduction: Complexities Abounding." *PMLA* 10.1 (1995): 7–16.

Jameson, Fredric. "Third World Literature in an Era of Multinational Capitalism." *Social Text* 15 (1986): 65–88.

———. "On Magic Realism in Film." In *Signatures of the Visible.* New York: Routledge, 1990. 128–52.

———. *Postmodernism, or the Cultural Logic of Late Capitalism.* Durham, N.C.: Duke University Press, 1991.

———. "Marx's Purloined Letter." *New Left Review* 209 (January–February 1995): 75–109.

Jauss, Hans Robert. "The Theory of Reception: A Retrospective of Its Unrecognized Prehistory." In *Literary Theory Today,* ed. Peter Collier and Helga Geyer-Ryan. Ithaca, N.Y.: Cornell University Press, 1990.

Kadir, Djelal. *Questing Fictions.* Minneapolis: University of Minnesota Press, 1986.

———. *The Other Writing.* West Lafayette, Ind.: Purdue University Press, 1993.

Kempton, Murray. "U.S. Sanctions for Salvadoran Atrocities." *Newsday,* May 19, 1993, 64.

Kubayanda, Josaphat. "Order and Conflict: Yo el Supremo in Light of Rama's *ciudad letrada* Theory." In *The Historical Novel in Latin America,* ed. Daniel Balderston. Gaithersburg, Md.: *Hispamérica* 15.45 (1986): 129–37.

Kusch, Rodolfo. *Geocultura del hombre americano.* Buenos Aires: F. García Gambero, 1976.

Laclau, Ernesto. *New Reflections on the Revolution of Our Time.* New York: Verso, 1990.

———, ed. *The Making of Political Identities.* London: Verso, 1994.

Larsen, Neil. *Modernism and Hegemony: A Materialist Critique of Aesthetic Agency.* Minneapolis: University of Minnesota Press, 1990.

———. *Reading North by South.* Minneapolis: University of Minnesota Press, 1995.

Lazarus, Neil. "National Consciousness and the Specificity of (Post)-

colonial Intellectualism." In *Colonial Discourse, Postcolonial Theory,* ed. Francis Barker, Peter Hulme, and Margaret Iversen. New York: Manchester University Press, 1994. 196–220.

Lechner, Norbert, ed. *Cultura política y democratización.* Buenos Aires: CLACSO, 1987.

Lewis, Tom. "The Politics of 'Hauntology' in Derrida's *Spectres of Marx.*" Unpublished manuscript.

Lowe, Lisa, and David Lloyd, eds. *The Politics of Culture in the Shadow of Capital.* Durham, N.C.: Duke University Press, 1997.

Ludmer, Josefina. "El coloquio de Yale: máquinas de leer 'fin de siglo.'" In *Las culturas de fin de siglo en América Latina,* ed. Josefina Ludmer. Buenos Aires: Beatriz Viterbo, 1994. 1–15.

Lyotard, Jean-François. *The Postmodern Condition: A Report on Knowledge.* Trans. Geoff Bennington and Brian Massumi. Minneapolis: University of Minnesota Press, 1984.

———. *The Differend: Phrases in Dispute.* Trans. Georges Van Den Abbeele. Minneapolis: University of Minnesota Press, 1988.

———. "The Sublime and the Avant-Garde." In *Postmodernism: A Reader,* ed. Thomas Docherty. New York: Columbia University Press, 1993 [1985]. 117–48.

Machín, Horacio. "Ángel Rama y 'La lección cultural de Marcha.'" In *Ángel Rama y los estudios latinoamericanos,* ed. Mabel Moraña. Pittsburgh: Instituto Internacional de Literatura Latinoamericana, 1997. 71–97.

Malinowski, Bronislaw. *Diary in the Strict Sense of the Term.* New York: Harcourt, Brace and World, 1967.

Mañach, Jorge. *Indagación del choteo.* Miami: Mnemosyne, 1969 [1928].

Mariátegui, Juan Carlos. *Siete ensayos de interpretación de la realidad peruana.* Mexico City: Ediciones Era, 1979.

Matos, Daniel., ed. *Teoría y política de la construcción de identidades y diferencias en América Latina y el Caribe.* Caracas: Nueva Sociedad, 1994.

Mbembe, Achille. "The Banality of Power and the Aesthetics of Vulgarity in the Postcolony." *Public Culture* 4.2 (1992): 1–30.

Mignolo, Walter. "Colonial and Postcolonial Discourse: Cultural Critique or Academic Colonialism?" *Latin American Research Review* 28.3 (1993): 120–31.

———. "Afterword." *Poetics Today* 15.4 (winter 1994): 205–20.

———. "Editor's Introduction." *Poetics Today* 15.4 (winter 1994): 1–8.

———. *The Darker Side of the Renaissance.* Ann Arbor: University of Michigan Press, 1995.

Mohanty, Chandra Talpade. "Epilogue: Colonial Legacies, Multicultural Futures: Relativism, Objectivity, and the Challenge of Otherness." *PMLA* 10.1 (1995): 108–18.

Monsiváis, Carlos. "Los milenarismos." In *Las culturas de fin de siglo en América Latina,* ed. Josefina Ludmer. Buenos Aires: Beatriz Viterbo, 1994. 164–83.

Moraña, Mabel. "De la ciudad letrada al imaginario nacionalista: contribuciones de Ángel Rama a la invención de América." In *Esplendores y miserios del siglo XIX: cultura y sociedad en América Latina,* eds. Beatriz González Stephan, Javier Lasarte, Graciela Montaldo, and María Julia Droqui. Caracas: Monte Avila/Ediciones de la Universidad Simón Bolívar, 1995. 41–51.

———, ed. *Crítica cultural y teoría literaria latinoamericana.* Pittsburgh: Instituto Internacional de Literatura Latinoamericana. 1996.

———, ed. *Ángel Rama y los estudios latinoamericanos.* Pittsburgh: Instituto Internacional de Literatura Latinoamericana, 1997.

Moreiras, Alberto. "Transculturación y pérdida del sentido." *Nuevo Texto Crítico* 3.6 (1990): 105–19.

———. "Pastiche Identity and Allegory of Allegory." In *Latin American Identity and Constructions of Difference,* ed. Amaryll Chanady. Hispanic Issues, vol. 10. Minneapolis: University of Minnesota Press, 1994.

———. "The Aura of Testimonio." In *The Real Thing,* ed. Georg M. Gugelberger. Durham, N.C.: Duke University Press, 1996. 192–225.

Moreno Fraginals, Manuel. *The Sugarmill: The Socioeconomic Complex of Sugar in Cuba, 1780–1860.* Trans. Cedric Belfrage. New York: Monthly Review Press, 1976.

Mudimbe, V. Y. *The Invention of Africa: Gnosis, Philosophy, and the Order of Knowledge.* Bloomington: Indiana University Press, 1988.

Norris, Christopher. *Paul de Man, Deconstruction and the Critique of Aesthetic Ideology.* New York: Routledge, 1988.

———. *Uncritical Theory, Postmodernism, Intellectuals and the Gulf War.* Amherst: University of Massachusetts Press, 1992.

———. *The Truth about Postmodernism.* Cambridge: Blackwell Publishers, 1993.

———. *Truth and the Ethics of Criticism.* Manchester: Manchester University Press, 1994.

Ortiz, Fernando. *Contrapunteo cubano del tabaco y el azúcar.* Havana: Consejo Nacional de Cultura, 1963.

Ortiz, Julio LeRiverend, ed. *Orbita de Fernando Ortiz.* Havana: UNEAC, 1973.

Ortiz, Maribel. "Modernidad conflictiva: Ángel Rama y el estudio de la literatura latinoamericana." Diss., State University of New York, Stony Brook, 1993.

Pérez Firmat, Gustavo. *The Cuban Condition.* New York: Cambridge University Press, 1989.

———. *Life on the Hyphen: The Cuban American Way.* New York: Cambridge University Press, 1994.

———, ed. *Do the Americas Have a Common Literature?* Durham, N.C.: Duke University Press, 1990.

Poblete, Juan. "Rama/Foucault/González Echevarría: el problema de la construcción del espacio discursivo del siglo diecinueve latinoamericano." In *Ángel Rama y los estudios latinoamericanos,* ed. Mabel Moraña, Pittsburgh: Instituto Internacional de Literatura Latinoamericana, 1997. 249–71.

Pratt, Mary Louise. *Imperial Eyes.* London: Routledge, 1992.

Rabasa, José. *Inventing America.* Norman: University of Oklahoma Press, 1993.

———. "Of Zapatismo: Reflections on the Folkloric and the Impossible in a Subaltern Insurrection." In *The Politics of Culture in the Shadow of Capital,* ed. Lisa Lowe and David Lloyd. Durham, N.C.: Duke University Press, 1997. 399–432.

Radhakrishnan, R. "Ethnic Identity and Post-Structuralist Difference." *Callaloo* 15.3 (fall 1992): 81–92.

———. "Postcoloniality and the Boundaries of Identity." *Callaloo* 16.4 (1993): 1080–1102.

Rama, Ángel. "El boom en perspectiva." *Escritura* 7 (1979): 1–85.

———. *Transculturación narrativa en América Latina.* Mexico City: Siglo XXI, 1982.

———. *La ciudad letrada.* Hanover, N.H.: Ediciones del Norte, 1984.

———. *Las máscaras democráticas del modernismo.* Montevideo, Uruguay: Fundación Ángel Rama, 1985.

———. *The Lettered City.* Trans. John Charles Chasteen. Durham, N.C.: Duke University Press, 1997.

Reguillo, Rossana. "Chiapas: la otra cara de la modernidad mexicana." *Nómada* 1 (1995): 3–10.

Richard, Nelly. *La estratificación de los márgenes.* Santiago de Chile: Francisco Zegers, 1989.

———. "Bordes, diseminación, postmodernismo: una metáfora latinoamericana de fin de siglo." In *Las culturas de fin de siglo en América*

Latina, ed. Josefina Ludmer. Buenos Aires: Beatriz Viterbo, 1994. 240–47.

———. "Cultural Peripheries: Latin America and Postmodernist Decentering." In *The Postmodernism Debate in Latin America,* ed. John Beverley, Michael Aronna, and José Oviedo. Durham, N.C.: Duke University Press, 1995. 217–23.

———. "Reply to Vidal (from Chile)." In *The Postmodernism Debate in Latin America,* ed. John Beverley, Michael Aronna, and José Oviedo. Durham, N.C.: Duke University Press, 1995. 307–11.

Rincón, Carlos. "The Peripheral Center of Postmodernism: On Borges, García Márquez, and Alterity." *boundary 2* 20.3 (fall 1993): 174–82.

———. *La no simultaneidad de lo simultáneo.* Bogotá, Colombia: Universidad Nacional de Colombia, 1995.

Rorty, Richard. *Objectivity, Relativism, and Truth.* Cambridge: Cambridge University Press, 1991.

———. "Tales of Two Disciplines." *Callaloo* 17.2 (1994).

Ruffinelli, Jorge. "Ángel Rama: la carrera del crítico de fondo." *Escritura: Revista de Teoría y Crítica Literarias* 8.5 (1983): 123–31.

Ruthrof, Horst. *Semantics and the Body: Meaning from Frege to the Postmodern.* Toronto: University of Toronto Press, 1997.

Said, Edward. *Orientalism.* New York: Pantheon, 1978.

———. *The World, the Text, and the Critic.* Cambridge: Harvard University Press, 1983.

———. "Representing the Colonized: Anthropology's Interlocutors." *Critical Inquiry* 15 (1989): 210–35.

———. *Culture and Imperialism.* New York: Knopf, 1993.

Santí, Enrico Mario. *Escritura y tradición: texto, crítica y poética en la literatura latinoamericana.* Barcelona: Laia, 1988.

Santiago, Silviano. "Reading and Discursive Intensities." In *The Postmodernism Debate in Latin America,* ed. John Beverley, Michael Aronna, and José Oviedo. Durham, N.C.: Duke University Press, 1995. 241–50.

Sarduy, Severo. *Escrito sobre un cuerpo.* Buenos Aires: Editorial Sudamericana, 1969.

———. *Barroco.* Buenos Aires: Editorial Sudamericana, 1974.

Sarlo, Beatriz. "Aesthetics and Post-Politics: From Fujimori to the Gulf War." *boundary 2* 20.3 (1993): 180–93.

———. *Jorge Luis Borges: A Writer on the Edge.* New York: Verso, 1993.

———. *Escenas de la vida posmoderna.* Buenos Aires: Espasa Calpe, 1994.

———. "Aesthetics and Post-Politics: From Fujimori to the Gulf War." In

The Postmodernism Debate in Latin America, ed. John Beverley, Michael Aronna, and José Oviedo. Durham, N.C.: Duke University Press, 1995.

Schwarz, Roberto. "Brazilian Culture: Nationalism by Elimination." *New Left Review* 167 (1988): 102–16.

Seed, Patricia. "Colonial and Postcolonial Discourse." *Latin American Research Review* 26.3 (1991): 181–200.

Shohat, Ella. "Notes on the 'Post-Colonial.'" *Social Text* 31–32 (1992): 99–113.

Silverstein, Ken, and Alexander Cockburn. "The Killers and the Killing." *Nation* 260.9 (1995): 306–11.

Slemon, Stephen. "Magic Realism and Post-Colonial Discourse." *Canadian Literature* 116 (1988): 9–24.

———. "Modernism's Last Post." In *Past the Last Post,* ed. Ian Adam and Helen Tiffin. Calgary: University of Calgary Press, 1990. 43–59.

Smith, Paul Julian. *The Body Hispanic.* New York: Oxford University Press, 1989.

Sokal, Alan. "Transgressing the Boundaries: Toward a Transformative Hermeneutics of Quantum Gravity." *Social Text* 46–47(1–2)(1996): 217–52.

Sosnowski, Saúl. "Ángel Rama: un sendero en el bosque de palabras." In *Ángel Rama: la crítica de la cultura en América Latina,* selection and prologue by Saúl Sosnowski and Tomás Eloy Martinez. Caracas: Biblioteca Ayacucho, 1985. ix–xxiii.

Spivak, Gayatri Chakravorty. "Poststructuralism, Marginality, Post-coloniality, and Value." In *Literary Theory Today,* ed. Peter Collier and Helga Geyer-Ryan. Ithaca, N.Y.: Cornell University Press, 1990. 291–344.

———. *The Post-Colonial Critic: Interviews, Strategies, Dialogues.* Ed. Sarah Harasym. London: Routledge, 1991.

———. "Can the Subaltern Speak?" In *Colonial Discourse and Post-Colonial Theory,* eds. Patrick Williams and Laura Chrisman. New York: Columbia University Press, 1994. 66–111.

———. "More on Power/Knowledge." In *The Spivak Reader,* ed. Donna Landry and Gerald Maclean. New York: Routledge, 1996. 214–29.

———. "Subaltern Talk." In *The Spivak Reader,* ed. Donna Landry and Gerald Maclean. New York: Routledge, 1996. 76–92.

———. "Teaching for the Times." In *Dangerous Liaisons,* ed. Ann McClintock, Aamir Mufti, and Ella Shohat. Minneapolis: University of Minnesota Press, 1997. 468–91.

Tabbi, Joseph. *Postmodern Sublime, Technology and American Writing from Mailer to Cyberpunk.* Ithaca, N.Y.: Cornell University Press, 1995.

Taibo, Paco Ignacio, II. "Zapatista! The Phoenix Rises." *Nation* 258.12 (1994): 25–38.

Taylor, Lucien. "The Same Difference." *Transition* 63 (1994): 98–111.

Thomas, Hugh. *The Spanish Civil War.* New York: Harper and Row, 1961.

———. *Cuba: The Pursuit of Freedom.* New York: Harper and Row, 1971.

Trigo, Abel. "De la transculturación (a/en) lo transnacional." In *Ángel Rama y los estudios latinoamericanos,* ed. Mabel Moraña, Pittsburgh: Instituto Internacional de Literatura Latinoamericana, 1997. 147–73.

Vargas Llosa, Mario. "Prologue." In Ángel Rama, *La ciudad letrada.* Hanover, N.H.: Ediciones del Norte, 1984. 1–8.

Vidal, Hernán. "A Perspective from Literary Criticism." *Latin American Research Review* 28.3 (1993): 113–19.

Villegas, Juan. "La estrategia llamada transculturación." *Conjunto* (July–September 1991): 36–42.

Williams, Patrick, and Laura Chrisman, eds. *Colonial Discourse and Post-Colonial Theory.* New York: Columbia University Press, 1994.

Wynter, Sylvia. "Beyond the World of Man: Glissant and the New Discourse of the Antilles." *World Literature Today* 63.4 (1989): 637–47.

Yúdice, George. "Marginality and the Ethics of Survival." In *Universal Abandon? The Politics of Postmodernism,* ed. Andrew Ross. Minneapolis: University of Minnesota Press, 1988. 220–38.

Yúdice, George, Jean Franco, and Juan Flores, eds. *On Edge: The Crisis of Contemporary Latin American Culture.* Minneapolis: University of Minnesota Press, 1992.

Žižek, Slavoj. *The Sublime Object of Ideology.* London: Verso, 1989.

Index

Compiled by Rich Calvin

and Latin Americanism, 60; and
Martí, 194; and multiculturalism,
164; and postcolonialism, 5, 8–12,
61, 155, 171, 194; and transnational
literacy, 166, 171, 194
subaltern, 10, 41, 44, 66, 82, 140,
170–71
subalternity and subaltern studies, 2, 4, 5,
6, 8, 9, 23, 27, 33, 110, 171

Tabbi, Joseph, 151, 155, 160
Taylor, Lucien, 105, 111
telenovelas, 64
testimonio: and Beverley and Zimmerman, 41–42; and Galeano, 43–44;
and Menchú, 3, 23, 80, 165; and
postcolonialism, 5; posthumanist, 24;
and postmodern, 6, 23–24, 80, 110;
and revolution, 41–42; and subalternity, 5–6, 23, 110; and travel narrative, 39; and women, 3
testimonial narrative: and Chiapas, 30;
and feminist, 170; Latin American, 2;
and Menchú, 2, 80, 165, 170; and
multiculturalism, 170; and postmodern canon, 2; and postmodernism, 30;
and transculturation, 80
Thomas, Hugh, 37
transculturation: and Arguedas, 76; and
border cultures, 68; and Caribbean
culture, 85; and Carpentier, 78; and
Clifford, 83; and cultural studies, 70,
72; and deconstruction, 65; and discursivity, 59; ethics, 151; and feminism, 65, 68, 83; and García
Canclini, 67, 69–70, 72, 75; and
globalization, 72; and hybridity,
65–66, 74, 83, 85; as intertextuality,
79, 124; Latin American, 27, 57; and
Latin American feminist articulations,
26; literary, 76–77; and magical realism, 78; and Malinowski, 66; and
mestizaje, 65, 74; and modernity,

65–66; and multiculturalism, 66, 70;
and neoliberalism, 72; and orality,
138; and Ortiz, 65, 74, 77, 79,
80–81; and performances, 26, 29, 76;
and performativity, 83–84; and popular culture, 67, 69; and postmodern,
65, 67; and postmodern history, 83;
and postmodernism, 3; and Rama,
66, 74–83, 121, 124, 138–39; and
revolution, 41; and semiological
doubt, 59; and Spanish narrative
forms, 139; and subaltern studies, 26;
and *testimonio,* 80; and transmodern,
57, 64; and women's writing, 27, 65,
83
Trujillo, Rafael Leónidas, 37
Tula, María Teresa, 80

underdevelopment, 24, 114, 151

Vargas Llosa, Mario: and boom, 3–4, 43,
71, 122, 129; and political commitment, 43; and postmodern canon, 30;
and Rama, 121–22
Vico, Giambattista, 57

West, Cornel, 114
Western canon, 6, 70, 145, 166, 171;
The Western Canon, 143–47, 161,
165
Wilson, Edmund, 121
women: and Benítez-Rojo, 112; and
Bloom, 143, 166; and Butler, 60; and
deconstruction, 164; and deconstructive practice, 61; and Fraser, 60; and
García Canclini, 73; and Glissant,
105; and performativity, 112; and
poststructuralist literary critics, 28;
and Rama, 77, 133; representations of
violence against, 51; as sign, 60; and
telenovelas, 64; and *testimonio,* 3–4,
6, 80; and transculturation, 27, 83;
writers, 3–4, 6, 80; women's issues,

Román de la Campa is professor of Latin American and comparative literature at the State University of New York, Stony Brook, where he chairs the Department of Hispanic Languages and Literature. He is the author of *José Triana: ritualización de la sociedad cubana* and *América Latina y sus comunidades discursivas.* He is also coauthor of *Contra viento y marea* (a book of *testimonio*), and coeditor of *Late Imperial Cultures,* a volume on contemporary cultural and literary theory.